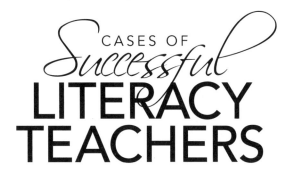

CASES OF
Successful
LITERACY
TEACHERS

To our children

Caroline

Grace

Sebastian

Andrea

And their fathers—Pete and Vic

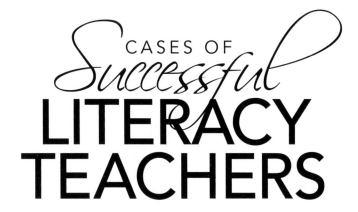

CASES OF *Successful* LITERACY TEACHERS

JAN LACINA & CECILIA SILVA

Texas Christian University

Los Angeles | London | New Delhi
Singapore | Washington DC

For information:

SAGE Publications, Inc.
2455 Teller Road
Thousand Oaks, California 91320
E-mail: order@sagepub.com

SAGE Publications India Pvt. Ltd.
B 1/I 1 Mohan Cooperative Industrial Area
Mathura Road, New Delhi 110 044
India

SAGE Publications Ltd.
1 Oliver's Yard
55 City Road
London EC1Y 1SP
United Kingdom

SAGE Publications Asia-Pacific Pte. Ltd.
33 Pekin Street #02-01
Far East Square
Singapore 048763

Printed in the United States of America

Library of Congress Cataloging-in-Publication Data

Lacina, Jan.
Cases of successful literacy teachers / Jan Lacina and Cecilia Silva.
      p. cm.
Includes bibliographical references and index.
ISBN 978-1-4129-5643-7 (pbk.)

   1. Language arts (Elementary)—Case studies. 2. Language arts teachers—Case studies. I. Silva, Cecilia. II. Title.

LB1576.L2425 2011
372.6—dc22   2009035795

This book is printed on acid-free paper.

10   11   12   13   14   10   9   8   7   6   5   4   3   2   1

Acquisitions Editor:	Diane McDaniel
Editorial Assistant:	Ashley Conlon
Production Editor:	Carla Freeman
Copy Editor:	Kristin Bergstad
Typesetter:	C&M Digitals (P) Ltd.
Proofreader:	Christina West
Indexer:	Diggs Publication Service
Cover Designer:	Gail Buschman
Marketing Manager:	Carmel Schrire

Brief Contents

Detailed Contents

4 Early Literacy Development

5 Vocabulary Development

8 Literacy Across the Curriculum: Strategic Instruction in the Content Areas   163

Preface

The celebrated children's author Patricia Polacco (1998) describes her struggles with dyslexia and learning to read in her autobiographical book, *Thank You, Mr. Falker*. In this book, Polacco brings to life her fifth-grade teacher, Mr. Falker, and the successful reading strategies he used to help her comprehend text. What impacted Polacco the most was Mr. Falker's belief in her, which changed her life forever. Excellent literacy teachers truly have the ability to change their students' lives—forever. The purpose of the present book is to highlight excellent literacy teachers, the Mr. Falkers across the United States. Our text provides teaching vignettes, cases for exploration, and research in the field that new and inservice teachers can use to reflect on effective instructional practices and how to best serve students in diverse schools across the nation. As a profession, we must find ways to mentor each other in order to recruit and retain the brightest and best teachers, and even more importantly to increase the academic achievement of all students. We must all strive to become the Mr. Falkers.

The Need for a Case Study Book

There is a great need for case study books at both the undergraduate and inservice levels in teacher education. Case study books allow for beginning and more experienced teachers to make connections between a problem in education and the research literature that can help them solve the problem. By connecting research to practice while intensively studying a case encourages teachers to become reflective practitioners. Studying cases provides teachers the opportunity to reflect on classroom dilemmas while discussing effective strategies.

Our book incorporates excellent teaching vignettes from classrooms across the United States, and connects these vignettes to a strong body of research. Each vignette is followed by a case for exploration to analyze this same research-to-practice connection. Our book is unique since we examine a wide variety of schools and programs. At the national level, millions of dollars were given to elementary campuses as a result of the Reading First legislation. With an emphasis on researched-based reading practices (Fletcher & Francis, 2004; McCardle & Chhabra, 2004; Shanahan, 2004), there is a need for case-based books that present reading practices that clearly connect research to actual classrooms. For that reason, this book can assist teacher education institutions and school districts to ensure that teachers understand, and implement, best reading practices.

This text was written for upper division undergraduate and graduate classes and inservice teachers who seek to connect literacy theory to practice in the classroom. The text is designed for college courses such as Early Literacy, Reading, Language Arts, and a variety of literacy-related courses.

Chapter Organization

Each chapter follows a similar format in order to provide cohesive chapter organization and to support a strong connection between research and teaching practice. Authors from different geographic regions wrote the *Inside the Classroom* and *Case for Exploration* sections of each chapter in order for us to include teaching vignettes and cases from a variety of states. The authors of these sections are:

- Chapter 2: Cynthia M. Schmidt and Catherine McMillan
- Chapter 3: Sandra Mercuri
- Chapter 4: James Salzman, Robyn Knicely, and Jeanne Schrumm
- Chapter 5: Patience Sowa
- Chapter 6: Donna Witherspoon and Julie Ankrum
- Chapter 7: Jan Lacina and Cecilia Silva
- Chapter 8: Theresa Harris-Tigg

Each chapter follows the following format.

Focus Questions: This section asks questions to help inservice and preservice teachers make connections between their prior background knowledge and experiences and the chapter.

Reading Research to Know: This section connects the vignette to research in the field of education.

Inside the Classroom: This section presents a vignette of how a teacher teaches a component of literacy. A detailed classroom vignette brings classroom instruction to life for the reader. Questions for discussion follow each vignette to help inservice and preservice teachers reflect on the teachers' instructional processes.

Summary of Strategies Used: This section helps the reader connect the vignette to classroom practice, while pointing out how to meet standards set forth in the International Reading Association's Excellent Reading Teacher Position Statement (2000).

Case for Exploration: This section presents a case, based on a situation that the vignette authors or their colleagues personally experienced. Each case presents a classroom scenario to stimulate discussion. Questions for discussion are listed at the end of this section to promote critical discussion of the case study.

Concluding Thoughts: This section summarizes the main points of the chapter for the reader.

Terms to Know: This section lists the specific educational terms introduced in boldface in the chapter.

Research That Works: This section includes a listing of current research in the form of books and journal articles that educators may want to read to investigate the chapter's topic in more depth.

Web Sites: This section includes exemplary Web sites that are helpful for educators interested in practical application.

The vignettes and case studies reflect research conducted in U.S. classrooms over a 2-year period. During that time, the vignette/case study writers interviewed many teachers and observed lessons taught at the elementary school level. The vignettes and case studies in this book reflect the whole of that experience. Some vignettes describe intact lessons observed; others reflect a variety of literacy strategies observed and discussed with teachers within a school.

The number of English language learners (ELLs) in elementary schools continues to increase. We strongly advocate that all teachers be prepared to meet the needs of ELLs within their mainstream classrooms. Throughout this book, we integrate strategies teachers can use to meet the academic, linguistic, and social needs of all children in their classrooms.

Acknowledgments

Cases of Successful Literacy Teachers would not have been possible without the mentoring and guidance provided to us by our SAGE editor, Diane McDaniel; her editorial assistant, Ashley Conlon; our production editor, Carla Freeman; and copy editor Kristin Bergstad. Diane walked us through the sometimes rough stages of revision, and provided detailed analyses of our work, while guiding us toward improvement. Thank you, Diane, for your detailed, thorough analyses of each chapter of our book.

We would like to thank the families from North Carolina, Pennsylvania, and Texas who allowed us to include photographs of their children in this book.

We also want to thank our graduate teaching assistants, who helped us with many different tasks as we wrote this book: Meaghan Burk, Ashlea Lambert, and Allison Haley. Thank you, too, to Petite Kirkendoll and Robin Shepherd at Texas Christian University, who also helped us with completing the book.

We are incredibly indebted to the reviewers of this text:

Kathryn L. Bauserman, Indiana State University

Diane Bottomley, Ball State University

Karen Bromley, Binghamton University

Karen Cameron, Nazareth College

Susan Jones, Longwood University

Jessica Kahn, Chestnut Hill College

Judith Lynne McConnell-Farmer, Washburn University

Audrey Quinlan, Seton Hill University

Jeannine Rajewski Perry, Longwood University

James Salzman, Cleveland State University

Elizabeth Saunders, Freed-Hardeman University

Patsy Self, Florida International University

Eleanore S. Tyson, University of Houston

Beth R. Walizer, Fort Hays State University

We also thank the teachers, children, colleagues, and our students who inspired this work—and the teachers and schools who welcomed us into their classrooms.

Jan Lacina and Cecilia Silva

CHAPTER 1

Introduction

Learning From Successful Literacy Teachers

I love my teachers! I want to give them a hug, Mama. I need to give all my teachers a hug.
—Grace Lacina, 3 years old (field notes, November 2007)

Grace recently, and quite often, has expressed her love for the teachers at the preschool fine arts academy that she attends. Teachers at her school emphasize reading, while focusing on good literature, each week of the school year. Children in the preschool classroom rotate from class to class, and excellent children's books are read and discussed in each content area (music, math/science, language arts, and art), with a common theme being emphasized throughout the curriculum. Students participate in plays about the books they read, while dressing in costume and acting out parts from the books. Grace recently enjoyed playing a goat in the *Three Billy Goats Gruff,* and her twin sister, Caroline, enjoyed acting as Mama Bear in the reenactment of *Goldilocks and the Three Bears.* The girls talk about literature after school, and ask for books at the library related to the thematic books they read in school. As a result, a love for reading permeates the school—and that love for reading transfers into early literacy success.

Besides an emphasis on reading and thematic teaching, this particular preschool recruits and retains excellent teachers. At the entrance of the school, prominently displayed on a large wall, are portraits of the teachers— with their years of service indicated below

Caroline and Grace participating in creative play

their pictures. Teachers in this school stay employed at the school for decades at a time because of the positive work environment, strong literature-based curriculum, teacher autonomy, and parental support. This school is an exception to schools across the nation, and offers a model that all preschools and elementary schools can use to achieve excellence.

Unlike in the school described above, new teachers often experience isolation (Levine, 2005; Little, 1982; Lortie, 1975; Waller, 1961), lack of resources, and the inability to manage a classroom of diverse learners—which often equates to burnout (Ashton & Webb, 1986; Farber, 1984; Fives, Hamman, & Olivarez, 2007; Friesen, Prokop, & Sarros, 1988; Tschannen-Morian, Woolfolk-Hoy, & Hoy, 1998). Educators refer to the high cost of teachers leaving the field of teaching after only a few years as the "teacher retention crisis" (Kersaint, Lewis, Potter, & Meisels, 2007). However, researchers also find that novice teachers, especially student teachers, who receive a high level of guidance and mentoring demonstrate lower levels of burnout (Fives et al., 2007). This book provides guidance, and mentoring, through the vignettes and case studies that illustrate effective literacy instruction throughout the elementary school grades. The following section describes why educators must begin to think of teaching as a profession instead of merely a job, and how this change in mind-set can change teaching into a profession.

Teaching as a Profession

Thinking about the types of teachers to highlight in this book, we reflected on the diverse academic, linguistic, and social needs children bring with them to the classroom. How can we prepare new teachers for teaching well in "hard to staff" schools, such as in urban and rural schools (American Federation for Teachers, 2007)? Teachers must be prepared for diverse classrooms with students with divergent needs, whether that includes social, linguistic, or academic needs—or any and all of these needs. As we considered the types of teachers to highlight in this book, we reviewed Csikszentmihalyi's (1990) important description of surgeons—and the very reason teachers, and more importantly the communities in which we live, must begin to think of teachers as more than transmitters of knowledge, but instead as professionals. Professionals stay current in their field—and meet the varying needs of the students they teach. Csikszentmihalyi (1990) describes the reasons why surgeons are viewed as professionals:

> But the surgeon has a chance to learn new things each day, and every day he
> learns that he is in control and that he can perform complicated tasks. The laborer
> is forced to repeat the same exhausting motions, and what he learns is most about
> his own helplessness. (p. 144)

The same can be said of good teachers and of the quality of schools in which they teach (Allington, 2006; Csikszentmihalyi, 1990). Excellent teachers find ways to learn new strategies and techniques to better meet their students' academic, linguistic, and social needs—to increase achievement. Besides learning about research-based strategies and techniques, excellent teachers find ways to implement this new knowledge to improve instruction (RAND Reading Study Group, 2002). Children's author Patricia Polacco (1998) explains the power of such a teacher in her autobiographical picture book, *Thank you, Mr. Falker,* as mentioned in this book's Preface. Polacco travels through her childhood, and shows readers the struggles she faced with dyslexia and learning how to read. This struggle continued throughout elementary school, until she met her fifth-grade teacher, Mr. Falker. Mr. Falker provided explicit and intensive reading instruction, but just as important, he developed a sense of community in his class. He built Patricia's self-confidence as a reader, and he taught her to love to read. Like Mr. Falker, good teachers find ways to blend research into effective practice in the classroom.

Society has long respected and valued the work of surgeons, and when that same respect and trust is placed in the hands of teachers, teachers can maintain a vigor and passion for teaching and learning (Day, 2000; Duffy, 1997). When administrators and school districts force prescriptive curriculum and policies on teachers and schools, teachers become laborers, with little passion and drive to teach and learn (Darling-Hammond, 1997)—and as a result, student achievement suffers.

Teacher Selection

The teachers highlighted in this book are the surgeons, or Mr. Falkers, of their schools, meaning they have a passion for teaching and learning, and the stamina to teach all students well. Just as important, they have a solid background and understanding of language and literacy. These teachers teach in both urban and rural schools, and work with diverse students with varying academic needs. We intentionally selected teachers from the following states: California, Florida, Missouri, Ohio, New York, Wisconsin, and Texas since these states offer a variety of school contexts. Teachers were nominated by building principals, district administrators, or by state Reading First centers. Exemplary teachers in this book taught in a wide variety of school contexts, and the list below describes the types of schools where they taught. Table 1.1 describes the type of schools we studied and notes the corresponding chapters that address each type of school.

TABLE 1.1 Types of Schools and Teachers Studied and Corresponding Chapters	
Type of School/Teacher	*Chapter Number*
National board certified: Teachers complete rigorous professional development training beyond state certification.	5
Reading First schools: Students in Reading First schools are typically from low-income families, based on the number of free and reduced lunches. These schools often have high teacher turnover rates, and receive federal money to implement interventions for struggling readers. They are located in both urban and rural areas throughout the United States.	4, 8

(Continued)

TABLE 1.1 (Continued)	
Type of School/Teacher	*Chapter Number*
Urban schools: Urban schools are located in an urban area and have high rates of poverty, high numbers of students learning English as a second language, and high numbers of students of color.	2, 3, 4, 7, 8
Suburban schools	5
Magnet school: Any student in the city can attend these schools. Typically, a lottery format is followed in which students' names are drawn—as a way to select the student population.	7
Rural schools: The National Center for Education Statistics defines rural schools as those serving small towns with a population of less than 25,000.	6

Excellent Reading Teachers

As we sought to recruit elementary school teachers who demonstrate excellence in the teaching of reading, we developed a list of qualities, based on the International Reading Association's (2000) *Excellent Reading Teachers: A Position Statement.* An excellent reading teacher makes a difference in a child's reading achievement and motivation to read (IRA, 2000), and for those preservice and new teachers who have not extensively observed such a master teacher, this book provides an in-depth examination of excellent reading teachers. For veteran teachers, this book provides current reading strategies and research support of the strategies and techniques teachers across the country use.

Excellent reading teachers possess a number of qualities that good teachers in general possess (IRA, 2000), such as ways to engage and motivate students while connecting students' prior background knowledge to current instruction. These teachers explicitly teach reading strategies to students, while scaffolding instruction when necessary (Allington, 2006; Frey, Lee, Tollefson, Pass, & Massengill, 2005). The many qualities possessed by excellent reading teachers are listed below, supported by a strong research base that we developed. We developed this comprehensive research base to correspond with IRA's *Excellent Reading Teachers* statements since the research to support the position statements was more than 7 years old (see Table 1.2).

1. Excellent reading teachers understand reading and writing development and believe all children can learn to read and write.

2. Excellent reading teachers continually assess children's individual progress and relate reading instruction to children's previous experiences.

3. Excellent reading teachers know a variety of ways to teach reading, when to use each method, and how to combine the methods into an effective instructional program.

4. Excellent reading teachers offer a variety of materials and texts for children to read.

5. Excellent reading teachers use flexible grouping strategies to tailor instruction to individual students.

6. Excellent reading teachers are good reading "coaches" (meaning that they provide help strategically) (IRA, 2000, p. 1).

TABLE 1.2 Excellent Reading Teachers Research Base	
Excellent Reading Teacher Characteristics (IRA, 2000)	*Research Base*
Understand the importance of the reading and writing process—and believe all children can learn	(Allington & Johnson, 2000; Anders, Hoffman, & Duffy, 2000; Blair, Rupley, & Nichols, 2007; Briggs & Thomas, 1997; Bukowiecki, 2007; Duffy, Roehler, & Herrmann, 1988; Haberman, 1995; Hoffman & Pearson, 1999; Knapp, 1995; Ladson-Billings, 1994; Metsala, 1997; Moll, 1988; Pederson, Faucher, & Eaton, 1978; Pressley, Mohan, & Raphael, 2007; Pressley, Rankin, & Yokoi, 1996; Ruddell, 1995; Sweet, Guthrie, & Ng, 1998; Taylor, Pearson, Clark, & Walpole, 1999; Tharp, 1997; Thomas & Barksdale-Ladd, 1995; Wharton-McDonald, Pressley, & Hampston, 1998)
Continually assess students—and link new material to prior knowledge	(Allington & Johnston, 2000; Blair, Rupley, & Nichols, 2007; Briggs & Thomas, 1997; Bukowiecki, 2007; Duffy, Roehler, & Herrmann, 1988; Fiene & McMahon, 2007; Gersten, Baker, & Shanahan, 2007; Haberman, 1995; Hoffman & Pearson, 1999; Knapp, 1995; Ladson-Billings, 1994; Metsala, 1997; Moll, 1988; Pressley, Mohan, & Raphael, 2007; Ruddell, 1995; Schumm, 2006; Sweet, Guthrie, & Ng, 1998; Taylor, Pearson, Clark, & Walpole, 1999; Tharp, 1997; Thomas & Barksdale-Ladd, 1995)
Know a variety of ways to teach reading, using successful research-based strategies	(Blair, Rupley, & Nichols, 2007; Bukowiecki, 2007; Duffy, Roehler, & Herrmann, 1988; Hoffman & Pearson, 1999; Knapp, 1995; Metsala, 1997; Pressley, Mohan, & Raphael, 2007; Ruddell, 1995; Sweet, Guthrie, & Ng, 1998; Taylor, Pearson, Clark, & Walpole, 1999; Tharp, 1997; Thomas & Barksdale-Ladd, 1995; Wharton-McDonald, Pressley, & Hampston, 1998)
Provide a variety of texts for students to read	(Allington & Johnston, 2000; Blair, Rupley, & Nichols, 2007; Briggs & Thomas, 1997; Bukowiecki, 2007; Duffy, Roehler, & Herrmann, 1988; Metsala, 1997; Moll, 1988; Taylor, Pearson, Clark, & Walpole, 1999; Thomas & Barksdale-Ladd, 1995; Wharton-McDonald, Pressley, & Hampston, 1998)
Use flexible grouping structures, and differentiate instruction to meet each student's needs	(Blair, Rupley, & Nichols, 2007; Briggs & Thomas, 1997; Bukowiecki, 2007; Fiene & McMahon, 2007; Gersten, Baker, & Shanahan, 2007; Metsala, 1997; Pressley, Mohan, & Raphael, 2007; Pressley, Rankin, & Yokoi, 1996; Ruddell, 1995; Schumm, 2006; Taylor, Pearson, Clark, & Walpole, 1999)
Provide strategic reading help to students	(Anders, Hoffman, & Duffy, 2000; Blair, Rupley, & Nichols, 2007; Briggs & Thomas, 1997; Bukowiecki, 2007; Duffy, Roehler, & Herrmann, 1988; Haberman, 1995; Ladson-Billings, 1994; McIntyre, 2007; Metsala, 1997; Moll, 1988; Pressley, Mohan, & Raphael, 2007; Taylor, Pearson, Clark, & Walpole, 1999; Tharp, 1997; Wharton-McDonald, Pressley, & Hampston, 1998)

SOURCE: Adapted from International Reading Association. (2000). *Excellent Reading Teachers: A Position Statement of the International Reading Association.* Newark, DE: Author.

Besides promoting a love for reading and writing, teachers must also explicitly teach reading and writing strategies to children. Across the nation, researchers find that teachers who hold a balanced literacy philosophy often do not devote enough time to the instruction and modeling of effective reading and writing strategies for students who are struggling to learn how to read and write (Frey et al., 2005). For more than a decade, researchers argued that successful literacy programs must balance teacher-directed instruction and student-centered activities (Au, Caroll, & Scheu, 1997; Freppon & Dahl, 1998; Pressley, Rankin, & Yokoi, 1996; Snow, Burns, & Griffin, 1998). Teachers in our text provide a balanced approach to teaching reading, while also explicitly teaching children research-based strategies that enable them to be successful readers and writers.

Ever since the publication of *Preventing Reading Difficulties in Young Children* (Snow et al., 1998), we have sought teachers who are exemplars of the teaching of reading because of the profound impact they can make in ensuring early reading success. Finding such a teacher for each of our preservice teachers was a challenge, and for each future teacher who was not placed with an excellent teacher, we felt as though we had failed. One of our former students, Sidney (participant self-selected pseudonym) describes why we must find cooperating teachers who not only understand how to teach reading, but are capable of teaching reading successfully to diverse groups of students. Sidney describes how she learned from her cooperating teacher how to teach reading strategies.

> We tell kids, "Remember the hand plan [previewing the text, stop and jot, one sentence summary, text evidence, and summarize] whenever you are going through and reading [benchmark tests]." My teacher takes ten points off if a kid does not use all five strategies. Some of those kids didn't actually need to [use the strategies] . . . and complain, "Miss this is a waste of time." But, you have to use the hand plan . . . or you lose the points. (interview transcripts, September 18, 2006)

In this description, you can see that the mandated use of specific reading strategies does not help children as they attempt to comprehend a story. The "hand plan" is an instructional strategy designed by local school district personnel as a way for students to remember five reading strategies: preview the text, stop and jot, one sentence summary, text evidence, and summarize. On each finger of the hand, the name of one of the reading strategies is listed. The instructional strategy is a good one; however, the way in which it is implemented in this classroom is not effective.

Sidney completed the student teaching experience at an urban school in the South. The school consisted primarily of African American (51%) and Hispanic students (43%); 89% of the students were labeled by the state as low income based on the high percentage of students receiving free or reduced-price lunch. Though the school received "acceptable" status from the state board of education, only 66% of the students passed the yearly reading assessment. Despite the teacher's familiarity with reading strategies, there was a disconnect between what research says about the teaching of reading strategies and how reading strategies were actually taught in this classroom. The teacher's requirement for students to use all five strategies when completing each reading passage indicates this misunderstanding.

Future teachers like Sidney need to be placed with an exemplary mentor teacher who knows how to teach researched-based reading strategies effectively; unfortunately, across the country, that does not always happen. Throughout the variety of vignettes in each chapter of this book, we showcase exemplary reading teachers from throughout the country, and the many ways these teachers met the academic needs of diverse student populations.

CHAPTER 2

Guiding Students' Literacy Success

Focus Questions

Prior to reading, try to answer the following questions:

1. What comes to your mind when you think of "literacy"?

2. Why and how do teachers assess students throughout a school year?

3. Think of an exemplary teacher you have observed teaching. How did he or she know if students were on track for their grade level—and how did this teacher differentiate instruction?

Reading Research to Know

As the era of No Child Left Behind comes to an end, the word *assessment* often invokes unpleasant thoughts of continuous testing and test-preparation instruction in schools (Allington, 2002). Since Reading First legislation, schools have been required to use standardized test results as a way for measuring **adequate yearly progress** (AYP). Schools that could not demonstrate AYP risked being restaffed and/or losing federal money to support their school programs. Many researchers question the validity of high-stakes testing since improvement on such assessments could be a result of more time spent on test preparation and students' ongoing familiarity with the test questions and procedures (Klein, Hamilton, McCaffrey, & Stecher, 2000; Koretz & Barron, 1998; Vacca & Vacca, 2008). More recently, Peter Afflerbach (2004) composed a policy brief for the National Reading Conference, which outlined research-based concerns for standardized testing—and how such testing does not give a clear picture of a child's reading capabilities. High-stakes testing also places English language learners (ELL) at a disadvantage since these tests do not take into consideration students' diverse language and cultural backgrounds (Gay, 2001; Gitlin, Buendía, Crossland, & Doumbia, 2003; Greenfield, 1997). For ELLs who have been in the country for only a few years, tests that are administered only in English present an unfair assessment of their learning and abilities (Lenski, Ehlers-Zavala, Daniel, & Sun-Irminger, 2006). For that reason, we are focusing this chapter on ongoing, and oftentimes informal and teacher-created assessments that can inform reading instruction. Such ongoing assessment gives teachers a full picture of a child's accomplishments and areas for improvement. Typically in literacy texts, the chapter that discusses assessment is left for the end of the book. As we discussed chapter organization and what preservice and novice teachers need to know about teaching literacy, we realized the importance of including such a chapter in the beginning. Teachers assess their students throughout the school year by using checklists, **anecdotal records, running records,** and **informal reading inventories**. While these terms are defined and explained further in the chapter, we want to emphasize the very importance of assessment since it guides instruction within exemplary teachers' classrooms. Based on the International Reading Association's (IRA's) position on excellent reading teachers, we examine the following aspects of assessment: use of flexible groups to differentiate instruction, continuous informal assessment of students, while linking new material to prior knowledge, and providing strategic reading help to students—by "listening in" to students (IRA, 2000).

Grouping and Learning to Read

Effective literacy teachers recognize the importance of grouping students for reading instruction, and such teachers often use **flexible grouping** to divide students into groups based on assessments of their instructional reading level and school district progress reports of reading. Effective teachers know they cannot teach children how to read effectively by relying solely on **whole-class instruction**, which is teaching a whole-class reading lesson in which all students are expected to read the same piece of literature at the same pace. New teachers often do not have the expertise to know how to group students, and frequently resort to whole-class instruction, or **ability grouping**. **Ability groups** are formed when teachers group students based on students' abilities or reading levels, and do not rotate group members. Twenty years of research document the negative results of whole-class instruction. When teachers teach using only whole-class instruction, individual student needs are not met; even more staggering, students are not given access to the material and knowledge that they need to learn (Goodlad & Oakes, 1988; Oakes, 1986, 1988; Opitz, 1998; Reutzel, 2003; Worthy & Hoffman, 1996). Whole-class instruction is a "one size fits all" form of teaching in which teachers teach students how to read using teacher-selected literature—usually from a basal textbook. All students read the same story, despite varying levels of success in reading and comprehending texts. Round-robin reading often occurs in such classrooms. **Round-robin reading** is when teachers have students read aloud from a text and move from student to student in a classroom—as each student reads aloud from the text. This type of instruction is not effective because students frequently focus only on their particular assigned oral reading and ignore the paragraphs read by their peers. Likewise, this type of instruction focuses only on oral fluency, and comprehension is disregarded.

In contrast, **ability grouping** places children in groups based on standardized test scores. Such groups are usually regarded as high, medium, and low reading groups—and teachers often give these groups names to try to conceal the different ability levels. Generations of adults remember the groups they were placed in during their early years of schooling, and such group names as Eagles, Robins, and Buzzards stick with children throughout a lifetime. No one wants to be a "buzzard." Despite creative naming of groups, children usually uncover the meaning of such groups—and learning that one is in the "low" group can be devastating and create lifelong self-concept issues (Eder, 1983; Hiebert, 1983; Rosenbaum, 1980). Just as in whole-class instruction, teachers often use round-robin reading in ability groups, and primarily select readings from class basals for students to read. As a result, students are frequently disengaged—while their self-image and peer groups are determined (Harp, 1989; Oakes, 1988; Wuthrick, 1990).

Flexible grouping is a way to group students into temporary groups based on their level of independence (Reutzel, 2003). Reutzel distinguishes the key differences between ability and flexible grouping strategies; these differences are highlighted in Table 2.1.

TABLE 2.1 Ability and Flexible Groups	
Ability Groups	*Flexible Groups*
• Identified based on standardized test scores. • Reading material is selected by the teacher, and reading revolves around basal texts. • Teachers give students low-level tasks. • Texts are read through round-robin reading. • Assessment decisions are based on standardized test scores.	• Independent reading in leveled books. • Reading material is chosen by the teacher and the student. • Use of leveled books and trade books. • Teachers give students a variety of high-level tasks. • Texts are read through guided reading and silent reading. • Assessment decisions are based on informal measures, such as running records, checklists.

Teachers use both leveled and trade books during **guided reading** instruction in their flexible groups. Guided reading instruction is one important component of flexible grouping. The next section describes what guided reading is and strategies for teachers to consider as they implement guided reading in flexible grouping.

Guided Reading

The term *guided reading* was coined by Irene Fountas and Gay Su Pinnell (1996, 2005). Guided reading is a way for teachers to support readers as they learn how to use new strategies for reading texts. In a guided reading group, the teacher works with a small group of students who are able to read similar texts at the same level. **Leveled text sets** are texts that have the same level of difficulty. A leveled text collection consists of set of books that range in difficulty from very easy books to books that have more complex plots and vocabulary.

A guided reading lesson begins with the teacher introducing the text and briefly discussing it. The teacher serves as a guide while the students read, noting the strategies students use to solve problems while reading the text. Teachers who use guided reading groups emphasize the importance of making meaning of the text while using reading strategies. Fountas and Pinnell (1996, 2005) describe the roles both teachers and their students take during guided reading, while noting the types of instruction used **before, during,** and **after reading**.

Before reading a text, the teacher chooses the text based both on how supportive it would be for the group of students and that it would present a few challenges. The teacher also spends time introducing the story—and poses questions for the children to think about while they read. At the same time, children are engaged in a conversation about the story, prior to reading. They make predictions about the text—and discuss questions they may have about the text.

During reading, the teacher "listens in" as students read the text. Effective literacy teachers "listen in" to students to assess children's reading fluency and comprehension while they read. These teachers help their students make personal connections to what they are reading—and talk in depth with the students about the story they have read. They also teach students how they can make connections to the text they are reading. One way to guide students to make such connections is to show them how to compare a story or a book to

Jessica Brown's prekindergarten dual language class, Westcliff Elementary, Fort Worth Independent School District

their own lives, making text-to-self connections. Other types of comparisons include text-to-text and text-to-world connections. Table 2.2 illustrates how children can examine a book and think of personal examples to connect to the book. Making connections helps guide students' understanding and comprehension of a text. While reading the text, the students read softly to themselves—and when they have a question they ask the teacher for help.

For students who are learning English as a second language, making personal connections to a text helps them connect their past experiences to the text they are reading. Lenski, Ehlers-Zavala, Daniel, & Sun Irminger (2006) emphasize the importance of teachers modeling to show students how to self-assess. These authors also suggest that students use a connections chart while reading a story or book, noting the connections they can make to other books, school learning, and to themselves. This strategy encourages students to read critically, making connections to their past learning, their selves, and books they have read in the past.

TABLE 2.2   Text Connections

What it is about . . .	What it reminds me of . . .
Owen & Mzee, by Isabella Hatcoff, Craig Hatcoff, and Paula Kahumbu It is about a baby hippo that everyone saves and how the baby hippo becomes friends with a turtle.	It reminds me of my best friend and how we do everything together. (t-s) It reminds me of the *Frog and Toad* stories because they are good friends too. (t-t)
What Happens to a Hamburger? by Paul Showers It is about what happens inside your body after you eat food.	It reminds me of eating somewhere like McDonald's. (t-s)
Mosquito Bite, by Alexandra Siy & Dennis Konkel It is about mosquitoes, how they grow, and what happens when they bite you.	It reminds me of when I am outside playing and get bit by a mosquito and my mom puts stuff on it so it won't itch. (t-s)
Actual Size, by Steve Jenkins It is about ways we can measure up against different animals.	It reminds me of the time I went to the zoo. (t-s) It reminds me of the article I saw in the newspaper about the really big tiger. (t-w)
Danger! Volcanoes, by Seymour Simon It shows many photos of volcanoes and lava.	It reminds me of when you shake a soda bottle and when you open the top, it explodes. (t-s) The lava reminds me of how bright the sun shines on a hot day. (t-s) It reminds me of the hurricane I saw on the news because they both can destroy property. (t-w)

t-s = text to self

t-t = text to text

t-w = text to world

After reading the text, the talk about the text continues. The teacher and children discuss their predictions—and they revisit the text to point out problems that need to be solved. During guided reading, teachers are continually assessing how students are reading, especially during and after the reading. As the teacher assesses student comprehension of the text and the strategies students use to solve problems when reading, the teacher makes decisions on how to instruct during guided reading.

In summary, effective literacy teachers model these important aspects of guided reading— before, during, and after reading with groups of students. Exemplary literacy teachers continually assess how students are reading, especially during and after the reading (IRA, 2000). As the teacher assesses student comprehension of the text and the strategies students use to solve problems when reading, the teacher makes decisions on how to plan future instruction.

Within a balanced literacy program, teachers teach reading and writing using a variety of reading methods and strategies. Teachers assess students continuously throughout the reading and writing process. Table 2.3 explains typical elements found in literacy classrooms throughout the nation. In such classrooms, teachers provide varying levels of support to their students. With kindergarten students there is a high level of teacher support, but as students progress and become more independent readers and writers, such support is withdrawn. The goal of such reading and writing elements is for all children to develop and become independent readers and writers. Researchers often refer to this event as a **gradual release of responsibility**. Table 2.3 shows the gradual release of the teacher's responsibility during literacy instruction—as students become increasingly independent readers and writers.

TABLE 2.3 Types of Reading/Writing and Levels of Teacher Support		
Reading/Writing Element	*Definition*	*Level of Support*
Reading aloud	The teacher reads a text out loud to children.	The teacher provides a high level of support while encouraging children to respond to the story and to pictures in the text.
Shared reading	Children read a text with the teacher. Typically, each child has his or her own copy of the text. Children often read the text chorally during rereadings.	There is a high level of teacher support; however, the students support one another as they find ways to read and make meaning of a text together.
Guided reading	Students are grouped in small, flexible groups—typically on the same reading level. The teacher selects and introduces a text, and the children read the text.	There is some teacher support, but less support is needed than with reading aloud and shared reading. Children problem solve as they read a new text— and they are mostly independent during guided reading.

Reading/Writing Element	Definition	Level of Support
Independent reading or silent sustained reading (SSR)	The children read silently to themselves or out loud to a partner.	Very little teacher support is needed—students are independent.
Interactive writing	Children "share the pen" with the teacher as they write. All children and the teacher participate in composing. Then, they read the text chorally—or together through a shared reading. Teachers often post the completed interactive writing in the classroom for further re-readings.	There is a high level of teacher support. The students decide on the message—and then each word (word by word) is composed by the entire group.
Guided writing	The teacher works one on one with a small group or the whole class by providing mini lessons on how to develop their writing. Such mini lessons could include: ways to develop crafting techniques (a lead, an ending, etc.), or ideas for developing content or refining mechanics.	There is some teacher support, but not as much as for interactive writing. The teacher acts more as a guide than as the instructional leader.
Independent writing	Students write on their own, independently.	There is little teacher support.

Teacher-Created Assessment

This section of the chapter will discuss how teachers can assess students' reading. We will not discuss fluency in detail in this chapter; however, we will examine informal reading inventories (IRIs) and ways that teachers can create classroom-based assessments. Additionally, we will discuss both why and how teachers keep running records, which allow teachers to keep track of students' reading progress throughout the year.

Informal reading inventories (IRIs) provide teachers with information about a student's reading level. IRIs do not provide a diagnosis; instead they inform classroom teachers which students can and cannot read well. IRIs have been used by teachers for at least 20 years, both those that are commercially published and ones that teachers have created themselves (Afflerbach, 2008; Paris & Carpenter, 2003; Pikulski & Shanahan, 1982; Walpole & McKenna, 2006). Commercially designed IRIs tend to have the following components: graded word lists, reading passages, and comprehension questions (Afflerbach, 2008). Many of these commercially prepared IRIs focus on **graded word lists**, which typically have between 10 and 30 words. The words on the lists are considered to be high-frequency words that need to be known for the grade level assessed. Key aspects of reading, based on No Child

Left Behind legislation, such as phonemic awareness, phonics, fluency, vocabulary, and comprehension, are also often assessed with commercially prepared IRIs. Graded word lists are usually the first section of a commercially prepared IRI. The words range in difficulty, and the purpose of the word list is to provide information on a student's decoding ability and sight word ability (Afflerbach, 2008). Based on a student's success or difficulty in completing the word list, teachers determine which reading passage the child will then read. This determination is often made based on a formula—and the specific formula seems to vary somewhat among the various reading inventories.

Next, teachers calculate the words that are correctly pronounced to determine the student's performance on the word list. The next section of the IRI is the reading passage, which focuses on students' ability to retell the story and to answer comprehension questions about the passage. Lastly, the silent reading and listening comprehension sections end the IRI assessment. This section of the IRI requires students to read and think independently from the teacher. Besides IRIs, there are a variety of other methods for keeping a record of student progress.

Anecdotal records are a way for teachers to keep track of student progress over a long period of time. They are also a way for teachers to note particular areas in which students need additional help or instruction. Typically, anecdotal records are brief and very focused. Comments are usually kept in chronological order—and over time a teacher can examine the comments to note areas of student strength and weaknesses. Table 2.4 shows a sample anecdotal record.

Anecdotal records are also an effective way for teachers to document "listening in" to students. "Listening in" is a way to monitor children's daily progress during guided reading.

TABLE 2.4	Anecdotal Record			
Day	*Kaitlin*	*Cate*	*Aiden*	*Jacob*
Monday	• Shared how she has developed a lead in her writing	• Prefers to work alone	• Having difficulty with memoir • Conference Wed.	
Tuesday	• Having difficulty generating ideas for writer's notebook			
Wednesday		• Does not want to share her writing with her table	• Working on sorting ideas • Prioritizing, outlining	
Thursday	• Found interesting ideas to write about in her writer's notebook; shared with her table			• Reviewed writing portfolio and evaluated his writing using the checklist for narratives

For example, during a guided reading lesson, a teacher may take anecdotal notes—noting whether students are able to identify chunks when they are decoding a word. The teacher may ask students to look at the word *har vest er,* to identify any *chunks.* **Chunks** are pronounceable parts of a word that can be recognized without an analysis of the word. When emergent readers examine chunks while reading a book, they are better able to pronounce polysyllabic words. When working with a guided reading group, teachers take notes on the strategies children use, and do not use, not only to decode words but also to comprehend text. Anecdotal records are an effective way to keep records of student progress.

Effective literacy teachers specifically monitor students' daily progress by "listening in" to oral reading and by taking running records to monitor students' word-solving strategies. **Running records** give teachers a way to analyze, record, and score a child's reading behaviors. Many teachers and researchers refer to Marie Clay's book, *An Observation Survey of Early Literacy Achievement* (2006), since Clay is credited with creating the idea and form of running records. Learning to take running records takes both time and practice, but such effort is worthwhile for both the teacher and the student.

How do you take a running record? First, you must find a quiet place to sit down one-on-one with a child. Typically, both the child and teacher have a copy of the text. While the child orally reads from a book that has already been read once or twice, the teacher records with a check mark those words that the child accurately reads. In some instances, the teacher will select a text that the child has not read before—especially in the context of a Reading Recovery program, which is a program that serves children who are struggling to learn to read and who need additional support from the teacher to achieve independent reading. In a mainstream classroom, keeping running records, the teacher records and codes the child's behavior while reading—and does not offer support or intervention while the child reads. The teacher serves as an observer in order to record the child's reading behaviors accurately. Teachers often find that keeping running records of students' ability to decode gives them a fuller picture of the strategies children know and the ones they need to know. For an in-depth examination of how to complete a running record, please refer to the reference section of this chapter. We provide a comprehensive list of Web sites, books, and articles that describe how to complete and score a running record.

Inside the Classroom:
Hawthorne Elementary School, Madison, Wisconsin

Cynthia M. Schmidt and Catherine McMillan

Like many urban schools, Hawthorne Elementary School is made up of children from diverse backgrounds: 30% Caucasian, 17% Asian, 14% Hispanic, 36% African American, 2% Native American, and 2% other ethnicities. Sixty-three percent of Hawthorne students qualify for free or reduced-price lunch. Administrators and staff are keenly aware that some of the linguistic and cultural differences among their students are often associated with lower standardized reading scores. However, the principal and teachers view the diversity in children's languages and cultures as strengths of their school community. They are concerned about students' reading scores, but assessment means much more than making adequate yearly progress (AYP) on standardized tests. Teachers at Hawthorne School use assessment as a tool to guide their literacy instruction.

The following vignette describes how one teacher uses her guided reading groups to connect meaningful assessment and instruction. Throughout this chapter, pseudonyms are used for all children to protect their privacy. Sarah Daines is a fourth-year teacher who is teaching a split second- and third-grade class with 17 students: 7 second graders and 10 third graders. Five of these children have individual educational plans (IEPs), one second grader receives additional reading instruction from a Title I teacher, and one child is in a talented and gifted program. Sarah team teaches with another second-/third-grade teacher, and they use flexible grouping to divide children from both class-rooms into reading groups based on quarterly assessments of each student's instruc-tional reading level and progress reports on the school district's Essential Outcomes in Reading (Opitz & Ford, 2001).

This quarter Sarah has three reading groups, all reading nonfiction books. Sarah has dif-ferent instructional goals for each group of readers, and she selects books from Hawthorne's extensive collection of leveled text sets to match curriculum goals and grade level outcomes, and to meet the needs and interests of children in each small group (Fountas & Pinnell, 2005).

During the 90-minute reading block, Sarah meets for 30 minutes with each of her three reading groups. At the beginning of the school year, Sarah worked hard to help her children learn classroom routines and develop the stamina to read and write independently while she works with one reading group at a time (Calkins, 2001). Some children are reading books in the library corner; some are reading and writing responses to books at small tables; others are reading along with books on tape to improve their fluency.

The general structure of a reading group involves an introductory teaching point or dis-cussion of the story, time for Sarah to "listen in" to individual readers, a final discussion to share thoughts about the text, and the introduction of the next text segment and a related comprehension strategy response sheet (Fountas & Pinnell, 1996). To an observer, the group time appears to have the natural rhythm of a conversation about the book; but Sarah uses the time efficiently and purposefully to teach and assess her readers. She uses three types of assessment tools to monitor children's daily progress during guided reading groups:

1. "Listening in" to oral reading and taking running records to monitor word-solving strategies

2. Taking notes related to students' comprehension and strategies used during discussions

3. Evaluating students' written products for evidence of strategies and understanding

After meeting with her groups, Sarah reflects on this information and writes anecdotal records related to the Essential Outcomes in Reading for each grade level. She keeps a checklist to help her organize and keep track of the anecdotal records related to these outcomes each week. Table 2.5 shows a sample list of Essential Outcomes in Reading.

TABLE 2.5 Essential Outcomes in Reading

Hawthorne 3rd Grade: Essential Outcomes in Reading

Uses reading strategies (rereads, reads on, self-corrects)

- Use multiple strategies
- Prior knowledge and context
- Apply all cues and text features to read for meaning

  - Apply punctuation cues
  - Self-correction strategies
  - Pictures, graphs, and diagrams
  - Information in the story
  - Titles and headings
  - Language structure
  - Apply phonetic principles

    Use knowledge of less common vowel patterns
    Use knowledge of letter-sound relationships

- Knowledge of different genres (e.g., less focus on absence of punctuation in poetry)

Applies comprehension strategies to independent reading

- Comprehend a variety of printed material

  - Make connections between previous experiences and prior knowledge, and reading selections
  - Make, confirm, or revise predictions
  - Ask and answer questions
  - Identify important ideas and provide support

- Compare and contrast settings, characters, and events

  - Recognize that characters can be stereotyped in a text
  - Organize information or events logically
  - Paraphrase information found in nonfiction materials
  - Use information to learn about new topics
  - Summarize important events/facts
  - Visualize
  - Infer
  - Determine importance
  - Synthesize

- Set a purpose for reading
- Preview and use text formats (e.g., headings, graphics, illustrations, indices, and table of contents)

  - Read text structures with fluency
  - Use story maps, Venn diagrams, webs, etc., to organize information
  - Select appropriate material and adjust reading strategies for different texts and purposes

- Identify author's and characters' points of view

(Continued)

TABLE 2.5 (Continued)

- Identify characteristics of different genres, including folk tales, biographies, social studies/science texts, poetry, etc.
  - Sequence plot in fiction texts
  - Compare and contrast characters in fiction stories
  - Compare and contrast lives of people in biographies and autobiographies

Reads aloud with fluency and expression

- Select appropriate material and adjust reading strategies for different texts and purposes
- Make connections between previous experiences and reading selections
- Apply prior knowledge and context clues
  - Read with expressive phrasing
  - Reread or slows to problem solve
  - Attend to punctuation
  - Attend to meaning
  - Apply knowledge of text features to interpret language structures
- Organize information or events logically
- Read text structures with fluency
- Identify the characteristics of different genres
  - Compare and contrast different genres

Reads books for enjoyment and information at an independent level

- Have stamina to read for at least 30–40 minutes
- Read from different genres, authors and topics
- Use information to learn about new topics
- Identify important ideas and provides support
- Set a purpose for reading
- Select appropriate material and adjust reading strategies for different texts and purposes

Reading Groups

Sarah convenes each reading group at the round table in the reading nook. Anchor charts describing the reading strategies they are working on this quarter are posted on the walls.

First Reading Group: Biographies

The first reading group consists of four girls who are reading biographies of famous women written at a fourth-grade level. We will hear more about this group of girls in the case study at the end of this chapter.

Second Reading Group: *Ant Cities*

The second group of children includes Jasmine, Stefan, and Marco, all second graders, who are reading *Ant Cities* by Arthur Dorros, written at a second- and third-grade level.

Sarah Daines, Hawthorne Elementary School, Madison, Wisconsin

Sarah explains her goals for this group:

We are working on the comprehension strategy of determining importance, but students in this group still need help in using their word-solving strategies. They get stuck on many words and have trouble coordinating their strategies, so I am working to help them monitor their understanding and use their strategies independently.

Sarah begins by asking students to summarize what they have learned about ants, but she spends most of her 30 minutes "listening in" to individual students reading. In the following scene, Sarah prompts Stefan to use his word-solving strategies:

Stefan: Their wings droop off.

Sarah: Does that make sense? Can you try that sentence again to see what word might fit?

Stefan: Their wings drop off.

Sarah: That's right. Now how did you know that word was "drop" and not "droop"?

Sarah praises Stefan for figuring out the right word, and she is also assessing his ability to explain his word-solving strategies. When Sarah "listens in" to Jasmine, she takes a running record of one page of text without prompting Jasmine to correct her miscues.

Finally, Sarah introduces the next section of the text, which students will read for tomorrow. "We are going to read about harvester ants." She writes *harvester ants* on the board, separated into syllables: "har vest er." She asks, "Do you see any chunks that you know? Can you say it with me?" Students read the word aloud together. Sarah explains that she has a text-to-self connection with harvester ants that she saw carrying off a dead beetle in her garden the other day (Harvey & Goudvis, 2007; Keene & Zimmerman, 1997). Jasmine and Stefan say that they have seen ants carrying bugs on the sidewalks.

Marco asks, "I wonder if harvester ants eat other ants or just different types of bugs?" Sarah responds, "Now that's an interesting question. Let's see if we find the answer when we read this next part of the book." Finally, Sarah introduces the response sheet for determining importance that students will fill out while they are reading the next section of text. (This response sheet is the same as the one listed below for group three.)

Later in the day, Sarah explains what she learned by monitoring children's oral reading and discussion today:

> Stefan corrected his miscue and was able to explain in his own words how he figured out the word was "drop" instead of "droop." I could see that he was using both graphophonic cues and meaning cues. That is an important goal for him; to self-correct and to take more control of his own reading strategies without prompting from me. I took a running record with Jasmine today because she does not seem to be making the kind of progress I expect in her word-solving strategies. I want to compare the running record with her other, more formal, quarterly assessments, to see if I can make a plan to help her improve during the remaining months this year. I was pleased that Marco asked an authentic question about whether harvester ants would eat other ants or just different types of insects. That shows me he is really thinking about what he is reading and making connections that are personal and appropriate.

Third Reading Group: *How You Talk*

The third reading group has one second grader, Erika, and three third graders: Cesar, Tanisha, and Daniel. This group is reading another nonfiction book at a second-/third-grade level related to science, *How You Talk,* by Paul Showers (1992). The book offers good material to support understanding of abstract processes; for example, drawings and explanations that are intended to help the reader understand concepts such as air flowing through the lungs. The children are all reading with reasonable fluency, and their word-solving strategies are in place. Consequently, Sarah spends less time listening to individuals read orally, and more time talking with the group about comprehension strategies for determining important ideas. The personal interactions among children in this group are more complicated than in the other two reading groups. Tanisha keeps looking around the room; Daniel is distracted by small noises; and Sarah has to work hard to engage the group in a worthwhile discussion.

Before meeting with the group, Sarah explains her focus for this lesson based on her monitoring of comprehension strategies used in recent group discussions:

When I ask them to retell, they just respond with random facts and they don't notice relationships among facts, so I am trying to get them to focus on the most important ideas . . . Sometimes, the problem is they are just not engaging or really connecting with what they are reading, so I am trying to make it relevant and interesting for them to learn about how sounds are produced when we talk.

In the following scene, Sarah tries to help students make relevant connections with the text by using their own bodies to follow the steps of breathing illustrated in the text. Sarah begins with a connection to their previous response sheets:

Some of you wrote on your response sheets that you liked the examples of experiments and diagrams in this book, so let's talk about one of those diagrams where the author compares how the air in your lungs moves in and out like the air in a balloon. How is the balloon in this diagram like your lungs?

There is no response from students, so Sarah asks students to "act out" the diagram in the text:

OK, let's look at the picture in the book, Now, everybody take a deep breath in. *[Everyone inhales.]* Point to your lungs. Now breathe out and point to your larynx. Can you feel how the air flows? *[Students are breathing in and out and touching their throats.]* Who can make a connection with this drawing?

Tanisha: I have blown up balloons.

Sarah: No, not just any connection, I want a connection that helps you understand this book.

Sarah is not getting the types of connections she wants from this discussion, so she shows students the response sheet she has already prepared to help them make stronger and more personal connections with the text. Table 2.6 is an example of such a response sheet.

TABLE 2.6 Determining Importance Response Sheet		
Determining Importance		
3 things I found out:	*2 interesting things:*	*1 question I still have:*
1.	1.	1.
2.	2.	
3.		

Sarah takes time when introducing this response sheet to emphasize the types of responses she expects through modeling and interactive dialogue with her students:

> Before we read on, let's talk about the type of thinking we want to show on our response sheets. In the first column, for three things I found out, let's write new things, not something you already know. Everyone write "Didn't Know Before" above the first column. Next, in the second column, two interesting things; let's put something that really surprised us. What should we write? Let's write "Wow!" in that column. Now, let's think of a really good question. What do you want to know about the larynx?

Cesar: I want to know everything.

Sarah: Try to think of just one thing that you really are interested in knowing or something that is confusing that you don't understand.

Daniel: How big is a larynx?

Erika: Can you talk without your larynx? I know someone who had an operation, and they put in a tube, and she couldn't talk.

Sarah: Now that's a good question, Erika. It is connected to something you know and something you are wondering more about.

Later in the day, Sarah explained what she noticed from monitoring this discussion and from reading students' written response sheets:

> During our group discussion, I noticed that Erika made a really good connection about someone she knew who had an operation. She was making the kind of text connection I want to see, one that is really helping her to understand the book. When I look at all the response sheets, I am still seeing some answers that are not thoughtful connections with the text. For example, all three facts that Tanisha wrote were about how babies talk. How babies talk is mentioned in this section, but it is not important, and it certainly isn't new information for her. When students write things like that I have to ask myself whether they are just not motivated to read and respond, or whether they do not see relevant connections in the text. At a basic level, the skill of "determining importance" is based on the types of connections they make while reading.

Both groups of students are working on determining importance in nonfiction texts. However, the conversations with Sarah show how she uses a more foundational comprehension strategy, making connections with texts, to teach and assess levels of quality in their comprehension of important information. Teachers at Hawthorne School have worked together to make assessment-based instruction more meaningful, and they use the rubric in Table 2.7 to guide their interpretations of students' comments and written work.

In this vignette, we see how Sarah changes the focus of her instruction for two different reading groups who are reading similar types of texts at the same instructional level. Although she follows a similar format for each group, she changes the focus of her instruction based on her continuing assessments of students in each group. Sarah keeps her instruction

TABLE 2.7 Rubric for Making Connections: Grades 2 and 3	
	Makes no attempt
Level 1 Minimal	Does not make connections with the text.
Level 2 Basic	Talks about what text reminds them of, but makes a superficial connection.
Level 3 Proficient	Makes a relevant/meaningful connection, but doesn't explain how it helps to better understand the book.
Level 4 Advanced	Makes a significant connection and explains a deeper understanding of the book.

focused by selecting only one or two teaching points for each guided reading lesson. She selects the teaching points based on her interpretations of the three assessment tools she uses to monitor progress for individuals in each group: "listening in" to oral reading, notes from discussions, and examples from response sheets. In conclusion, Sarah explains how she uses assessment to monitor children's daily progress and to guide her instruction:

I have learned how to use the Essential Outcomes as a general guide, and I have also learned how to listen and watch for important evidence that children are using their strategies to become more thoughtful readers. I write quotes and comments in my anecdotal records that show evidence of the type of growth I am looking for. Are children making important personal connections with books? Are children using their reading strategies for their own purposes? I want my children to grow as real readers.

Questions for Discussion

1. Sarah limits herself to one or two teaching points for each guided reading lesson. How does Sarah use evidence from the three types of assessment tools to determine her teaching points for the lessons in this vignette?
2. Notice the differences in the way Sarah plans and carries out instruction in two of the reading groups. Both groups are reading nonfiction books at the same reading level. What are the differences in these lessons?
3. How does Sarah use the Essential Outcomes to guide assessment and instruction?
4. How does Sarah use the Rubric for Making Connections to guide her assessment and instructional choices?

Summary of Strategies Used

Sarah Daines uses many effective strategies for monitoring students' reading progress. Similar to the International Reading Association's (2000) position statement describing excellent teachers, Ms. Daines continually assesses students, while linking new material to prior knowledge. She likewise provides a variety of texts for students to read, while focusing on the importance of reading and understanding nonfiction texts. Just as important, as noted in the IRA's (2000) excellent reading teacher position statement, Ms. Daines uses flexible group structures in her classroom to differentiate instruction to meet the academic needs of each child within her class. The strategies and methods for ongoing assessment are explained in detail in the next section of this chapter.

Case for Exploration:
Hawthorne Elementary School, Madison, Wisconsin

Cynthia M. Schmidt and Catherine McMillan

We have already been introduced to Sarah Daines and her classroom at Hawthorne Elementary School. This case study focuses on Sarah's first reading group, four girls whose quarterly assessments indicate that they read with good comprehension and fluency at third-/fourth-grade reading levels as they approach the end of the school year. Despite the similarities in their instructional reading range, we will examine the differences among individual students and the challenges they face as they read a book that is appropriate for their grade and instructional reading levels. All four girls are motivated readers. Rayna is a second grader; Colette, Eileen, and Kangying are third graders. Kangying is comfortable conversing with her friends in English, but Hmong, her first language, is spoken at home.

As you read this case, notice how Sarah works to develop thoughtful understanding rather than simply checking to see if students have a basic or literal comprehension of the text. Also notice how she differentiates her instruction for individuals while still maintaining a shared experience with the book.

All students are reading nonfiction books in guided reading groups this quarter, and Sarah has selected biographies of famous women for this group of girls. The girls have just finished a book about Helen Keller, and she is introducing a new book: *Georgia O'Keeffe,* by Linda Lowery (1996). This book will present challenges for the girls because there are many types of inferences to be made about the character's motivations. The author uses flashbacks, changing scenes and time periods, and there are many idioms and figures of speech describing the artist and her art. In the following scene, Sarah introduces the new biography to the girls.

Sarah:	Why do you think I would choose this book for us to read next?
Rayna:	It's about another famous woman.
Sarah:	That's right. Have any of you heard of Georgia O'Keeffe?
Eileen:	We will go to Georgia O'Keeffe Middle School for sixth grade.
Colette:	I think she is an artist.
Sarah:	You are both right. Georgia O'Keeffe was a famous painter and she was born near us in Sun Prairie, Wisconsin; and that's one reason the school is named for her. Now let's look at the book. Notice what the author shows us about the

setting at the beginning of each chapter. The first chapter starts, "New Mexico, August 1930." The second chapter starts, "South Carolina, October 1915." First of all, how do those dates connect with the life of Helen Keller?

The girls comment that both are women and they lived at about the same time. Sarah encourages the students to look through the book to see how the chapters are organized. Students notice that the first and last chapters are set in the 1930s, but chapters in the middle go back to earlier times in Georgia O'Keeffe's life.

Sarah: Have you read a book or seen a movie where the time changes like that?

Eileen: I saw a movie about a time machine.

Sarah: Well, no, this is different. Have you seen a movie where it starts at one point, and then goes back to an earlier time in someone's life?

Sarah explains how authors use flashbacks to tell a story about someone's life, and she and the girls talk about some movies they have seen that use flashbacks.

Colette: Like in Harry Potter?

Other students nod in agreement. Sarah asks the students to begin reading, and she "listens in" while Kangying reads.

After a few minutes, Sarah reconvenes the group for discussion. She begins, "Kangying asked a good question when she was reading. What does it mean on page 18, 'She pulled out her black charcoal sticks.' What are charcoal sticks?" Colette remembers that they made some charcoal drawings in art class. The girls talk to each other about those drawings and infer that charcoal sticks must be similar to the black chunks they used in those drawings. This group is comfortable talking about texts with each other; they respond to each other without much direction from their teacher.

In the next scene, Sarah introduces the girls to their first response sheet for this book. As we noticed in the earlier vignette, Sarah's students are accustomed to using reader response sheets to practice comprehension strategies and to document their thinking during reading. Table 2.8 is a sample of a reader response sheet.

> Your response sheet *[Sarah refers to the response sheet shown in Table 2.8]* asks you to write about three of the comprehension strategies we have been using, but I especially want you to focus on visualizing the scenes in this story because we are reading about an artist, and I think it will help us understand her story. There are some illustrations, but I want you to pay attention to the descriptive words that the author chooses and use your imaginations. *[Sarah directs their attention to the anchor chart on the wall that identifies different senses that might be triggered while trying to visualize a story.]*
>
> Remember that when we use the strategy of visualizing, we are talking about imagining with all our senses, not just seeing (Harvey & Goudvis, 2007; Keene & Zimmerman, 1997). Notice how the author uses words that appeal to your sense of hearing, smelling, tasting, and touching. What images does the author paint in your mind?

TABLE 2.8 Comprehension Strategies Response Sheet		
Comprehension Strategies *List the page number, story quote, and a note describing the strategy you used.*		
Connections (t-s, t-t, t-w)	My Questions	Visualizing

t-s = text to self

t-t = text to text

t-w = text to world

After this introduction, the girls collect their books and response sheets and move to their tables while Sarah convenes the next reading group. Later in the day, Sarah reflects on the discussion.

My main goal with this group of girls is to help them integrate their use of comprehension strategies. That is why I used the response sheet that includes three strategies we have been practicing. I am looking for evidence of their thinking during reading. As I was introducing this story, I wanted to be sure that they were not confused about the sequence of events because the author changes the settings and time periods using flashbacks. I used Kangying's question about charcoal sticks because I knew the girls could make connections to their own art projects, and I like to take opportunities for them to practice making personal connections. Also, I think Kangying learns more when there is group discussion among her peers. Kangying can decode many words, but she isn't always willing to ask about the meanings of unknown words. It helps her and all the others when we talk together about the meanings of unusual words. This book is tricky for everyone because of figurative language; for example, when Georgia O'Keeffe is painting pictures of apples, Alfred (Stieglitz) says Georgia has "apple fever." That will confuse all the girls.

The next day, Sarah showed me their response sheets, and explained her interpretations of their responses for each of the comprehension strategies: visualizing, asking questions, and making connections (Harvey & Goudvis, 2007; Keene & Zimmermann, 1997).

Visualizing

Despite Sarah's review of different sensory images, all students commented only on things they could see, and none of the visual images seemed to add to their understanding of the scene or the story. Sarah knows that the girls are able to visualize during reading in some texts, but they have not demonstrated their best abilities in this response sheet. Their responses are listed below:

Colette: Georgia's picchers are butufale.

Kangying: I can see the apples in the photographs.

Rayna: I can visualize Georgia painting the apples.

Eileen: I can see her paintings.

Asking Questions

Sarah was more satisfied with the quality of the questions the girls reported on their response sheets, because these questions gave Sarah better insights into what the girls were wondering and thinking about during reading. Some questions focus on the character's intentions, one focuses on the author, and Kangying's question indicates that she is wondering how to interpret the text. These questions give Sarah good ideas for the next lesson. Their questions are listed below.

Colette: Why does she think she is going mad? like crase?

Kangying: Are the shapes supposed to be real, like moving around?

Rayna: Why did it go back in time and then front in time?

Eileen: Why did she paint cow bones?

Making Connections

Sarah was not at all satisfied with the text connections her students wrote on their response sheets. The students identified differences among the types of connections they have studied: text-to-self (T–S), text-to-text (T–T), and text-to-world (T–W). However, their connections were not powerful, and they did not make connections that would extend their understanding of the text (see Table 2.7, "Rubric for Making Connections"). Three girls made connections to the previous story about Helen Keller, but the qualities of their text-to-self and text-to-world connections were superficial, indicating that students were not making meaningful connections when reading on their own. Notice the connections listed below.

Colette: T–S I feel like I go mad when my brother bugs me.

T–W Some people think they are mad (crazy).

T–T Georgia and Helen both have a problem.

Kangying: T–S I like painting.

T–W Her paintings are real.

T–T Georgia has courage too (like Helen Keller).

Rayna: T–S I think the flowers she painted look like firecrackers.

T–W A lot of artists paint flowers.

Eileen: T–S I like flowers.

T–W Georgia and Helen Keller lived at the same time.

When Sarah meets with the girls today, she decides to reread parts of the story with them to see if she can help them focus on Georgia O'Keeffe's problem as an artist and how she feels as she struggles to find her own unique style. She believes that the students need scaffolding to make meaningful connections with Georgia.

Sarah asks the girls to reread a passage from the text, as she read it aloud:

She noticed that this painting was made to please a teacher. . . . Other paintings looked just like the work of famous European artists. Not one painting was simply hers. She had no idea how to paint like Georgia O'Keeffe. (Lowery, p. 11)

Sarah asks, "Now what does the author mean by that when she says, 'She had no idea how to paint like Georgia O'Keeffe?'" At first the girls are silent, but Sarah continues to probe: "How do you think Georgia is feeling about her paintings?"

Rayna: She doesn't like her paintings.

Sarah: Why not? What's wrong?

Colette: She doesn't want to paint just like other people.

Sarah: That's right. She is trying to find her own unique style. Let's talk about that word *unique*. . . . What does it mean?

Sarah pulls out a dictionary and reads some synonyms for unique: "original, or different from others . . . special."

Rayna: Oh yeah, like she is trying to discover her style.

Sarah: That's right, Rayna. She is trying to discover her style. Now, let's read ahead and think about how Georgia feels when she is trying to develop this style.

Night after night, Georgia worked until the charcoal crumbled in her hand. Her fingers got so sore she could hardly hold a pen to write to Anita. "Am I completely mad?" she wrote. She wondered if drawing such strange shapes meant she was insane. Maybe this was not art at all. Maybe it was just crazy scribbles. (Lowery, p. 22)

Sarah: So how does Georgia feel?

Colette: She feels mad, but not like angry, sort of like when my brother makes me go crazy.

Sarah: That's a great connection, Colette. Her problem is that she is doing something new and original and she feels so discouraged that she thinks she is going crazy. When you finish reading this book, let's see if she solves her problem of trying to paint in her own unique style.

After this discussion, Sarah explains why she focused on rereading and interpreting those two sections of the text:

> I always try to return to the story itself, to reread confusing parts and work together to help students interpret and understand the text. I think that Georgia's emotional struggle to express her art is central to this story, but I have to find a way to help students make a personal connection. I knew that everyone was confused about "going mad." I had worked with Colette individually on that phrase and helped her think of a time when "something drove her crazy." She had an authentic connection with her younger brother, so I focused on that part to let Colette explain it to the others in her own words. After reading their response sheets, I could see that they were not making good personal connections with the character in this story, and that they couldn't understand or interpret her actions and motivations. This was the most important teaching point for today's lesson. Without a clear understanding of Georgia O'Keeffe, they will not be able to practice other strategies, such as visualizing or inferring themes.

Sarah knows this book presents comprehension difficulties. It provides an example of a typical dilemma that teachers face when selecting appropriate texts for their students. This book is interesting to the girls, because Georgia O'Keeffe is a famous woman who was born in their state. The book fits the curriculum requirements, a nonfiction text that is written at their instructional reading level. Students can recognize most of the words in this book, but the figurative language is confusing and the theme—Georgia O'Keeffe's struggle to express her own painting style—is elusive to these young girls. Each girl in this group brings her own personal experiences to this book, and the teacher is committed to supporting all her learners. Sarah explains her decision to use this text. "I know this book is challenging for the girls. On the other hand, I feel like we are working through some of the challenges that they will continue to face in their reading."

Questions for Discussion

1. Based on quarterly assessments, all four girls are reading third-/fourth-grade stories with reasonable fluency and comprehension. What differences do you notice among students? Are individual differences apparent in their response sheets? (Refer to Table 2.7, "Rubric for Making Connections," when you evaluate their responses.)

2. Sarah needs to make individual assessments of her readers, but she also wants to build community within the reading group. How does she balance these two competing needs in this case; for example, addressing vocabulary development with her ELL student?

3. Review the instructional decisions that Sarah makes in this case. How does her instruction respond to the evidence of assessment from discussions and written responses? Would you focus instruction differently? Why or why not?

Concluding Thoughts

Our nation and the individual states must consider giving the voice of student progress back to the classroom teacher. Teachers know which students are progressing, which are not, and what instructional decisions need to be made to help students better understand what they are reading. When teachers are given a greater role in this process, they can better impact student academic progress. Schools must allow teachers to look at the whole child when making educational decisions. Teachers can do this by keeping ongoing records of student progress, not merely basing educational progress on state-mandated assessment tests. Teachers like Sarah Daines use many effective strategies for monitoring students' reading progress throughout the school year. Her school encourages teachers to examine the progress of the whole child, and that child's progress throughout a school year. With such examination of the whole child, teachers make note of the ways the child decodes words, comprehends text, and makes connections to what he or she is reading. Based on such ongoing assessment, teachers make informed decisions about how best to plan instruction. Flexible group structures in these teachers' classrooms help them differentiate instruction to meet the academic needs of each child within a class. The strategies and methods for ongoing assessment should be a component of all elementary school classrooms—and for this to happen, states must rethink the dominant role of high-stakes testing in our nation's schools.

TERMS TO KNOW

Ability grouping	Graded word lists
Adequate yearly progress (AYP)	Gradual release of responsibility
After reading	Guided reading
Anecdotal records	Informal reading inventory
Before reading	Leveled text sets
Chunks	Round-robin reading
During reading	Running records
Flexible grouping	Whole-class instruction

RESEARCH THAT WORKS

Afflerbach, P. (2008). *Understanding and using reading assessment K–12*. Newark, DE: International Reading Association.

Cooter, R. B., Sutton Flynt, E., & Spencer Cooter, K. (2007). *Comprehensive reading inventory: Measuring reading development in regular and special education classrooms*. Upper Saddle River, NJ: Pearson.

Denton, C. A., Ciancio, D. J., & Fletcher, J. M. (2006). Validity, reliability, and utility of the observation survey of early literacy achievement. *Reading Research Quarterly, 41*(1), 8–34.

Fountas, I. C., & Pinnell, G. S. (2006). *Leveled books K–8: Matching texts to readers for effective teaching.* Portsmouth, NH: Heinemann.

Gottlieb, M. (2006). *Assessing English language learners: Bridges from language proficiency to academic achievement.* Thousand Oaks, CA: Corwin.

International Reading Association. (1999). *High-stakes assessments in reading: A position statement of the International Reading Association.* Newark, DE: Author.

Israel, S. (2007). *Using metacognitive assessment to create individualized reading instruction.* Newark, DE: International Reading Association.

Johnson, P. H. (2000). *Running records: A self-tutoring guide.* York, ME: Stenhouse.

McKenna, M. C., & Walpole, S. (2005). How well does assessment inform our reading instruction? *Reading Teacher, 59*(1), 84–86

Opitz, M. (2006). Assessment can be friendly! *Reading Teacher, 59*(8), 814–816.

Reutzel, D. R., & Cooter, R. B. (2007). *Helping every child succeed* (3rd ed.). Newark, DE: International Reading Association.

WEB SITES

Informal Reading Inventory: **http://lrs.ed.uiuc.edu/students/srutledg/iri.html** is a Web site designed by a classroom teacher. It is an incredibly helpful site for teachers interested in creating their own IRIs. The author leads viewers through specific steps for choosing books, determining levels, creating questions, and scoring the inventory.

Reading a–z.com: **http://www.readinga-z.com/assess/runrec.html** provides an easy-to-read description of how to keep running records. A coding system for keeping running records is shown and described in detail.

Southwest Educational Development Laboratory (SEDL): **http://www.sedl.org/cgi-bin/mysql/rad.cgi?** searchid = 194 offers a comprehensive chart comparing commercial informal reading inventories. The Web site presents solid research and materials helpful to teachers interested in learning more about reading assessments.

CHAPTER 3

Oral Language Development

Prior to reading, try to answer the following questions:

1. What are the basic components of language?

2. How might an understanding of language variation support teachers in creating rich oral language development environments?

3. What is the role of the teacher in supporting oral language development?

Reading Research to Know

The International Reading Association (2000) begins its position statement on the qualities that distinguish excellent reading teachers by identifying how these teachers understand reading and writing development and believe that all children can learn. Undergirding this understanding is the teacher's awareness of the ways in which oral language supports the development of reading and writing (Cook-Gumperz, 2006; Dickinson & Neuman, 2006; Dickinson & Tabors, 2001; Roskos, Tabors, & Lenhart, 2004). We begin the discussion of oral language by highlighting its key components. We then look at the role of the teacher in promoting oral language, and discuss three strategies that support its development in the classroom. We end the discussion with a focus on English language learners (ELLs).

Pragmatics, Semantics, Syntax, and Phonology

To promote language development, Wong Fillmore and Snow (2000) contend that classroom teachers must possess a basic knowledge of linguistics. This includes an understanding of the language systems involved in oral language acquisition: **pragmatics, semantics, syntax,** and **phonology.** While in the following discussion these components of language are presented in isolation, language users draw simultaneously from all systems when they engage in speaking or listening.

35

When children acquire the **pragmatic system of language**, they are developing the rules that govern the functions, uses, and intentions of language (Freeman & Freeman, 2004b; Kucer, 2009; Wong Fillmore & Snow, 2000). Children learn that in order to communicate they must take into consideration how language use varies depending on the participants and the social circumstances. Children's progressive development of the ability to use language to serve a wide range of human needs—**language functions**—has been well documented by Halliday (1973; see also Webster, 2004). Focusing on how children use language to accomplish different purposes, Halliday notes that children develop the following functions:

1. **Instrumental** (I want): Language to meet needs (e.g., child says "bottle" while pointing and reaching for a bottle)

2. **Regulatory** (Do as I tell you): Language used to control others (e.g., child says "bye-bye" while taking his dad's hand and moving toward the door)

3. **Interactional** (You and me): Language used to build personal relations (e.g., child says "I love you")

4. **Personal** (Here I come): Language used to express individuality (e.g., child says "pretty girl" when referring to herself)

5. **Heuristic** (Tell me why): Language used to learn about the environment (e.g., child says "What is this?")

6. **Imaginative** (Let's pretend): Language used to pretend (e.g., child uses language while engaging in pretend play)

7. **Informative** (I've got something to tell you): Language used to impart information (e.g., giving a report or writing a paper)

Children develop functions related to the exploration of self (**instrumental, regulatory, interactional,** and **personal**) from interactions in the home environment. The language functions associated with the exploration of the objective environment are learned to meet linguistic demands expected within the school environment (**heuristic, imaginative,** and **informative**). Effective teachers must take into consideration variations in children's linguistic experience and provide multiple opportunities for children to develop this wide range of language functions in the classroom. **Activity centers,** as we discuss later on, can be structured so that they provide children with the environments necessary to engage in language that supports the development of these functions. Furthermore, teachers understand their role in supporting children in learning those functions of language that are more tightly linked to schooling.

When children develop oral language they also develop the **semantic system of language**. This system governs the meaning relations among words, phases, or sentences (Freeman & Freeman, 2004b; Kucer, 2009; Wong Fillmore & Snow, 2000). As children come across four-legged, furry animals, for example, they develop the concept of dog. These encounters with dogs then become the basis for developing the word *dog*. With more experiences with dogs, children can understand that a *boxer* can also be a *dog* and that in some contexts, this four-legged animal might also be referred to as a *canine*. Semantic development also involves being able to understand how different words evoke different meaning (e.g., beautiful, gorgeous, attractive, pretty).

Excellent teachers understand that social contexts and experiences influence semantic development. Hart and Risley's (1995) work highlights the disparity in vocabulary between children from families with low socioeconomic status and children from higher socioeconomic families. These researchers followed 42 families—professional, working class, and welfare—for 2½ years. Comparing vocabulary growth among 3-year-olds, Hart and Risley found that the average child from a professional family had a cumulative vocabulary of 1,100 words, while the average child from a welfare family had 500 words. What is important about this research is that reading teachers understand that children from low-income families do not lack the ability to learn, but need more opportunities to develop the conceptual knowledge that leads to the vocabulary gains of their more affluent peers (Neuman, 2006).

Morphology refers to the study of words (Freeman & Freeman, 2004b; Kucer, 2009; Wong Fillmore & Snow, 2000). **Morphemes** are the smallest units of meaning in a language. In English, the word < dog > represents one morpheme. Morphemes that can stand alone, such as < dog >, are referred to as **unbound morphemes**. **Bound morphemes**, on the other hand, are those morphemes that must be attached to unbound morphemes. The bound morpheme /s/ is attached to the unbound morpheme /cat/ to signify plural. In English, morphemes can play various roles, depending on whether they modify syntactical information (e.g., *dogs*) or semantic information (e.g., *unhealthy*).

Teachers need to be aware that morphemes function differently across dialects and languages (Freeman & Freeman, 2004b; Wong Fillmore & Snow, 2000). For example, the morpheme < s >, used to signify third person, singular in English (e.g., *runs*) is often dropped in vernacular African American English (Wolfram & Schilling-Estes, 2006). Some languages have one morpheme per word. In Chinese, plural is expressed through a separate morpheme (Jia, 2003). Teachers who understand how dialects and languages vary also understand that these variations are not the result of linguistic deficits among their students.

The **syntactic system of language** sets the rules that govern how words are arranged within a sentence (Freeman & Freeman, 2004b; Kucer, 2009). While the main elements of a sentence include a noun and a verb phrase, each of these is further composed of other elements such as nouns, adjectives, and verbs. Knowledge of the syntactic system allows children to generate a great number of sentences (e.g., *The boy saw the girl. The girl saw the boy. Did the boy see the girl?*).

Syntax specifies which combination of words might be acceptable or not in a particular language. For example, using what he or she knows about Spanish, a child might say *the house red,* not knowing that in English that is not an acceptable way of structuring these words. Understanding syntax, however, is different from knowing the rules of grammar. Knowledge of grammar rules generally is the result of schooling activities.

The **phonological system of language** involves the rules that govern how sounds can be combined in any particular language (Freeman & Freeman, 2004b; Kucer, 2009; Wong Fillmore & Snow, 2000). **Phonemes**—the smallest units of sound that can signal differences in meaning—vary across languages. English has approximately 44 phonemes. Differences in phonemes allow English-language users to understand meaning differences: for example, the difference between /p/ and /b/ in **p**in and **b**in.

Dialects and languages can differ in terms of phonemic patterns (Freeman & Freeman, 2004b). Native English speakers from the South, for example, do not differentiate the vowel phoneme in /pin/ and /pen/. These speakers rely on context to distinguish these two homonyms. Similarly, because Spanish speakers do not distinguish between /d/ and /ð/, words such as *den* and *then* might be pronounced the same. Knowledge of phonology can help classroom teachers understand variation in children's pronunciation. Knowledge of phonology can also help teachers understand why phonemic awareness exercises can be difficult for some children.

Language Variation

Excellent reading teachers use their understanding of pragmatics, semantics, syntax, and phonology to understand language variation. Over the past 20 years research in sociolinguistics has been important in helping teachers understand the difference between **Standard English** and **non–Standard English** (Gumperz & Cook-Gumperz, 2006). Standard English refers to the variation of English that is socially accepted. Some consider Standard English to be the "correct" variation of English. From a linguistic perspective, however, all dialects— whether they are considered to be standard or not—are rule governed. In this sense, there is no such thing as right or wrong forms of English (Kucer, 2009). Standard English, instead, reflects the dialects of the dominant groups in U.S. society. Non–Standard English is considered a socially inferior dialect. Researchers focusing on language variation also use the term **stigmatized dialects** when making reference to dialects that are devalued in schools, business, government, and the media (Godley, Sweetland, Wheeler, Minnici, & Carpenter, 2006). Further, these same researchers document the damage that negative responses to stigmatized dialects have on teacher expectations of their students and on student academic achievement.

Excellent literacy teachers build on the linguistic diversity of their students to support the development of Standard English forms. They understand that adding a new dialect does not require that children abandon their home dialects. Teachers who understand dialect from this perspective support Ebonics speakers in acquiring an additional variation of English (Perry & Delpit, 1998). In the United States, the term **Ebonics** is commonly used to refer to Black English or African American Vernacular English. Effective classroom teachers, rather than judging Ebonics speakers as deficient or constantly attempting to correct them to use Standard English, validate students' home language. Delpit (1997) proposes that as part of the curriculum for all students, children engage in the study of linguistic diversity. Acting as "language detectives," children listen to radio and television programs and identify patterns in the ways different people talk. These can then be analyzed for similarities and differences. A similar activity can be conducted with children's books. For children's books that contain examples of dialect variations, please refer to the Banks Street Library Web site in the "Web Sites" section at the end of this chapter. To further support children in using Standard English, teachers can also make use of role-play or puppet shows.

An understanding of linguistic diversity is at the core of bilingual education programs. These programs aim at serving ELLs, one of the fastest growing student populations in the United States. Dual language programs, as we will see in our vignette and case study, aim to support children from different language backgrounds, English and Spanish in our examples, to become not only bilingual but also biliterate.

Role of the Teacher

Teachers play a critical role in supporting oral language development in the classroom. Teachers provide children with the opportunities for social interaction that are necessary for language development. Excellent reading teachers are particularly aware of the way in which they create **zones of proximal development** (Vygotsky, 1978). Vygotsky referred to the difference between what children can do with the guidance of an adult and what they can do by themselves as the **zone of proximal development.**

Structuring oral language development within this framework, teachers initially provide children with the amount of language support needed to accomplish a task. For example, in a science observation, the teacher might ask the children to predict which objects sink or float and initially provide the language to describe the event they are observing. As the children engage in the activity and understand the concept, the teacher removes himself or herself from the activity and the children continue to discuss and perform the task on their own.

A common thread among the research examining oral language development is the focus on the role of the teacher in promoting **real discussion** (Cazden, 1988). Real discussions, Cazden warns, are easy to imagine but difficult to do. When engaged in real discussions, teachers support children in exploring ideas and engaging in more talk. Real discussion also involves providing children with opportunities to decide when to speak and to address their peers directly. Real discussion contrasts with the teacher-talk behaviors most often observed in the classroom: asking known-answer questions—questions to which teachers already have the answers, spending more than two thirds of the time talking, and allowing children to speak only when called on. Teachers like Joey Mantecon, a first-grade teacher at Alice Carlson Elementary School in Fort Worth, Texas, create a literacy community by encouraging students to determine topics of conversation for classroom meetings. In these classroom meetings, children and their teacher discuss student concerns and formulate strategies or solutions to the concerns.

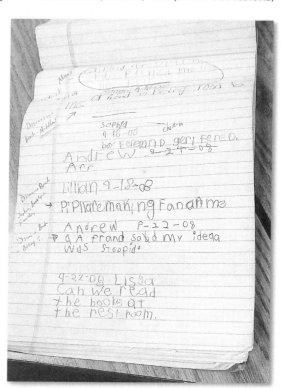

Student-created classroom meeting agenda

Supporting Oral Language in the Classroom

Excellent reading teachers facilitate oral language development in various ways. In the following discussion we highlight the role of **activity centers,** the use of **literature,** and the development of **thematic units** of instruction to enhance oral language development.

Activity centers support the development of oral as well as written language (Doctoroff, 2001; Neuman, Copple, & Bredekamp, 2000; Pellegrini & Galda, 1991, 2000; Petrakos & Howe, 1996). Classroom environments often provide children opportunities to engage in a variety of interest centers. Teachers vary the props that they make available at each interest center in order to promote the development of a wide range of language functions (Morrow & Rand, 1991; Petrakos & Howe, 1996). Play centers can be structured to reflect different environments where language is used (e.g., home center, bakery, restaurant, post office, library, etc.). Other play centers provide students with opportunities to manipulate materials (e.g., block corner, water or sand tables). A third type of center can engage children in oral language through the exploration of themes related to various content areas: art, language arts, science, social studies, music, and mathematics. Table 3.1 provides examples of how different language functions might emerge during work at activity centers.

TABLE 3.1 Language Functions and Examples	
Language Function	*Language Examples*
Instrumental: Language to meets needs	Asking for materials needed to engage in play or complete a project
Regulatory	Giving direction on how to build a structure in the block center
Interactional	Inviting others to participate in play or center activity
Personal	Sharing personal experiences
Heuristic	Conducting an experiment in the science center
Imaginative	Creating imaginary plays with puppets in the language arts center
Informative	Describing what happened during an activity at any center

Starpoint students at Texas Christian University discussing thematic-related vocabulary and concepts

Literature provides young children with limitless opportunities for developing oral language. Listening to the teacher read aloud not only is a comforting activity for the children, but it provides them with opportunities to hear language in its natural context and to develop vocabulary. A conversation around books is one of the timeless strategies that underpins language arts instruction for young children (Lapp, Flood, & Roser, 2000). The ability to read well aloud, Galda and Cullinan (2000) emphasize, requires some practice. These authors suggest that prior to a read-aloud, teachers become familiar with the book and practice reading it to develop quality oral interpretation skills (natural voice, inflections, enunciation, projection).

While teachers vary in their read-aloud styles, they often invite children to respond and discuss the book being read. These invitations provide teachers and children with the opportunity to engage in the real discussion that Cazden (1988) proposes. Kelly (1990) suggests three questions to begin such discussions: (a) What did you notice about the story? (b) How did the story make you feel? and (c) What does the story remind you of in your own life? Kelly documents how responses to these questions increase length and depth of student discussion.

In selecting classroom literature, teachers need to include **culturally relevant books** (Alanis, 2007; Freeman & Freeman, 2004a). Culturally relevant books relate to the children's background. Culturally relevant books allow children to more easily make predictions and inferences about the story being read. More important, students become fully engaged in the reading of the story when teachers use culturally relevant texts. Freeman and Freeman suggest that, in choosing culturally relevant texts, teachers and students ask themselves the following questions: (a) Are the characters in the story like you and your family? (b) Have you ever had an experience like one described in the story? (c) Have you lived in or visited places like those in the story? (d) Could this story take place this year? (e) How close do you think the main characters are to you in age? (f) Are there main characters in the story who are boys/girls? (g) Do the characters talk like you and your family do? (h) How often do you read stories like this? Please refer to the Web site section in this chapter for Web links to bibliographies with culturally relevant texts.

Thematic units of instruction provide another avenue to support oral language development. Classrooms that organize the curriculum around themes have the potential to provide children with access to academic **discourse**. Gee (2008) points out that, in spite of the emphasis on decoding skills in schools, children fail not because of their inability to decode but because of difficulties in handling **academic language.** The need to understand why children—linguistically and culturally diverse students in particular—are failing school, has propelled the education community to begin to understand ways in which children develop the language of schooling. Thematic units support teachers in helping students bridge everyday language and academic discourse.

Working With English Language Learners

Reading teachers today, similar to Mrs. Lee in the case study that follows, will often have the opportunity to work with ELLs in their classrooms. ELLs enrolling in schools today reflect different levels of English oral language proficiency. While some ELLs entering elementary schools might be at the beginning levels of language development, others enter with native-like language proficiency. In an attempt to ease the tracking of students' progress, one of the major professional organizations working with ELLs, the association of Teachers of English to Speakers of Other Languages (TESOL), described students' language development in terms of five levels (TESOL, 2006). Table 3.2 highlights key listening and speaking characteristics of language performance at each level. Excellent reading teachers understand that instructional activities must be differentiated so as to provide language growth opportunities to students at different levels of language development. Group work and the use of thematic units provide such oral language development opportunities.

TABLE 3.2	Levels of Language Proficiency
Level	Description
1	*Starting:* Students have little or no ability to understand or speak English. They respond to simple commands or questions and use single words or phrases to communicate.
2	*Emerging:* Students can understand and communicate through the use of short phrases or sentences. Discussions focus on familiar topics and situations.
3	*Developing:* Students understand more complex speech than they can produce. Students use simple sentences to communicate.
4	*Expanding:* Students understand most day-to-day communications. They communicate well in most situations. They might still have difficulty with academic concepts.
5	*Bridging:* Students understand language spoken in social and academic contexts with minimal support. They use language to express themselves in a variety of contexts.

SOURCE: Adapted from TESOL. (2006). *TESOL Revises PreK–12 English Language Proficiency Standards.* Alexandria, VA: Author.

In addition to considering levels of language development, teachers working with ELLs understand that, depending on the contexts in which language is being used; children demonstrate different types of proficiencies. Cummins (2000) uses the terms **conversational** and **academic language** proficiency to distinguish between the language proficiency that is required to carry on conversations in everyday situations and the language proficiency needed to perform well on school tasks. Research in second language acquisition demonstrates that ELLs will develop conversational fluency in 2 to 4 years, while the development of the advanced language competencies associated with academic language proficiency might require 5 to 9 years (Hakuta, Butler, & Witt, 2000). Classroom teachers who understand the difference between conversational and academic language proficiency use linguistic strategies and mediations to support ELLs in succeeding in school.

The role of the teacher in language development becomes even more critical in second-language learning settings. **Instructional conversations**, a model developed by Tharp and Gallimore (1991), aims at helping classroom teachers in moving forward with instructional goals while supporting children's participation in classroom discussions. The model, as the name implies, presents five instructional and five conversational elements. The instructional elements of the model include (a) a thematic focus, (b) activation of background knowledge, (c) direct teaching of skills or concepts, (d) strategies for eliciting more complex language, and (e) strategies for assisting students in supporting their arguments or positions. The conversational elements focus on the quality of the discussion and include: (a) few "known-answer" questions, (b) teacher response to student contributions, (c) discourse that connects across the discussion, (d) an atmosphere that challenges but does not threaten students, and (e) and teacher encouragement of participation without determining turn taking.

A strategy proposed by Mohr and Mohr (2007) to support oral language in the classroom asks that teachers "beckon, broaden, and build" (p. 447). After observing that newcomers were reluctant to participate in class discussion and their teachers were reluctant to engage them in class discussions, Mohr and Mohr developed a response protocol that sought to value student participation while providing teachers with scaffolds to develop more sophisticated language use in their responses. Scaffolds within this response model included the use of praise. Students were always asked to elaborate on their responses, and teachers who were faced with silent students were asked to provide longer wait time or to move on to ask other children to contribute to the response before returning to the silent student.

One of the ways teachers usually provide opportunities for ELLs to engage in talk is through the use of group work (Gibbons, 2002). Group work provides learners with opportunities to hear more and use more language. In addition, it provides redundancy, so that ELLs can hear similar ideas expressed in different ways. Teachers in second language learning classrooms often integrate cooperative learning models such as the one developed by Kagan and Kagan (2009) to apply the three principles considered essential to successful cooperative structures: simultaneous interactions, positive interdependence, and individual accountability.

Teachers working with second language learners also rely on the use of thematic instruction as an avenue to support language development. While thematic activities provide children with opportunities to use language for various purposes and functions across content areas, they also provide teachers with opportunities to engage students at various levels of language proficiency in common curriculum conversations (Kucer, Silva, & Delgado-Larocco, 1995). For example, in an inquiry theme focusing on erosion, all students can participate in similar experiments, yet the teacher can scaffold language differently to support students at different levels of language acquisition. A classroom that focuses around themes also provides opportunities to create language-rich environments where literature is at the core of all activities.

Inside the Classroom:
A. Doyle Elementary School, Central Valley, California

Sandra Mercuri

Mrs. Lee is a third-grade teacher in the dual language program at A. Doyle Elementary School, an inner-city school that serves approximately 1,000 students in a city in the Central Valley of California. The student population is 70% Hispanic, 18% Asian, 6% African American, and 6% White not Hispanic. Approximately 53% of the students are considered

ELLs. Teachers at this school have an average of 11 years of teaching experience, and 98% of the teachers are fully credentialed.

Doyle Elementary has two different program models to serve the needs of its students: English-only classes and dual language classes. Dual language classrooms integrate native English speakers with native Spanish speakers for academic instruction. Together they learn both English and Spanish, the native language of the ELLs. It is expected that all students enrolled in the dual language program will become bilingual, biliterate, and bicultural (Lindholm-Leary, 2002). Approximately 250 of the students at Doyle Elementary participate in the dual language program. Parents who wish to enroll their children in the program must undergo an application process. Many of the English-only families taking part in the program do not reside to the neighborhood and must also go through an inter- or intra-district approval process in order to have their children join the program.

Mrs. Lee's classroom is organized around thematic units of instruction. Words and ideas, thoughts and language, are inseparable in this classroom (Vygotsky, 1978). In Mrs. Lee's classroom some of the students are at the early stages of oral language development while others are more proficient. She is aware that the research on classroom talk not only shows its importance to the learning process but also documents how little talk actually occurs in classrooms (Nystrand, 1997). This is not the case in Mrs. Lee's classroom. Oral language development as well as reading and writing skills are part of her daily planning and instruction. Reflecting the research on effective practices, Mrs. Lee's classroom is engaged in a discussion that enables them to discover new ideas, see issues from new perspectives, and learn new strategies to deal with challenging concepts. Looking into Mrs. Lee's classroom we can see how she uses the classroom environment as a tool for learning and the ways in which she provides multiple opportunities for talk and interaction for the students of both language backgrounds.

Entering Mrs. Lee's Classroom

It is 10:00 a.m., and I am walking toward Mrs. Lee's classroom. I can hear the sound of classical music playing through the speakers around the school. As I enter the classroom I immediately feel welcomed. Respect and commitment to learn is the motto of this classroom. Mrs. Lee has created a community of learning in which each member is respected and valued. Every member of this community shares the desire to learn and to achieve great things together.

Mrs. Lee is the guide for this adventurous group in their explorations of the world. I sit quietly in the corner while the group engages in a discussion about plants:

T: In English we call this graphic organizer a tree map. The title is forest. If you are doing a listing you need to use a brace but not in this case because I am going to write a description of a coniferous forest. That's why we need to use a tree map. Which is the number one? How can we describe a coniferous forest?

S: It is cold . . . with coniferous trees. . . .

T: It's cold, dry. According to what it says on the board . . . it has coniferous trees, and . . . what else?

T: What are coniferous trees?

S: They have cones. . . . *[Barely audible]*

T: What would you write next on the tree map? What's the next forest?

S: Deciduous forest.

Aware that the classroom provides ELLs with the environment to develop academic discourse, she uses the science theme to support children in developing **content-specific vocabulary** or technical words that relate to a particular academic field (Freeman & Freeman, 2009).

Mrs. Lee's third-grade classroom includes 20 bubbling 8- and 9-year-old bilingual students with a language distribution of two to one (two Spanish speakers for each monolingual English speaker). The physical environment of the classroom promotes literacy and learning (Schifini, 1997). Each area of the classroom has been created for oral language development opportunities and has reading and writing materials related to the theme of instruction accessible to students at all times. The classroom includes a plethora of good children's books that are available for free voluntary reading, several computers, a smart board close to the rug area for quick lectures and read-aloud time, and several areas around the room for students to work comfortably. Four groups of tables are placed at the center of the classroom, where most of the learning and group work happens. The classroom pets—a fish, two turtles, and a crawfish—are placed at the center of the tables.

The room is filled with professional and teacher-made posters, class-made books, chants, and poetry charts. Materials are used by students and the teacher to further develop the academic linguistic abilities of the students as they discuss topics of interest, revise their own work, or engage in language experiences that enhance the oral skills of students at different proficiency levels.

In addition, well-defined content areas around the classroom are used for specific purposes. As you move clockwise around the room, you find a computer station and a whiteboard that students use to carry out research on topics of interest around the theme of study. This area is next to a language arts corner where students display their work and graphic organizers in both English and Spanish. This is also where they gather to receive language instruction. The teacher and students meet at the guided reading table every day to read and discuss literature corresponding to the students' reading abilities and interests. Through these activities, Mrs. Lee reinforces and further develops the oral language skills of her students.

In the science corner students find literature related to the topic of study. During this particular unit of study, the science corner is transformed into the Rainforest Corner (see photo on next page). Here students encounter a replica of the rainforest where hanging paper and photographs are used to represents the different layers. Photographs of animals and plants are attached to the different layers to indicate their habitat within the rainforest. On the wall to the right are maps where students locate the rainforests around the world. The thematic library on the wall to the left provides students with books in both English and Spanish. Reflecting an inquiry-based approach to science teaching, resources are used by the students for independent research on the theme they are studying. The back wall displays the graphic organizers that students created as a whole class during the introduction of new science concepts. This wall also serves to

Science corner in Mrs. Lee's classroom: rainforest

display student writing samples and includes research reports about rainforest animals or plants that students have self-selected to investigate.

A unique spot in this classroom is the student research corner. The research corner is used to display the students' science research. The teacher introduces the theme and provides resources for students to work on topics that are part of the science standards. The goal of the project is twofold. First, it focuses on writing a science report. Second, it requires an oral presentation. Academic presentations on individual research projects are used as an informal assessment tool by the teacher and provide students with the opportunity to use the academic language learned in front of the audience of the classroom. Classmates are expected to write down ideas presented by the researcher and ask questions at the end of each oral presentation. Opportunities for oral language development provide the foundation for more advanced reading and writing skills. Once the research is completed, students' papers are displayed. The classroom belongs to the students.

Oral Language Development in the Science Classroom

This teaching event starts with the students gathering at the rug to begin a science lesson about seeds. Mrs. Lee begins the lesson with a review of what the students have learned about plants in different habitats:

I want you to take a moment to share with your partner what we have learned about plants in different habitats. Using voice level 2, share with the partner you have been assigned to work with at the rug area one of the characteristics of plants that live in a specific habitat. Then, after you finish sharing, we will share a few ideas with the rest of the class to expand our knowledge about the topic. This will also help us when we are working with informational texts about the theme in reading and writing.

Mrs. Lee believes that social interaction is critical for oral language development and organizes her classroom to capitalize on the use of **simultaneous interaction** (Kagan & Kagan, 2009). By asking students to work with a partner to share what they know about habitats, she guarantees that at any one time half of the class is talking—or simultaneously interacting. Mrs. Lee further supports interaction by bringing into the classroom the management strategies that provide students with parameters for participation. She asks students to use voice level 2 when working with a partner at the rug, but reminds them to use voice level 3 to speak to the entire class so that everyone can hear. Voice level 1 refers to a soft voice so that other children are not distracted while partners work together.

Once the students have shared with each other, the teacher brings them back as a whole group to share with the class some of the characteristics of the plants that grow in different habitats (see Table 3.3). This opportunity to use academic language in an environment where they are more willing to take risks allows students to internalize vocabulary and be able to speak like scientists before tackling the science textbook. The foundation for reading was built through the oral discussion. The ideas shared by students and teacher during the oral discussion were organized in a chart under the big question: How do we distinguish plants that come from different habitats?

TABLE 3.3 Classroom Chart: How Do We Distinguish Plants From Different Habitats?			
Desert	*Tropical Rainforest*	*Coniferous Forest*	*Aquatic Habitat*
Cactus	Ferns	Pine trees	Rattan
Endure drought.	Diferentes plantas viven en distintas capas del bosque.	Existen diferentes tipos de pinos en el bosque.	Viven sumergidas en el agua.
Live in dry and hot weather.	Live in hot and wet weather.	Live in cold and snowy weather.	Live in humid weather.
Store water inside to survive during periods of drought.	Need high humidity and water to live.	Use water they need from melted snow.	Use the nutrients they need from the aquatic habitat in which they live.

This categorization activity has a double purpose. First, it focuses on the use of academic language by reviewing the academic concepts learned in the area of science. Second, it provides opportunities for students to review or expand their prior knowledge on the topic and to develop higher order thinking skills as they compare information on the different habitats through the oral discussion. Oral language development is a big part of all Mrs. Lee's instructional routines. Throughout the day, students have endless opportunities to discuss their knowledge or share what they have read with each other, modeling the language and enhancing their own language skills in different content areas.

Mrs. Lee also provides constant opportunities for vocabulary development, starting with oral language and then moving into reading and writing. Activities consciously planned for oral language development are the foundation for vocabulary acquisition. Mrs. Lee's oral language development part of the day always starts with a review of the previous day's introduction to key vocabulary.

Mrs. Lee's learning community did not just happen. The instruction, activities, and opportunities for interaction provided by the teacher with a focus on academic language development show that Mrs. Lee has drawn on her understanding of second language acquisition, bilingual education, biliteracy, and her experiences in the bilingual classroom.

Questions for Discussion

1. How does Mrs. Lee organize the classroom environment to support oral language development?

2. Mrs. Lee uses science themes to organize her curriculum. What are the advantages of using this type of curriculum organization to support first and second language acquisition?

3. Mrs. Lee structures opportunities for teacher talk and for student talk throughout the day. How might she decide when it is appropriate to use teacher talk? Student talk?

Summary of Strategies Used

The International Reading Association (2000) begins its position statements by acknowledging that excellent reading teachers understand reading and writing development. While the position statement does not explicitly acknowledge the relationship between oral language and literacy development, it is clear that Mrs. Lee understands that a classroom rich in oral language development supports reading and writing development. Mrs. Lee's curriculum and classroom environment provide a springboard for oral and written language development. Her curriculum is carefully orchestrated to support children in developing the language and literacy skills they need to deal with everyday living as well as with academic content. The International Reading Association also recognizes that excellent reading teachers offer children a variety of materials and texts. Mrs. Lee's classroom reflects this characteristic of an excellent reading teacher. In addition to making a great number of books available to the students, Mrs. Lee has carefully organized the classroom environment so that children have opportunities to encounter print everywhere, including her classroom walls. And in this classroom, books and print support all children in becoming biliterate in English and Spanish.

Case for Exploration:
A. Doyle Elementary School, Central Valley, California

Sandra Mercuri

Research has consistently shown that when compared to other models of second language instruction, students in dual language programs surpass others in their development of functional proficiency (Genesee, 1987). In dual language programs, second language teaching is embedded in a rich, meaningful communicative context. Dual language programs focus on the acquisition of language skills for academic purposes through the implementation of an integrated curriculum. In these settings students acquire second language skills and academic knowledge of the content areas.

Lisseth is a third-grade teacher with 13 years of experience teaching second language learners. For the past 10 years, she has taught in a dual language program in which she uses both English and Spanish. Spanish, her mother tongue, is used 80% of the day, and English, her second language is used during the remaining 20%.

Lisseth organizes the curriculum around themes that connect similar ideas and provides multiple opportunities for students to use the academic language of the disciplines during the day. Research has shown that teaching language through themes is an effective way to provide access to high-level content in the second language to students in dual language settings (Freeman, Freeman, & Mercuri, 2005). Because Lisseth understands how to support students at various stages of language development by using academic content as the medium of instruction, students develop an increasing competency for communicative purposes in her classroom.

Even though Lisseth's students are doing fairly well in acquiring both languages, there is a small group of students that is falling behind their peers in the development of academic language in Spanish. These students are unable to use the academic vocabulary introduced to the class in their oral presentations or in their written assignments. Lisseth knows that these students need extended opportunities to engage in academic classroom discourse in order to acquire language production skills. Lisseth understands that these students need more authentic opportunities for language use and knows that science inquiry supports this type of interaction and language development (Ellis, 1994).

Research has shown that the use of instructional strategies and activities that foster active oral discussions among learners and teachers are likely to be beneficial for the academic language development of all learners and more specifically for those students who are learning in two languages (Genesee, 1994). Staab's (1986) research has shown that teachers often become so focused in keeping to the planned routine, finishing the textbook, or preparing students for standardized tests that they forget about the relationship between oral language development and thinking skills. Consequently, they do not provide enough opportunities for the development of critical thinking skills that are so important for academic success. In well-constructed oral language activities students are able to develop oral communication skills, critical thinking, and reasoning abilities at the same time (Aiex, 1990). This is the case in Lisseth's classroom.

To enhance the acquisition of the academic vocabulary of science around the theme of plants and habitats, Lisseth organized several oral language activities with different scaffolds.

To introduce the textbook's key vocabulary she wrote the words on different-color paper (see Table 3.4). Content-specific vocabulary was written on blue paper. **General academic vocabulary** was written on yellow paper. General vocabulary, in contrast to content-specific vocabulary, cuts across disciplines (Freeman & Freeman, 2004b, 2009). While content-specific vocabulary refers to the specialized vocabulary of each discipline—such as *photosynthesis, anarchy,* or *plot*—general academic vocabulary refers to academic terms that appear across disciplines, such as *label, essay,* or *furthermore*. The words in the first group are easy to identify and are the ones teachers tend to teach more often because they are connected to a specific theme of study. The second group of words is more difficult for all learners, but especially for second language learners because they cannot be connected to any particular concept or theme. Content-specific words are usually presented with a different font in textbooks and are explained in a glossary at the end of the chapters. While content-specific vocabulary is needed for academic success, general academic vocabulary is even more important because it is used across all the subject areas. General academic vocabulary words do not show conceptual relationships that could make their comprehension and acquisition easier.

TABLE 3.4 Color-Coded Content-Specific and General Academic Vocabulary

Cotyledon	Esporas	Embryo	Germinate	Photosynthesis
Forms	Size	Cereals	Herbs	Cells

Lisseth applied what researchers, such as Linda Hoyt (2002), call **frontloading**, the process of introducing new vocabulary and discussing concepts before reading or writing about academic content. According to Hoyt, frontloading means learning about something, talking about it, wondering about it, and finally reading and writing about it. In this sense, frontloading helps students develop ideas instead of focusing on the words themselves. Frontloading is more than a cursory look at a few words before beginning a lesson. Frontloading provides background knowledge and understanding before attempting new learning. In an interview, Lisseth explained why she used color-coded information to help students understand and/or differentiate concepts that are abstract or difficult to grasp:

> It is important that students are exposed to different types of words, to learn about the meaning of words in different contexts and to be able to use them in the discipline or across disciplines effectively. I color-coded the information so it is easy for the students to identify the type of words we are discussing.

Mrs. Lee also refers to the complexity of teaching academic vocabulary in her interview:

> In academic discourse we find different types of words. Some words are specific to the subject matter and are easier to learn. Other words that are used in different content areas are more difficult to internalize because their meanings

may change in different contexts. These differences in vocabulary need to be explicitly taught and discussed with students starting at an early age. This is not easy for me as a second language teacher but I understand its importance and I am conscious about when I plan and as I instruct them. I always teach language, discuss about language and engage my students in meaningful practice of language contextualized in the teaching and learning of subjects such as science and social studies.

Lisseth is thoughtful in planning and delivering instruction. She focuses on using multiple scaffolds, especially with students who have not demonstrated the acquisition of the academic vocabulary. She provides the students with an engaging strategy to practice the academic vocabulary introduced during whole class discussions. Lisseth uses verbal–visual word association cards (see Figure 3.1) to support students in developing academic language. This activity requires students to select one or two vocabulary words from the content-specific or general academic vocabulary discussed as a whole class. Once students have created their cards, the oral language development activity starts. First, students are asked to use the think, pair, share cooperative learning strategy (Kagan & Kagan, 2009). Each student selected a partner to share and discuss the term they have defined, drawn, and

FIGURE 3.1 Verbal–Visual Word Association Card	
Word: **Germination**	**Drawing that represents the meaning of the word:**
Definition: When the seed starts to grow, the embryo pushes down into the soil, from which it absorbs water and minerals. The stem and new leaves push toward the light to continue to grow. The plant needs water, warmth, and nutrients from the soil as well as light to continue to grow.	**Word or words that remind you of the definition of the word:** Begins to grow Sprouts

thought about when making their verbal–visual word association card. During this exercise, students orally used the academic vocabulary of science as well as developed higher-order thinking skills. Working in pairs allowed students from different language proficiencies to work more comfortably with one another before they were required to share with the rest of the class. Lisseth further supported oral language development by asking students to participate in an inside–outside circle cooperative learning strategy (Kagan & Kagan, 2009). She asked the class to form two concentric circles, facing each other. Working with the person facing them, the students were asked to orally present and discuss their terms and answer questions from their partners about the vocabulary selected. After each pair completed this exchange, Lisseth asked the students in the outer circle to move clockwise and work with a second partner. Here the students again discussed their cards.

Once both students had the opportunity to share their cards, the teacher requested the outer circle students to move once again and share their cards with a third partner. This activity provided multiple opportunities for students to develop their oral language proficiency focusing on the academic vocabulary of science. This is an effective way for teachers to capitalize in both language and content development needed for school success.

Questions for Discussion

1. Lisseth has students at different levels of language development. What challenges might this present to a classroom teacher? How might teachers differentiate lesson plans for students at various levels of language acquisition?

2. Lisseth *frontloads* language. How is this different from teaching vocabulary?

3. Why might it be important to explicitly teach content-specific and general academic vocabulary?

Concluding Thoughts

In this chapter, we have focused on oral language development. We began by examining how language is composed of different systems and looking at language variation in terms of linguistic variations across these systems. We discussed the role of the teacher as critical to the development of oral language, and identified classroom structures to support children in developing a range of language functions. We then stepped into Mrs. Lee's and Lisseth's classrooms to see how these excellent reading teachers worked with linguistically diverse children at various levels of language acquisition.

TERMS TO KNOW

Academic language	Content-specific vocabulary
Activity centers	Conversational language
Bound morphemes	Culturally relevant books

Discourse

Ebonics

Frontloading

General academic vocabulary

Heuristic

Imaginative

Informative

Instructional conversations

Instrumental

Interactional

Language functions

Literature

Morphemes

Morphology

Non–Standard English

Personal

Phonemes

Phonological system of language

Phonology

Pragmatics

Pragmatic system of language

Real discussion

Regulatory

Semantics

Semantic system of language

Simultaneous interaction

Standard English

Stigmatized dialects

Syntactic system of language

Syntax

Thematic units

Unbound morphemes

Zone of proximal development

RESEARCH THAT WORKS

Diffily, D., Donaldson, E., & Sassman, C. (2001). *The Scholastic book of early childhood learning centers (Grades PreK–K)*. New York: Scholastic Professional Books.

Gibbons, P. (2002). *Scaffolding language, scaffolding learning*. Portsmouth, NH: Heinemann.

Isbell, R. (1995). *The complete learning center book*. Beltsville, MD: Gryphon House.

Kagan, S., & Kagan, M. (2009). *Kagan cooperative learning*. San Clemente, CA: Kagan.

Kucer, S. B., Silva, C., & Delgado-Larocco, E. L. (1995). *Curricular conversations: Themes in multilingual and monolingual classrooms*. York, ME: Stenhouse.

Staab, C. (2001). *Oral language for today's classroom*. Markham, Canada: Pippin Publishing.

WEB SITES

Annenberg Media: **http://www.learner.org/about/aboutus.html** provides multimedia resources to support language instruction.

Banks Street Library: **http://streetcat.bnkst.edu/html/dialectbib.html** provides a list of children's literature that contains dialect variations.

Colorín Colorado: **http://www.colorincolorado.org/educators/content/oral** outlines a step-by-step procedure for implementing Total Physical Response (TPR) to support ELLs in the beginning stages of language acquisition.

Do You Speak American? **http://www.pbs.org/speak/** documents linguistic variation across the United States.

Multicultural Children's Literature: **http://www.lib.msu.edu/corby/education/multicultural.htm** provides Web links to a number of culturally relevant book resources.

National Capital Language Resource Center: **http://www.nclrc.org/essentials/speaking/spindex .htm provides** language teachers strategies and assessments for listening and speaking.

Rethinking Schools Online: **http://www.rethinkingschools.org/archive/12_01/ebdelpit.shtml** features an article by Lisa Delpit on Ebonics; the article includes culturally responsive classroom strategies.

Teaching Diverse Learners: **http://www.alliance.brown.edu/tdl/elemlit/orallanguage.shtml** provides oral language considerations for ELLs and concrete examples of ways in which teachers can model language in the classroom.

Early Literacy Development

Prior to reading, try to answer the following questions:

1. How did you learn how to read?

2. What are some strategies that teachers use when teaching young children to develop as readers?

3. How do teachers teach a class that includes students at various reading levels?

Reading Research to Know

For more than 40 years, researchers have debated how best to teach young children to read (Chall, 1967; Goodman, 1965; Kim, 2008; Literacy Task Force, 1997; Pearson, 2004; Snow, Burns, & Griffin, 1998). Instead of focusing on the differences in positions, we have organized this chapter according to recommendations from the two leading international organizations: the International Reading Association (IRA) and the National Association for the Education of Young Children (NAEYC). In its position statement regarding the research-based qualities that distinguish excellent reading teachers, IRA recognizes that these teachers know a variety of ways of teaching reading and know how and when to use different reading methods to provide effective instructional programs. IRA further strengthened this position statement when joining NAEYC (NAEYC & IRA, 2005) to consider practices aimed at supporting beginning reading instruction. Excellent reading instruction, they emphasize, "must be appropriate and effective for *young* children, not just adaptations of what may work in the later grades" (p.1).

Learning to Read

Learning strategies for reading should begin before kindergarten; however, today's kindergarten classrooms include a diverse group of students with varying background experiences and abilities. Some kindergartners may be reading prior to kindergarten, whereas some students in the same kindergarten class may not know the letters of the alphabet yet. In kindergarten classes across the country, English language learners (ELLs) make up many prekindergarten and kindergarten classes. Because of the diverse experiences and backgrounds of today's young children, teachers must be prepared to teach reading to children at varying spectrums. The question that many novice teachers may ask is "How do I teach a class with students at various reading levels?" This section of the chapter will provide an overview of important literacy terms and methods for teaching early literacy.

Reading aloud to children and exposing them to a print-rich environment serves as a background for future success in school. The NAEYC/IRA (2005) position statement explains that there is no one method that is superior for all children; however, "Approaches that favor some type of systematic code instruction along with meaningful connected reading report children's superior progress in reading" (p. 13). For that reason, it is important for teachers to understand factors that influence reading competency, such as alphabetic principle, phonemic awareness, phonological awareness, phonics and word study, fluency, vocabulary, and comprehension. Besides these competencies, excellent reading teachers must know a variety of ways to teach reading (IRA, 2000), such as the importance of developing a print-rich environment and including the scaffolding of various reading strategies within the early literacy classroom for both monolingual and ELL students. Because vocabulary and comprehension are discussed in great depth in other chapters in this book, the following paragraphs will discuss in detail print-rich environments, strategies for scaffolding reading, phonological awareness and phonemic awareness, phonics, word study, and fluency. Likewise, the vignette and case study will take you into two elementary classrooms in different geographic regions of the United States to bring early reading instruction to life.

Past Literacy Perspective

Before we begin discussing the components of successful early reading programs, it is important to understand the former perspectives of teachers. Teachers of the past often had a readiness view of reading development (NAEYC & IRA, 2005), which means that children are ready to be exposed to reading and writing only at a certain stage of maturity. Teachers who held this viewpoint believed that exposing children to reading/writing before they were ready was a waste of time and even harmful to the child. In contrast, the NAEYC–IRA position statement describes this type of viewpoint as failing children because it places limits on what children can learn. Such outdated practices as only whole class reading instruction, isolated skills practice, and relying only on the reading basal are unfortunately still present in schools across the country (NAEYC & IRA, 2005). The following paragraphs will explain literacy development and effective practices based on solid research support.

Print-Rich Environments

Excellent reading teachers provide children with **print-rich environments**. Print-rich environments are known for the abundance of opportunities for children to develop an awareness of how written language works in a variety of contexts. In print-rich classrooms,

Environmental print in Joey Mantecon's first-grade classroom, Fort Worth Independent School District

teachers read to children and encourage the children to read a wide range of books—narratives, informational texts, poetry, and so on—and continue to support children in using environmental print to recognize words.

Teachers who seek to support children's literacy development are well aware of the need to make **literacy centers** a focal point of print-rich environments. Literacy centers provide individuals or small groups of children with the opportunity to participate independently in reading and writing activities. Well-designed literacy centers are packed with materials that promote reading and writing. Kindergarten, first-, and second-grade classrooms often have writing, library, poetry, puppet, listening, game, and technology centers. Children self-select the centers in which they want to work during the time the teacher has allocated to center time. Well-developed centers require that children work collaboratively and use language to communicate and engage in reading and writing activities (Neuman, Copple, & Bredekamp, 2000).

Effective teachers understand the importance of **environmental print** for young children, who can read words they encounter in familiar contexts—*McDonald's* on the sign for the restaurant or *Cheerios* on the cereal box (Kuby & Aldridge, 2004; Orellana & Hernandez, 1999). **Labels and directions** organize the classroom environment and also become part of the environmental print that supports literacy development.

Student-created labels in a first-grade classroom, Fort Worth Independent School District

Teachers, for example, make use of labels to identify literacy centers and the materials stored within the centers. In some kindergarten classrooms, rather than calling on children to take attendance, teachers ask that they write their names on index cards and place them on an attendance chart as they walk into the classroom in the morning. Bloodgood (1999) documented the value of such name-writing activities in promoting literacy development. Children apply information they know about their names when attempting to read other words that have the same letters. Name writing supports children in developing knowledge about the alphabet, word recognition, and concept of word. Directions can also easily become part of the environmental print in the classroom. For example, posted directions might provide information on how to use classroom equipment (starting the computer or CD player) or remind children of expected behaviors (Wet paint, do not touch!). What is important here is that the teacher supports the children in understanding how reading and writing are used on a daily basis and fulfill a wide range of human needs.

Excellent reading teachers extend the classroom's print-rich environment into the school community. Visitors walking into print-rich schools are immediately struck by the many ways in which teachers help children understand how reading and writing are used on a daily basis. At one of the elementary schools where we often work, kindergartners are in charge of labeling the "visitor" badges that are handed out in the office. As we move

Student-created recycling reminders, Alice Carlson Elementary School, Fort Worth Independent School District

through the hallways, children-made signs direct us to the library, the auditorium, and other key school locations.

Literacy is evident even in unlikely environments. In the bathroom, not only did we find signs that reminded us to wash our hands, but we were also able to read a child's explanation for fighting disease-causing germs. Similarly, at another school where we often work, each classroom has a mailbox and the kindergartners are in charge of delivering the school mail.

A print-rich environment can also extend into the children's homes through the use of FunPacks (Kokoski & Patton, 1997; Powell-Mikle & Patton, 2004). Best described as traveling learning centers, the FunPacks were conceptualized as a way to replace traditional paper-and-pencil homework and aimed at engaging students and their families in meaningful, hands-on literacy experiences. FunPacks are developed around a particular theme and contain children's books and all of the materials a family would need to engage in hands-on activities related to the book's theme. In addition, FunPacks include a journal to provide the families with a means to reflect and share their experiences as they engage in the readings and activities.

FunPack

Daily Routines

A print-rich environment becomes part of the learning experience only when teachers consciously lead children to engage with the available print through the development of daily routines. Three classroom routines often used with young children to highlight reading and writing include **morning message**, **word walls,** and **independent reading.**

Morning messages are developed as the children gather to talk about important events that are occurring in their lives (Payne & Schulman, 1998). The students watch as the teacher transcribes their message and makes observations about the written text as he or she is writing. Often the teacher has the children notice how several words might begin or end with similar letters. Such demonstrations are critical in supporting emergent readers in developing **sound–letter correspondence.** The acquisition of sound-letter correspondence requires that children understand how letters (**graphemes)** in written language correspond to sounds (**phonemes**) in oral language. In English, 26 letters represent approximately 44 sounds (Kucer, 2009). After transcribing the morning message, the teacher reads the message and invites the children to chime in as they recognize words that they know. In addition to highlighting letters and sounds, the teacher also takes advantage of these writing demonstrations to point out other spelling and punctuation patterns.

Word walls support children in learning to read and write **high-frequency words.** These are words that appear often in written text (e.g., *the, of,* or *and*) but are difficult for children to remember because they have no meaning (Cunningham, 2000). To create word walls, teachers divide a large wall or a bulletin board into sections; each section is headed by a letter of the alphabet. Teachers select about five high-frequency words to add to the word wall each week. In selecting words for the word wall, teachers often take into account those words that children repeatedly need when writing. What is critical here, Cunningham (2000) emphasizes, is that teachers not just display the words on the wall: "Teachers who 'do' word walls (rather than just have word walls) report that ALL their children can learn these critical words" (p. 60). To "do" word walls, teachers spend about 10 minutes each day writing, clapping, chanting, sorting, and engaging in a variety of games with the words that appear on the wall.

Another avenue to maximize reading opportunities in the classroom is through the implementation of independent reading. **Sustained silent reading** (SSR) or Drop Everything and Read (DEAR) are examples of independent reading programs. SSR and DEAR programs provide children—and teachers—with regular opportunities to engage with self-selected reading materials. These programs are well documented for their effectiveness in motivating and encouraging children to read (Krashen, 2004; Pilgreen, 2000). Essential to the success of self-selected reading programs is that the children have access to a variety of books and that they are provided with reading times on a regular basis.

Sustained Silent Reading at Starpoint School, Fort Worth, Texas

Scaffolding Reading Instruction

While programs such as SSR and DEAR provide opportunities for independent reading, excellent reading teachers know that they must structure the learning environment so that children move from most to least mediation and support. The following paragraphs discuss strategies for scaffolding reading to offer varying levels of teacher support—such as scaffolding through read-alouds, shared reading, and guided reading.

The single most important activity in the early years of schooling for future reading success is the amount of time children are exposed to books—and the amount of time these books are read aloud to children (Beck & McKeown, 2001; Bus & Van Ijzendoorn, 1995; Neuman, 1999; Wells, 1985). Children need to be exposed to a wide variety of literature, both fiction and nonfiction. For many children, literacy development begins early, while curled up on the lap of parents, as they spend many hours reading and rereading their favorite books. Excellent reading teachers capitalize on this natural interest and make story time an important part of the class schedule. **Reading aloud** is the most highly recommended activity for encouraging the development of language and literacy.

Read-alouds support readers in acquiring **concepts about print** (Clay, 1979, 1991; Holdaway, 1979; Stanovich & West, 1989; Teale, 1984). Concepts about print, a term coined by Clay (1991), refers to the elements about language and print that young children develop as they interact with books. These include the ability to understand that print carries a message and that there is a difference between print and pictures. Children who have developed concepts of print also understand that when reading, readers hold the book upright, turn pages one at a time, and read front to end, top to bottom, left to right. These children can also identify the book's title, author, and illustrator, and they understand the concept of word and the purpose of punctuation.

Read-alouds provide teachers and caregivers opportunities to involve children in actively discussing the book. Teachers can encourage children to experiment with language through creative drama and reenactments of favorite books, reading and writing together, and reading and writing individually. Pleasure and engagement, Sipe (2002) reminds us, must not be forgotten when using read-alouds. Sipe's research highlights five strategies to engage children in active participation: (1) dramatization, (2) talking back to the story (e.g., children shouting "Watch out" when Little Red Riding Hood encounters the wolf), (3) critiquing/controlling (children suggesting alternative plots, characters, or settings during a read-aloud), (4) inserting oneself (children assuming a role in the story), and (5) talking over (talking over the text and manipulating for one's own purposes, often involving humor).

Shared reading refers to the process by which the teacher and the children read a book together (Holdaway, 1979). Shared reading is often done with **big books**—oversized books that allow all children to see the print and illustrations and easily follow the reading. Teachers will generally read and reread a book a number of times over a span of several days. During shared reading, teachers invite children to make predictions about the text. As the children become comfortable with the text, they are also invited to chime in and read parts of the story. Shared readings allow teachers to demonstrate a number of reading strategies and language skills while enjoying a reading activity.

Guided reading (Fountas & Pinell, 1996, 2006), different from read-alouds or shared reading, provides children with instructional scaffolds that allow them to read text on their own. Working in small groups, students engage in texts that, while of interest and comprehensible to the children, provide them with opportunities to come across words or ideas that are unknown or not readily understood. The texts should provide children with the opportunity to develop and use problem-solving strategies while being supported by the teacher. We refer to these as instructional-level texts in the following discussion on fluency. Prior to having students read the book selection, the teacher introduces or reviews a strategy that they can use when encountering difficult text. Strategies focus on the use of all three cueing systems. Strategies can support children in using **graphophonic cues** and invite children to explore sound–letter patterns and other print conventions such as punctuation and directionality. Strategy instruction can also support children in using **syntactic cues**. When examining syntactic cues the teacher asks that students focus on what they know about English language structure and grammar to see evaluate if what they are reading *sounds right*. To focus on **semantic cues,** teachers ask that students use what they know in terms their own background knowledge and the context of the text. Here students are asked to evaluate whether what they are reading *makes sense* given the context in which it appears. Throughout this process, the teacher informally assesses her students, their literacy strengths, and areas that need improvement. Based on informal teacher observations, the school curriculum, state standards, and possibly state adopted informal reading inventories, the teacher then decides whether there is a need to plan and deliver explicit instruction in the area of phonological awareness, phonics, and fluency.

Phonological Awareness

Early experiences with print also support children in developing phonological awareness. The **phonological system of language** involves the rules that govern how sounds can be combined in any particular language. Phonemes—the smallest units of sound that can signal differences in meaning—vary across languages. Even thought humans can produce a large number of sounds, English has approximately 44 phonemes (Kucer, 2009). Differences in phonemes allow English language users to understand meaning differences, for example the difference between /p/ and /b/ in **p**in and **b**in.

   Phonemic awareness, a narrower concept within a discussion on phonological awareness, refers to the ability to focus on and manipulate language. In its final report, the National Reading Panel (National Institute of Child Health and Human Development, 2000) stresses the relationship between phonemic awareness and reading achievement. Children who have developed phonemic awareness are capable of (a) isolating phonemes: Tell me the first sound in *bear?* /b/; (b) identifying phonemes: What sound is the same in *bear, brown,* and *blue?* /b/; (c) categorizing phonemes: Which word does not belong: *bear, boat,* or *play?* (*play*); (d) blending phonemes: What word is /b/ /u/ /s/? (bus); (e): segmenting phonemes: How many phonemes are there in *cat?* (three /c/ /a/ /t/); (f) deleting phonemes: What is *sand* without the /s/? (*and*).

   Though most researchers and educators agree that there is a relationship between phonemic awareness and reading development, they disagree in terms of the best approach to support children in developing this awareness. Based on its review of the research, the National Reading Panel supports the use of direct instruction of phonemic awareness. While cautioning readers to make instructional decisions based on "reason, moderation, and situational factors" (National Institute of Child Health and Human Development, 2000, pp. 2–42), the National Reading Panel also highlights how children in effective reading programs did not spend more than 20 hours on phonemic awareness instruction.

The National Association for the Education of Young Children and the International Reading Association (2000) question the appropriateness of direct approaches for teaching phonemic awareness with young children. These professional organizations instead propose that rather than relying on formal training, preschool children should be sensitized to phonemic awareness through "listening to patterned, predictable texts while enjoying the feel of reading and language" (NAEYC & IRA, 2000, p. 8). In a publication of the NAEYC, Neuman et al. (2000) recommend that teachers use materials that are already part of early childhood settings—nursery rhymes, rhyme books—to promote phonemic and phonological awareness. The use of common classroom routines—such as dismissing children whose name starts with the same sound as *bear* and *brown* to go to centers—support the development of phonemic awareness. Other recommended activities include singing, finger plays, jumping rhymes, and clapping to syllables. Teachers, however, need to be intentional in integrating phonemic awareness tasks in the daily life of the classroom.

Phonics

As with phonemic awareness, the literature surrounding the teaching of **phonics** presents two different perspectives. Paralleling its findings on phonemic awareness, the National Reading Panel (National Institute of Child Health and Human Development, 2000) concluded that the use of explicit, systematic phonics instruction is fundamental to learning to read and an essential component of effective reading programs. Phonics instruction focuses on learning the **alphabetic principle** that involves knowledge of letter–sound correspondence and spelling patterns. The report supports phonics instruction in kindergarten or first grade and with children with reading difficulties. In a subsequent publication, three common reading programs are specifically identified as nonsystematic in terms of their approach to phonics instruction: literature-based programs, basal reading programs, and sight-word programs (National Institute for Child Literacy & National Institute of Child Health and Human Development, 2001). In response to these publications and federal government reading initiatives, many school districts adopted two commercial reading programs: Open Court and Direct Instruction (International Reading Association, 2007).

Example of student-created rime activity, Alice Carlson Elementary School, Fort Worth Independent School District

In its position statement on phonics, the International Reading Association (1997) acknowledges the need for learners to attend to the sound–symbol relationships as a strategy for word recognition. The IRA also raises concerns regarding prescriptive phonics programs that restrict teacher judgment in making instructional decisions as to what is best for students. Neuman et al. (2000) again propose that teachers take advantage of daily activities to teach recognition of sound–letter and spelling patterns. One way to do so is by drawing the student's attention to word families and some basic rules. Moustafa's (1997) work with **onset** and **rime** supports the notion of using word families. Onset refers to the part of the syllable that precedes the vowel in oral language, for example, /m/ in the word *man*. Rime refers to the vowels and consonants after the onset; in this case, /an/. Beginning readers, Moustafa argues, use knowledge of onsets and rimes to figure out unfamiliar words. This, Moustafa stresses, is done within the context of stories familiar to the children.

Building Fluency

For more than a decade, national experts have noted the importance of fluency and early reading success (Cassidy & Cassidy, 2005; Hasbrouck & Tindal, 1992, 2006; National Institute of Child Health and Human Development, 2000; Samuels & Farstrup, 2006). Each year, leading national reading experts vote on "what's hot" and "not hot" in the field of reading. For at least 5 years in a row, fluency was a "hot" topic in reading—and even noted by the experts as a "should be hot" topic (Cassidy & Cassidy, 2005, 2006, 2007, 2008).

What is **fluency?** Fluency means that children can easily decode words while reading, and use appropriate intonation and expression while reading. A student who struggles decoding word after word while reading, is not a fluent reader. For example, a student who reads a word such as "mat" as /m/, /m/, /ma/, /ma/, /mat/ and other words in a passage in the same way may be struggling with fluency. Children need to develop fluency in order to read words quickly and accurately—and this is important in order for students to eventually begin comprehending text (Samuels, 2002; Samuels & Flor, 1997). Fluent readers read words automatically and quickly, and can focus on making meaning of the text (Vaughn & Linan-Thompson, 2004). Why is fluency important? Researchers find that students who struggle with fluency also struggle with text comprehension since they focus on decoding words while reading, instead of finding ways to make meaning of the text (U.S. Department of Education, National Center for Educational Statistics, 2003). Fluency is an important component of the complex process of learning how to read. However, Hasbrouck and Tindal (2006) warn that raising a student's fluency score should never be the primary goal for reading instruction. They note that fluency is only one component involved in learning to read—and students should not be pushed to reach a particular percentile for their grade level.

To improve fluency, students need to work with texts on their independent reading level. How do you determine a student's reading level? First, have the student read a text that you think may be appropriate for her or him. Time the student reading for one minute, and place a slash (/) or bracket (]) after the last word the child reads in one minute; however, continue to allow the child to finish reading the passage. Then, calculate the total number of words the child read in one minute (WPM) (University of Texas, http://jabba.edb.utexas.edu/mainstep/orf/) and count the number of errors made by that child in one minute. Finally, subtract the number of errors from the WPM. The resulting number is the words read correctly in one minute—the WCPM. To calculate the percentage of words read, divide the WCPM by the WPM and then multiply by 100. The percentage of words read correctly is what teachers use to determine a student's reading level for a passage, the independent, instructional, or frustrational level.

Detailed information, videos, and practice in calculating students' reading level is available from the University of Texas's Mainstep Project, http://jabba.edb.utexas.edu/mainstep/orf/. The formula below is helpful for calculating the percentage of text students read accurately:

WPM (minus) Errors = WCPM

WCPM (divided by) WPM (times) 100 = %

Once students are familiar with the procedure for timed readings, they can begin recording their own progress on a chart.

When teachers are knowledgeable about their students' reading levels, they are able to use flexible grouping strategies to tailor instruction to individual students, as noted by IRA's (2000) *Excellent Reading Teachers*. **Independent-level texts** are those that students can read and comprehend with 95% accuracy. When working with students in a guided reading lesson or through one-on-one instruction, they can read **instructional-level texts**, which are texts that they can read with 90% to 94% accuracy. **Frustrational-level texts** are those that students read with 89% or less accuracy because too much time is spent struggling with decoding words. Students should not work with frustrational level texts (Vaughn & Linan-Thompson, 2004).

How do teachers find good books at a student's independent or instructional level? There are numerous Web sites that provide book lists for leveled readers. For example, McCarthy-Towne School in Acton, Massachusetts, has a well-developed leveled books site, http://home.comcast.net/~ngiansante/, that organizes books by authors' names and includes two or three different sets of levels within each grade. Reading A–Z also has a large selection of leveled books and downloadable leveled books at their Web site: http://www.readinga-z.com. The best-known list of leveled books is the Fountas and Pinnell Leveled Books K–8 Web site: http://www.fountasandpinnellleveledbooks.com. There is a fee for this site; however, they provide over 18,000 leveled books that can be sorted based on grade level, genre, series, or publisher. These authors include video clips of guided-reading classrooms and numerous activities that support the acquisition of fluency.

Activities That Build Fluency

There are multitudes of ways that teachers can plan instruction to build reading fluency. We will begin by describing the most effective and the strategies that we believe students are most engaged and motivated to do. In following Pressley, Gaskins, and Fingeret's (2006) recommendations, teachers should use a "try and monitor" approach when deciding on what methods of instruction to use and continue. In their study of the Benchmark School in Media, Pennsylvania, a school that uses evidence-based teaching to help struggling readers in Grades 1–8, the authors find that teachers in this school are successful since they are continually monitoring the methods for instruction they are implementing—and what works with their students and why. If a particular strategy for developing fluency does not work, these teachers try something else. As you read the following methods for fluency building, keep the advice of Pressley et al. in mind: Find the particular approaches that work for your students, and vary the approaches used to keep students engaged and interested in instruction.

First, **choral reading** is a simple and fun way to build fluency. Choral reading is when a group of students, or even an entire class, reads a text or passage together. Choral readings can involve reading a **Readers Theater** script, which is a story broken into individual parts for different characters. This is a fun and engaging way to read and to improve fluency for young children (Martinez, Roser, & Strecker, 1998/1999; Rasinski, 2000, 2003, 2006).

Carrick (2006) describes the many benefits of incorporating Readers Theater across the curriculum to build fluency. Readers Theater's repeated reading of a text helps children develop automaticity (Samuels, 1979), develop prosodic cuing (Schreiber, 1980), and additionally builds the lifelong skill of working with others through the cooperative learning (Johnson & Johnson, 1985; Slavin, 1987) effort of reading the theater script. In all, there are many benefits to incorporating choral reading and Readers Theater into the classroom, but most important is that these activities are a way for students to build better reading skills in order to become independent and lifelong readers.

Partner reading, or buddy reading, is another way for students to build reading fluency. This type of reading occurs when a child reads and rereads a text or passage with a peer. Other examples of reading with others includes **echo reading,** which means when a less fluent reader "echoes" a more fluent reader while he or she reads—and shared reading, which is when the teacher does most of the reading but children contribute to repeated lines or words throughout the reading. All of these methods for reading text are powerful ways to build fluency, and comprehension is also strengthened when students stop at selected times during the reading to discuss the text with one another or their teacher.

Teaching children common **sight words** is an additional method to help children build reading fluency. There are numerous ways that teachers can help students develop sight words to build fluency. Historically, Edward Dolch (1939, 1941, 1945, 1951, 1960) explained that children should be taught the words they see most often in text as sight words. He believed that learning sight words helped students develop automaticity, which is the ability to recall and recognize a word quickly and accurately (LaBerge & Samuels, 1974). Through extensive research, Dolch identified 220 words that made up between 50% and 75% of texts that children read—words like *the, a, and* in addition to common pronouns, prepositions, and verbs. Likewise, he found 95 nouns that are commonly used within texts for children (Pressley et al., 2006). As a result, these words became part of a large list of 1,000 of the most common words that children encounter in texts that they read.

Reutzel (2006), a noted scholar in the area of reading instruction, developed a hands-on method for teaching fluency—the **fluency development workshop**. Using the guidelines of the National Reading Panel (National Institute of Child Health and Human Development, 2000) and what students need to know to be fluent, effective readers, the following guidelines were established. Children need the following:

- Explicit, systematic explanation and instruction about the elements of reading fluency
- Rich and varied modeling and demonstrations of fluent reading
- Guided oral reading practice and appropriately challenging and varied texts on a regular basis
- Guided repeated and multiple rereadings of the same text
- Assessment and self-monitoring of oral reading fluency progress

- Information on how to "fix up" faltering reading fluency
- Genuine audiences and opportunities for oral reading, performance (Reutzel, p. 71)

There are many benefits to using Reutzel's model. First, the explicit nature of the model allows teachers to model and demonstrate fluent reading—while at the same time move beyond a teacher transmission model to a shared responsibility of learning with the students. Similarly, Reutzel's model was designed with the **gradual release of responsibility** model (Pearson & Gallagher, 1983), in which the teacher gradually releases the responsibility of explicit teaching as students become more fluent readers and writers. Researchers have well documented the importance of repeated readings, as discussed earlier in this chapter—and some researchers have even noted that those students who read a passage twice or more outperform their peers who read a passage only once on fluency and storytelling ability (O'Shea, Sindelar, & O'Shea, 1987; Sindelar, Monda, & O'Shea, 1990; Vaughn & Linan-Thompson, 2004). Group practice allows students, particularly the less independent readers, to learn this effective reading skill from the more fluent readers.

There are many instructional resources for teachers who are searching for fluency building lessons. The Vaughn Gross Center for Reading at the University of Texas provides free online resources as well as a wealth of materials teachers can purchase. For example, *Essential Reading Strategies for the Struggling Reader: Activities for an Accelerated Reading Program* (Allen, 2007) provides a wealth of activities that draws from strong early reading research (Snow et al., 1998), including the following components: fluency, phonological awareness, word study/spelling, and progress monitoring. There are many other commercial resources available for schools to purchase, as noted in detail in the Web sites and resources listed at the conclusion of this chapter. Additionally, there are many commercial fluency assessments used throughout the country; see Table 4.1 for a brief description of three of the most popular fluency assessments.

TABLE 4.1   Fluency Assessments

Assessment	Publisher	Description
Reading Fluency Monitor	Read Naturally	A progress monitoring system that allows teachers to follow students' fluency development through weekly assessments using grade-level passages. This is a onetime expense; it is easily implemented and requires minimal training.
National Assessment of Educational Progress (NAEP) Fluency Scales	National Center for Educational Assessment	A way to report a student's oral reading fluency. This measurement is divided into levels that provide descriptors of reading fluency such as phrase length and expressive interpretation.
Dynamic Indicators of Basic Early Learning (DIBELS)	University of Oregon	A set of strategies for assessing the acquisition of literacy skills for students in kindergarten through sixth grade. These short (1-minute) measures are used as a form of consistent, regular monitoring.

Working With English Language Learners

Second language learners benefit from the same print-rich environments as their native-English-speaking peers. Teachers working with second language learners, however, ought to take into consideration the following points.

Children who have the opportunity to develop literacy in the home language use their knowledge of the first language to support the development of reading in the second language. In its review of the research literature, the National Literacy Panel on Language-Minority Children and Youth (Francis, Lesaux, & August, 2006) identified three specific areas where language transfers: "Rather than confusing children, as some have feared, reading instruction in a familiar language may serve as a bridge to success in English because decoding, sound blending, and generic comprehension strategies clearly transfer between languages that use phonetic orthographies" (p. 397). Similarly, bilingual readers are capable of transferring strategies they use to process text from the first to the second language. Regardless of the language, children use background knowledge to make reading predictions, they make inferences and they draw conclusions while reading (Jiménez, Garcia, & Pearson, 1996; Kucer, 1995). While reading teachers are not generally in the position to make policy decisions as to the types of programs offered to English language learners in schools, it is important that they understand that a child's first language can support the development of the second language.

When teaching reading in the second language, teachers working with ELLs are particularly mindful that these students are acquiring a new language and learning how to read at the same time. While instruction that integrates reading, writing, listening, and speaking undergirds the curriculum in monolingual early literacy settings, teachers working with ELLs know that they must magnify these opportunities in order to support children in developing both language and literacy. ELLs benefit from activities that support them in developing the background knowledge needed to make sense of written English. Here we again emphasize the effectiveness of read-alouds, shared reading, and guided reading as instructional structures to support the mediation of language and literacy. These strategies provide ELLs with ample opportunities to focus on meaning, while engaging in rich discussions around text and providing opportunities to develop reading strategies.

As with teaching reading to monolingual English speakers, the role of phonemic awareness and phonic instruction is also a matter of debate within second language learning settings. Schools receiving funds from the federal government for the implementation of early literacy programs must include programs that systematically and explicitly focus instruction on phonemic awareness and phonics (U.S. Department of Education, 2008). While narrowly focused programs are widely implemented, the limited research available does not offer wide support for their implementation. For example, the National Literacy Panel on Language-Minority Children and Youths report states, "Clearly, five small studies of phonological awareness and phonics are far from sufficient to allow a determination of the most useful instructional methods for meeting the early literacy needs of English-language learners" (Shanahan & Beck, 2006, p. 427). Researchers recommend that the teaching of these linguistic features occur within the context of reading through the use of strategies that support children in exploring letters and sounds while focusing on meaning (de la Luz Reyes, 1991; Freeman & Freeman, 2004b; Kucer & Silva, 1999, 2006). As these students become more proficient in English, teachers can engage them in strategies to examine letter–sound generalizations rather than focusing on phonics rules.

One strategy often used to support ELLs' reading development not mentioned in the discussion thus far, and also applicable to monolingual emergent readers, is known as the **language experience approach** (Peregoy & Boyle, 2005). Within this approach the teacher generally begins the lesson by providing children with an experience that will generate material for a rich discussion. Experiences can be as involved as a trip to the zoo or they can focus on activities within the daily life of the classroom, such as a science experiment or the retelling of an event or a story. Following the discussion, the teacher records what the students dictate about the experience. As each statement is transcribed, the teacher takes the opportunity to **think aloud** and draws the children's attention to concepts of print and exploring letters and sounds. When the children have completed the dictation, the teacher reads the statement back to the students. The students then read and reread their own statements. This approach is most supportive of ELLs in that it taps into the students' own experiences. It also allows readers to see how they can put into print and then read statements that they can express orally.

In the following vignettes, you will read about successful reading programs in two very different parts of the country. The first vignette examines fluency instruction at a Reading First School in Ohio, while the second vignette describes a very different school, an exemplary university laboratory school in Florida. Both schools are racially and linguistically diverse, and they both showcase ways that teachers work with individual students to develop fluency and phonological awareness. By closely examining two diverse vignettes from different parts of the country, one can see the connection between effective practice and exemplary teaching.

Inside the Classroom, Vignette I:
Masson Elementary School, Lorain, Ohio

James Salzman and Robyn Knicely

Lorain City Schools (LCS) is a large, urban district located near Lake Erie, just west of Cleveland, Ohio. Masson Elementary School, a Reading First School, is one of the largest elementary schools in the LCS system. It has approximately 490 students, which includes the largest population of ELL learners as well as special needs students in the district. It is a K–6 building, where approximately 80% of the students are eligible free or reduced-price lunch. The teaching staff is made up of dedicated, mostly veteran teachers who care deeply about their students. Despite the dedication, this school fails consistently in academic improvement on achievement scores year after year according to the Ohio Department of Education (ODE). What does this mean for teachers at Masson Elementary? They must work harder to get their students' scores up! Four years ago, Masson Elementary was selected to receive Reading First funding from the federal government because of its low achievement scores.

At 8 a.m., the students scurry down the hallway, ready to begin their day, the bell clanging in their ears. Mrs. Shreve's third-grade students grab their breakfast and pour into the classroom anxious to start their day. The students know the routine. It's 8:30 a.m. and they are now seated at their desks chomping at the bit to read their poetry for the morning. Mrs. Shreve pulls up her collection of poems on the interactive whiteboard and tells the students they are going to read "Food Fight," by Ken Nesbitt (2005). The students break into a loud cheer.

"I like that one."

"That's sooo funny."

"I like when the food splattered."

Penny Shreve holds up her hand and the squeals cease. The poem, "Food Fight," is on the Smart Board and the students in Penny's room listen quietly as she reads the poem aloud to them.

Mrs. S: "We'd never seen the teachers/ in a state of such . . . "*[Points to the word distress in the poem]* Raise your hand if you know how to pronounce this word. *[Several students raise their hands.]* Jullian, how do you say this word?

Jullian: The word is *distress*. Distress is when someone is upset.

Mrs. S: That's right, Jullian. How did you figure that out?

Jullian: I saw the principal was yelling and the lunchroom was messy, so I figured the teachers would be upset. . . . And sometimes my mom says she gets distressed and that's when she's mad. *[Jullian smiles, and Mrs. S and a number of students laugh.]*

Mrs. S: Who can tell me what Jullian did that good readers do when they may not know a word?

While she says this, Mrs. Shreve points to a chart she has posted in the front of her room that depicts the things good readers do when they are reading (see Table 4.2).

Mrs. S: They go back and reread the text to see if they can make sense of the meaning of the word. Remember that knowing how to pronounce a word and what it means will help us to be more fluent readers of the story or poem.

TABLE 4.2   *Characteristics of Good Readers*

WHAT DO GOOD READERS DO?

✓ **Read with expression.**

✓ **Read at the right pace.**

✓ **Follow punctuation marks.**

✓ **Words flow together.**

NO ROBOT READERS! READ WITH EXPRESSION!

The lesson continues, and Penny reads the poem until they come to another word in the text that may prove difficult for the students to understand. The word is *innocent,* and she stops and follows the same procedure as before. After going through the whole poem in this fashion, the students are better able to understand the meaning of the poem. It's now time to reread to practice their fluency. Penny takes them back to the beginning of the poem again, and she then reads it one stanza at a time. The students are instructed to read the stanza after she reads it. She reads. They read. She reads. They read. And so it goes until they have completed the poem. The students have now learned the difficult words, the flow and rhythm of the poem, and have also comprehended its meaning. Penny has modeled for them the importance of reading text and rereading for meaning and fluency. It is now time to practice it all together.

Mrs. S: Are we ready, now? Remember, we don't want to "race-read." We don't get any extra points by reading it fast and we lose the meaning and the funny parts. Give me a thumbs-up if you understand? *[All the students put their thumbs in the air.]* One more thing, I want you to listen to each other and let's all try to stay together as a class. Ready, set, let's begin. . . .

The students start reading, but soon they are at all different parts of the poem.

Mrs. S: Let's stop, please. I can't understand you. I'm hearing some race-reading. Here's one thing that I think is causing us problems. *[She points to a comma on the Smart Board.]* What should we do when we see this mark? Everybody?

Class: Pause.

Mrs. S: What does it mean to "pause"? Alejandra?

Alejandra: Have a little stop.

Mrs. S: That's right. And what do we do when we see this? Everybody? She points to a period.

Class: Big stop.

Mrs. S: That's right. Let's try it again. Ready, set, begin. . . .

They start off well and follow the cadence, but then halfway through; the voices become gibberish again. Penny patiently stops them once again and explains to them what has happened. She reads a section, and then has them repeat it. They do this a few times and now they are ready to try the entire poem again. This time, they make it through in unison, using the correct pausing techniques.

Mrs. S: That was very good. Now, I want you to break off with your reading pal and practice it just like we've done before. What does that mean? Albert?

Albert: First my partner reads and then I do.

Mrs. S:	That's right. And what should the person who is not reading be doing while the partner is reading?
Albert:	The partner should listen to make sure they are saying the right words.
Mrs. S:	Very good. Now, when you've each had a chance to read twice, close your books and fold your hands so that I know you are done. Begin.

Getting the Students Involved

It should be obvious that Penny believes in student involvement. This is exhibited in many ways in her room. After a few months, the students have learned dozens of poems. They have learned to select them from their teacher's computer files and show them on the Smart Board. They take turns working in small groups reading the poems together and rehearsing their prosody. They also mimic their teacher's modeling of highlighting words and defining them. Many of the fluent students help the students who are struggling, but they do not realize this is what they are doing. All of the students have been trained to work collaboratively as a team. They mimic the teacher's "talking with" each other. The environment is a comfortable and relaxed one. While some of the students work together on their fluency at the Smart Board, others are reading from a selection of many leveled books that are in baskets in the classroom. They know what level they can read independently and proceed to select a book from the appropriate basket. These baskets have many genres of books so the students can be exposed to many different types of stories. Tiara, a student who has been working one-on-one with the reading coach, is anxious to sit down and read with the coach. She has been practicing her fluency and wants to share her accomplishment. Her confidence as a reader is much higher now than it was just a few weeks ago. Meanwhile, in the back of the room, Penny is working with her students one-on-one. She is **progress monitoring** them for fluency. Penny regularly checks her students' progress in both the accuracy and rate of their reading, as well as their ability to read with expression. Individual students read three passages of text at their grade level as Penny uses her PDA (personal digital assistant) to mark their accuracy. She stops after each passage and shows the students what their fluency rates and accuracy are for each passage. After the last passage, she shows them their average and has them color it in on their fluency graph. In most instances, the students improved and they are progressing. Many show the reading coach their graphs and talk about their improvements. Their confidence is soaring.

Scaffolding the ELL learners is also in the back of the teacher's minds as they plan their daily lessons. It takes place working in small groups as students help each other with words and meanings, as they reread books and poems, and individually when Penny continues to help these students understand words and meanings with pictures, explanations, actions, modeling, or using the Spanish equivalent of the words or meanings they are struggling with. Because the ELL learners are immersed in such a rich language environment, with teachers who are so dedicated to helping them with various strategies, these learners often take off quickly. They have lots of support, but they are taught they must take over the responsibility of learning.

Questions for Discussion

1. What did you find most interesting about this vignette?

2. What connection do you see between vocabulary development and fluency?

3. In what way did Penny turn ownership of the fluency instruction over to her students?

4. In your own teaching situation, or one that you have observed, what are the challenges in trying to teach this way? What did Penny do to try to be proactive in overcoming some of those challenges?

Inside the Classroom, Vignette II: Henry S. West Laboratory School, Miami, Florida

Jeanne Schrumm

It was time for read-aloud. The classroom teacher drew the students' attention by saying, "ice cream." The students replied in unison, "cone." Then at the teacher's direction the first-grade students tiptoed to the reading center at the front of the room. After reminding the students to sit "crisscross apple sauce," Susana Ramirez proceeded with a big build up for the story they would hear today, *The Wonderful Pigs of Jillian Jiggs* (Gilman, 1993). After an animated and enthusiastic oral reading, she then asked her students, "How did you 'feel' about this story?"

One student replied, "It's like a little song. All of the rhymes are at the end."

After the discussion, Susana led the students into a follow-up activity involving a rhyming contest—students working in pairs were asked to generate lists of words in the –ig family. As they were working with the timed activity Susana coached her students, "Put your thinking caps on! . . ." "You can do it—oh yes, you can! . . ." "You get extra power working with a partner!" The lesson ended with a "create a pig" art project. Clearly, students knew classroom routines and were on task and engaged with all phases of the lesson.

Susana Ramirez is a 13-year veteran teacher at Henry S. West Laboratory School. Although Susana has taught a variety of grade levels over the years, she is currently teaching 22 first-grade students. Since 1954, "West Lab" has been affiliated with the University of Miami and serves as a research and development site for the university's School of Education as well as a field placement site for preservice teachers. While the school is located on university land, the building is the property of Miami–Dade County Public Schools, and the school district governs the school's policy and procedures.

West Lab is a "school of choice" in that parents apply for their children's admission to the school through the school district. A lottery system is used to select incoming students. The school population roughly represents the demographics of the schools system as a whole, with 23% of students being White, non-Hispanic; 26% Black non-Hispanic; 49% Hispanic; and 2% Asian/Indian/Multiracial. Approximately 20% of the students are on free and reduced-price lunch. Even though the school is housed in an affluent neighborhood, the student population represents a cross-section of students in the district. The school has consistently remained an "A" school based on the state of Florida's school grading system. However, the challenge of maintaining ongoing progress to meet annual yearly progress (AYP) standards becomes more formidable each year.

For most of her 13 years of teaching, Susana has been at West Lab. With respect to phonological awareness instruction, the National Reading Panel report with its emphasis on the direct teaching of the sounds of language in the early grades has influenced curriculum in first grade. To keep her professional development up to date, Susana attended a University of Miami Summer Reading Institute and several school-district–sponsored workshops to learn more about research and instruction regarding phonological awareness. She learned about the key components of phonological awareness instruction (i.e., onset, rime, segmentation, blending, phoneme manipulation), as well as strategies for students to get "physically involved" with segmentation and blending (e.g., clapping, down the arm and grasp, Elkonian boxes).

Ongoing assessment and monitoring of students is essential to make certain that individual student needs are identified and addressed. In addition to weekly benchmark skill tests from the basal reader, Susana administers the Dynamic Indicators of Basic Early Literacy Skills (DIBELS; Good, Kaminski, Simmons, & Kame'enui, 2001) and STAR Early Literacy Tests (Renaissance Learning) three times a year. Susana is assisted with DIBELS assessment by a team of professionals that includes the school counselor and media specialist. As Susana puts it, "We have moved to data-driven decision making. We monitor students closely and when problems arise I provide extra instruction during small-group guided reading lessons." Susana supplements assessment with informal instruments and those included in the school district's basal reading series.

Susana recognizes that the teaching of phonological awareness is essential for her students' future success as readers and writers. What she is quite successful in accomplishing is making learning of the different aspects of phonological awareness fun and engaging.

First, it would be difficult for learning not to be fun in Susana's classroom. Her organized, ordered classroom defines a print-rich environment. Her face is always lit by a smile. She constantly monitors the whole group and individual students and knows how to reel students in when necessary. Moreover, Susana has an uncanny intuition for what will "turn students on" and get them excited about learning.

Like most first-grade teachers, at the beginning of the school year Susana is faced with a wide range of student differences in terms of students' knowledge of phonological awareness. Some students have moved beyond phonological awareness and think of such instruction as "so baby." Others have forgotten over the summer what they learned in kindergarten. Therefore, she provides differentiated instruction depending on where students begin and when they need to go to meet school-district benchmarks. "I use the DIBELS scores and teacher judgment to group students."

Susana agrees with Heacox (2007), who defines differentiated instruction as, "changing the pace, level, or kind of instruction in response to learners' needs, style, and/or interests" (p. 1). To provide this differentiation, she plans small-group guided reading lessons, instructional centers with hands-on activities, and computer programs to offer students a variety of teacher-directed, cooperative learning groups and independent activities. She moves her students beyond workbook pages to a range of learning opportunities that are aligned with the curriculum she teaches, meet individual needs, and capture students' attention. When possible, Susana enlists the assistance of university preservice teachers to assist with individual and small groups of students. Students assist with creating center activities that offer them multileveled learning opportunities to practice phonological awareness.

Most of the intensive concentration of phonological awareness instruction occurs at the beginning of the first-grade school year, with reinforcement throughout the year. Susana reinforces phonological awareness when she conducts morning message, introduces spelling words each week, and with weekly choral readings of poetry focused on different rhyming and alliteration patterns. As the example at the beginning of this case indicates, literature connections are a primary way that Susana uses to reinforce phonological awareness. Phonological awareness activities are an important component of classroom instruction, and through children's literature, word sounds and patterns come alive.

Susana keeps her focus on students and "their needs, style, and/or interests" (Heacox, 2007, p. 1); she has thus created a supportive environment for the teaching of phonological awareness—and to make it meaningful and fun.

Questions for Discussion

After reading this chapter, consider the following questions:

1. How does Susana use a variety of activities to promote student engagement?
2. What are resources and activities that you might use to create hands-on learning centers to teach phonological awareness?
3. What additional strategies could Susana use to make phonological awareness instruction meaningful and fun?
4. Susana relies on poetry and children's literature to reinforce phonological awareness. What are some resources you could use to do the same?
5. How can you differentiate instruction for students who have varying needs in developing phonological awareness?

Summary of Strategies Used

Based on the International Reading Association's *Excellent Reading Teachers: A Position Statement* (2000), it is evident that Penny and Susana are excellent teachers. In particular, Penny explicitly teaches reading strategies to students, while scaffolding instruction when necessary. Just as important, Penny continually assesses children's individual progress and relates reading instruction to children's previous experiences. Likewise, Susana reinforces phonological awareness—and like Penny, she explicitly teaches reading strategies to students. For example, to reinforce phonological awareness, she delivers morning messages, introduces spelling words each week, and incorporates weekly choral readings of poetry focused on different rhyming and alliteration patterns.

In summary, both Penny and Susana are excellent reading teachers because they find ways to meet the individual needs of each student in their class.

Case for Exploration:
Masson Elementary School, Lorain, Ohio

James Salzman and Robyn Knicely

Penny Shreve is a third-grade teacher at Masson Elementary School in Lorain, Ohio. She has been teaching for more than 10 years and currently teaches part-time while "job sharing" with her teaching partner, Sandra Peloquin. Penny teaches the language arts portion of the curriculum in the morning, and Sandra takes over the math, science, and social studies curriculum with the class in the afternoon. In addition to Penny and Sandra, the students also have a third teacher, Lydia Guerrieri, who assists them. Lydia is the third-grade ELL teacher in the building; her third-grade ELL students are mainstreamed into Penny and Sandra's room nearly full-time. These three teachers use a common philosophy of education that allows them to work efficiently as a team, to plan and to meet the needs of all of their students. They each believe that all students can learn to read, that fluency is a necessary but not sufficient skill to being a grade-level reader, and that their explicit and systematic teaching of fluency skills with opportunities for student practice will facilitate their students' unlocking of the code to reading. They further implement this message to the students by the way they interact with each other during the lesson of the day.

Daily Fluency Lessons

Because these teachers are in a Reading First school, they also have the benefit of a reading coach, Robyn, who has provided training and modeling of different fluency strategies and techniques. Penny, who has taught third grade for several years of her career, is anxious to try some of these new techniques this year. In addition to the professional development in her school, Penny attended some fluency building workshops. A few months into the school year, Robyn came into Penny's classroom to see how things were going with the new techniques she learned at the workshops.

"I've been using daily fluency lessons, and my students really appear to be responding. I think their reading skills have improved and they seem excited about reading."

"So, what have you done that's different from other years?" Robyn asked.

"Well, I have a collection of poems on my computer that I pull up on the Smart Board. We talk about fluency as a class and why it is important. I read the poem through for them and we take time to talk about the difficult vocabulary words in the poem. Then it's their turn to read it through, line by line."

From past conversations, Robyn knew that Penny's focus this year was to have as many students as possible reading on benchmark—as measured by their DIBELS—so that they will have a better chance of passing the Ohio Achievement Test at third grade. The research indicates that the more fluent readers are, the better they will do on statewide tests. She is determined to use daily fluency lessons as her springboard to helping her students attain benchmark.

This is the first year all of the third-grade ELL students have been mainstreamed into a regular classroom, and Penny feels these daily fluency lessons have helped them as well. "I just can't believe how well my ELL students are reading! They have really gotten the hang of the rhythm of the poetry and the sounds of the words. When we work on the vocabulary meanings in the poem, it allows them to understand not only the words better, but the poem too!"

Robyn's weekly consultations with Penny show that Penny is charting her student's progress, using data from all assessments that she gives. To remind her of the purpose of fluency assessments, Robyn occasionally asks her teachers, "What is your goal for charting this student's data?"

In response, Penny stated,

> Well, my first goal is to see which students need some extra help and to diagnose what gaps I might need to intervene on, so I keep all of the data on each student in a notebook. But, I'd be less than honest if I didn't also say that I am trying to predict which students will pass the state reading test. That way I can go back and look and see if they are improving.
>
> For instance, Maria and Jackie, two of my ELL students, are mainstreamed all day, but they started the year struggling with their fluency. Their oral reading fluency scores were 40 and 61, respectively, on the first benchmark test. The girls were struggling to sound out words that were unfamiliar to them. Lydia [the ELL teacher in third grade] told me that it's hard for ELL students to sound out words that they have never encountered. But she also said it's important for them to be exposed to the vocabulary at this stage so they can build their knowledge. We just have to work harder to help them incorporate these words into their knowledge base.

"How do you do that?" Robyn asked.

Both Penny and Lydia, an additional teacher, agree they need to use a lot of picture clues, gestures, stories, one-on-one help, and a print-rich environment to help these students gain more vocabulary information:

> For instance, in the poem "Food Fight," by Kenn Nesbitt, the word "hurling" comes up. The students commonly refer to this word as "throwing-up," but we had to explain in this instance it meant throwing something across the room. We used gestures as we repeated the word over and over in the sentence to allow the ELL students time to think about it and its meaning. The students learned to interpret the word differently, allowing the ELL learners, struggling readers and visual learners to "see" the word's definition as well as "hear" the definition.

Questions for Discussion

After reading this chapter, consider the following questions:

1. What did you find most interesting or surprising when reading the case?
2. What does research tell us about teaching fluency to students?
3. Can you think of any other way for Penny to assess her student's fluency?

4. If Penny wants to increase literacy instruction further with her ELL students, what would you recommend to her?

5. Share strategies you have used for fluency instruction.

Concluding Thoughts

In this chapter, you learned that effective teachers use a variety of instructional strategies to meet the needs of the diverse learners within their classrooms, as also noted by the International Reading Association (2000) position statement on excellent reading teachers. Likewise, you learned that effective teachers use both informal and formal assessments to monitor student progress. As the teachers from the vignette, Penny and Susana, demonstrated, they are excellent reading teachers because they find ways to meet the individual needs of each student in their class while also varying instructional strategies and making learning fun and relevant to students from diverse backgrounds.

TERMS TO KNOW

Alphabetic principle

Big books

Choral reading

Concepts about print

Echo reading

Environmental print

Fluency

Fluency development workshop

Frustrational-level texts

Gradual release of responsibility

Graphemes

Graphophonic cues

Guided reading

High-frequency words

Independent reading

Independent-level texts

Instructional-level texts

Language experience approach

Literacy centers

Morning message

Onset

Partner reading

Phonemes

Phonemic awareness

Phonics

Phonological awareness

Phonological systems of language

Print-rich environment

Progress monitoring

Read-alouds

Reading aloud

Readers Theater

Rime

Semantic cues

Shared reading

Sight words

Sound–letter correspondence

Sustained silent reading

Syntactic cues

Think aloud

Word walls

RESEARCH THAT WORKS

Beers, K. (2003). *When kids can't read: What teachers can do.* Portsmouth, NH: Heinemann.

Cappellini, M. (2005). *Balancing reading and language learning.* Portland, ME/Newark, DE: Stenhouse/International Reading Association.

Cooter, R. B., Flynt, E. S., & Cooter, K. S. (2007). *Comprehensive reading inventory: Measuring reading development in regular and special education classrooms.* Columbus, OH: Pearson.

Davenport, M. R., & Lauritzen, C. (2002). Inviting reflection on reading through over the shoulder miscue analysis. *Language Arts, 80*(2), 109–118.

Fang, Z. (2008). Going beyond the fab five: Helping students cope with the unique linguistic challenges of expository reading in intermediate grades. *Journal of Adolescent & Adult Literacy, 51*(6), 476–487.

Hudson, R. F., Lane, H. B., & Pullen, P. C. (2005). Reading fluency assessment and instruction: What, why, and how? *Reading Teacher, 58*(8), 702–714.

Lapp, D. Fisher, D., & Grant, M. (2008). "You can read this text—I'll show you how": Interactive comprehension instruction. *Journal of Adolescent & Adult Literacy, 51*(5), 372–383.

Li, X., & Zhang, M. (2004). Why Mei cannot read and what can be done. *Journal of Adolescent and Adult Literacy, 48*(2), 92–101.

Opitz, M. F. (2002). Children's books to develop phonemic awareness—For you and parents, too! In International Reading Association, *Evidence-based reading instruction: Putting the National Reading Panel Report into practice* (pp. 77–82). Newark, DE: International Reading Association. (Reprinted from *The Reading Teacher, 51*, 526–528, March 1998)

Pritchard, R., & O'Hara, S. (2008). Reading in Spanish and English: A comparative study of processing strategies. *Journal of Adolescent & Adult Literacy, 51*(8), 630–688.

WEB SITES

Literacy Organizations and Resources

CIERA: **http://www.ciera.org./index.html** states that their main goal is to distribute information to those who can make a difference in the reading abilities of young children through many different types of pedagogical practices. This site has links to several research articles about effective reading instruction and PowerPoint presentations that can be used to instruct teachers about specific teaching strategies for topics such as reading comprehension. This site is quite extensive.

Florida Center for Reading Research: **http://www.fcrr.org** uses applied research to provide assistance to educators in areas such as curriculum and instruction, assessment, and interventions for struggling readers. This site also provides resources in the form of presentations, recommended publications, and professional development supports.

National Institute for Literacy (NIFL): **http://www.nifl.gov** offers research information, programs, and services to improve reading instruction for children, adolescents, and adults. There is also a discussion board and program reviews to allow teachers to share information they have gained about specific literacy tools and their usefulness.

National Reading First: **http://www.ed.gov/programs/readingfirst** provides information and resources regarding the National Reading First program. It also answers FAQs about Reading First as well as providing contact information for educators who wish to implement the program in their school or community.

National Reading Panel (NRP): **http://www.nationalreadingpanel.org** is a Web site devoted to analyzing and presenting the most effective strategies for teaching children how to read. It includes a few informational resources, such as a research study conducted by the NRP about effective teaching practices, and answers several specific frequently asked questions about reading instruction such as, "What is phonemic awareness?"

Pacific Resources for Education and Learning (PREL): **http://www.prel.org** emphasizes programs, services, and products to promote educational excellence within multicultural and multilingual environments. PREL works throughout the educational community including school systems, classrooms, and administrations as well as collaborating with local governments, businesses, and communities.

Vaughn Gross Center for Reading and Language Arts: **http://www.texasreading.org** is a research center within the College of Education at the University of Texas at Austin. The center works to improve reading and mathematics skills through scientifically based research for all students, especially English language learners (ELLs), special education students, and struggling readers.

What Works Clearinghouse: **http://ies.ed.gov/ncee/wwc** has a great deal of information about beginning reading, character education (including behavior, academic achievement, knowledge, attitudes, and values), dropout prevention, early childhood education, elementary and middle school math, English language learners, improving adolescent literacy, and has an extensive glossary of terms. It also provides intervention reports and practice guides for these topics.

Word Walls

4 Blocks Literacy Framework: **http://www.k111.k12.il.us/lafayette/FourBlocks/word_wall_chants .htm#In%20The%20Seat** shares several classroom chanting activities to assist students in learning the five weekly words. It provides directions for many chants and cheers done in the seat, standing, and sung to aid students in memorization of sight words and extensive other word wall activities with directions that can easily be followed by the teacher. It also provides extensive guidelines for guided reading to increase student comprehension and exposure to literature as well as several segments for teaching writing through modeling.

Interactive Word Wall: **http://www.teachnet.com/lesson/langarts/wordwa11062599.html** provides the goals for word walls as well as explicit instructions and guidelines for using word wall activities in the classroom.

Interactive Word Walls: **http://www.theschoolbell.com/Links/word_walls/words.html** provides a detailed summary of what a word wall is, demonstrates the types of words to use, and includes a weekly schedule of how to incorporate an interactive word wall into your daily work.

Word Wall Activities: **http://www.teachingfirst.net/wordwallact.htm** was put together by a first-grade teacher. The site tells about "red words" or sight words that do not follow normal patterns and must simply be memorized and how this teacher presents these words to her students. It also describes, in detail, over 15 interactive activities to play with young children to help them review the red words they have learned each week so that they do not forget this information.

Word Walls for Elementary, Middle, and High Schools: **http://www.santarosa.k12.fl.us/ reading/WordWall.htm** provides guidelines for how to choose the most effective words for a wall word and includes pictures of different examples of word walls.

Word Walls That Work: **http://content.scholastic.com/browse/article.jsp?id = 4380** contains six detailed tips on how to use a word wall smoothly and effectively in the classroom, which words to select (make the words memorable, useful, practical, etc.), and presents the possible pitfalls for each of the tips that can prevent students from using the wall.

Word Wall Use in Kindergarten: **http://www.calicocookie.com/wordwall.html** features activities to use with the word wall in a kindergarten classroom. This site contains a sample list of sight words for students at this level and provides reinforcement activities.

Language Experience

Literacy Connections: In Their Own Words: **http://literacyconnections.com/InTheirOwnWords .php** describes how the language experience approach can be used in multiple language settings to motivate apathetic or struggling readers. It also provides additional articles that detail how others have used the language experience approach.

Digital Language Experience Approach: Using Digital Photographs and Software as a Language Experience Approach Innovation: **http://www.readingonline.org/electronic/elec_index .asp?HREF = labbo2/index.html** details how children with different literacy levels can be even more engaged in the language experience approach when it is combined with digital photography and software. An outline of Digital Language Experience Approach, classroom implications, and related postings are also available.

Centers

Can Teach: Math Centers**: http://www.canteach.ca/elementary/mathcentres.html** lists ideas for math centers by subject, including numbers and equations, geometry, measurement, and patterns.

Classroom Centers: **http://www.mrsmcdowell.com/centers.htm** gives examples of multiple content centers for first-grade students, including centers focusing on the arts and motor skills. It offers links for center resources, organizational strategies, and centers for small spaces.

Math and Science Center Activities: **http://www.coollessons.or**g offers ideas and brief descriptions for math and science centers by subject, including computation, file folder activities, math games, and measurement.

The Teacher's Cafe: **http://www.theteacherscafe.com/Teacher-Directory/Free-Online-Art-Holiday-Activities.htm** contains ideas for centers, lesson plans, activities, and online art for all content areas K–12. This site also addresses additional subjects, such as management and assessment, by providing links to resources with tips, lessons, and literature that offer further support.

Teaching Heart's Learning Centers Page: **http://www.teachingheart.net/LC.htm** explains how one teacher integrates multiple types of literacy centers within her elementary classroom. Pictures, links to literature, printable worksheets, and a discussion board are also included.

Using Big Books

Kinder Friends: Big Books: **http://www.kinderfriends.com/bigbooks.html** presents tips for creating and using teacher-made big books in the elementary classroom as well as links to sample teacher-made books and commercial resources.

Learning From Books: Big Books and Predictable Books: **http://www.sasked.gov.sk.ca/docs/ ela/e_literacy/learning.html** provides example procedures and activities for using big books and predictable books to help support students' understanding of such concepts as letters, words, sentences, and punctuation by using rhymes and repetitions throughout a text.

Onset–Rime

Onset and Rime Activities: **http://fds.oup.com/www.oup.com/pdf/elt/catalogue/9780194375993 -c.pdf** is a two-page document that introduces the concepts of onset, rime, and word families by providing directions for class activities, including time, materials, preparation, and follow-up activities.

Reading Rockets: Tuning Into the Sounds in Words: **http://www.readingrockets.org/article/273** details games children can play to develop phonemic awareness. This resource also provides strategies for segmenting words to prevent children from mispronouncing individual sounds within words.

ReadWriteThink: K–2 Lesson Plan: **http://www.readwritethink.org/lessons/lesson_view.asp?id = 264** provides a lesson plan for using song writing to teach rhyme.

Student Center Activities: Phonological Awareness**: http://www.pblunit10.com/k-3Reading/PA_ Final_Part2.pdf** is an activities packet created by the Florida Center for Reading Research. The third section is devoted to rhyme and onset–rime and includes games and worksheets to practice onset–rime.

Fluency

Developing Reading Fluency: **http://www.auburn.edu/ ~ murraba/fluency.html** explains reading fluency and offers strategies for increasing reading fluency in students.

5 Surefire Strategies for Developing Reading Fluency: **http://content.scholastic.com/browse/ article.jsp?id = 4367** explains five strategies (model fluent reading, do repeated readings in class, promote phrased reading in class, enlist tutors, use Reader's Theater in class) to increase fluency in the classroom and suggests books for Reader's Theater and repeated readings.

Reading Rockets: Fluency: **http://www.readingrockets.org/helping/target/fluency#do_teachers** provides several links to extremely helpful articles for teachers and parents to help identify if a child is not fluent and strategies for how overcoming fluency difficulties.

CHAPTER 5

Vocabulary Development

Prior to reading, try to answer the following questions:

1. What does it mean to know a word?

2. What are some methods you use to learn new words?

Reading Research to Know

Many adults can recall how, as elementary school students learning new vocabulary, they were asked to spend time copying dictionary definitions that made little sense. Fortunately for children today, classroom teachers understand that current research does not support the use of this practice (Farstrup & Samuels, 2008; Hiebert & Kamil, 2007; Wagner, Muse, & Tannenbaum, 2007). Exemplary reading teachers are aware that vocabulary development is more complex than learning definitions, and consequently use a wide range of teaching strategies to support its development. Above all, teachers today understand that vocabulary development requires language-rich classrooms where students have opportunities to engage in verbal interaction, but most significantly, where they are encouraged to engage in extensive reading (Beck & McKeown, 2003; Blachowicz, Fisher, Ogle, & Watts-Taffe, 2006; Krashen, 2004; Marzano, 2004; Pressley, Disney, & Anderson, 2007).

Word Meaning

But what does it mean to know a word? An important point to consider in a discussion on vocabulary development is that **word meaning** is different from **word recognition**. Word recognition, Stahl and Nagy (2006) clarify, involves only the ability to recognize the written form of a word. Acquiring word meaning refers to the way students develop (a) a new concept or (b) a new word for a familiar concept. Acquiring a word such as *photosynthesis,* we might expect, would require that children not only develop a language label but a new concept. With a word like *goslings,* on the other hand, children already familiar with *goose* and the concept of plural only need to acquire a new label for baby geese. Beck, McKeown, and Kucan (2002) further explain that to know a word is not a matter of "all-or-nothing" (p. 9) and place understanding of word meaning along a continuum (see Figure 5.1).

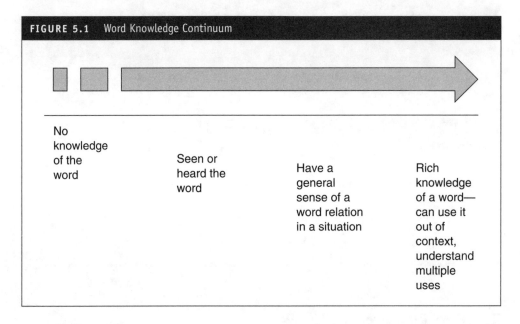

FIGURE 5.1   Word Knowledge Continuum

No knowledge of the word

Seen or heard the word

Have a general sense of a word relation in a situation

Rich knowledge of a word— can use it out of context, understand multiple uses

Allen (2007) suggests that students use a similar continuum to self-assess their own understanding of a word by using the following statements: (a) I've never heard the word, (b) I've heard the word, but I don't know what it means, (c) I think the word means or is related to . . . , and (d) I know the word.

Researchers examining vocabulary development also note that effective teachers vary vocabulary strategies in terms of word utility (Beck et al., 2002; Phythian-Sence & Wagner, 2007). **Word utility** refers to the range of frequency and usage a word might have (Beck et al., 2002; Marzano, 2005). Consequently, reading teachers carefully judge which words they select to teach in their classrooms. When visiting schools, we frequently hear teachers and students talk about vocabulary tiers or levels.

For Beck and colleagues (2002), Tier Three vocabulary instruction includes words that have low-frequency use and are limited to specific domains. At this level children might encounter a word such as *alluvial fan.* Tier Three words are found and best learned within each content area. Tier Two vocabulary includes a larger number of high frequency words that cut across domains. Instruction focusing on Tier Two vocabulary goes beyond just learning new synonyms. It supports children in developing new words to more precisely refer to ideas that they have already developed. Words such as *bellowed* and *muttered,* depending on the students' background, might be representative of this category. Eunice Davis and her second grade students at Bruce Shulkey Elementary School (Fort Worth Independent School District) spend time considering such differences. While these second graders are familiar with the word *said,* they learn to use new words that more precisely express its meaning. Tier One vocabulary, the final level, consists of words that are familiar to students and do not require instruction in school.

Words for *Said*

Stahl and Nagy (2006) further develop the notion of word utility by stressing the teaching intensity required to teach words at each level. These authors conceptualize vocabulary instruction in terms of a pyramid. Level III, at the top of the pyramid, involves the most intense teaching. While Level III might have the fewest words—key content vocabulary and high-utility words—it requires more time and effort on the part of the teacher and students. Instruction at this level leads students to use the word in writing as well as understand its meaning in multiple contexts. The photo on the next page illustrates one of the ways in which kindergartners in Gracie Escovedo's classroom at Alice Carlson Elementary (Fort Worth Independent School District) learn Level III mathematics content vocabulary related to geometric shapes. Level II, in the middle of the pyramid, consists of the vocabulary that children need to know in order to read unfamiliar words they encounter in books. The meanings of these words can be partial and the words might be recognized only within their context. Level II vocabulary requires more effort and time than Level I, but is not as intense as Level III. Level I, at the base of the pyramid, consists of the vocabulary that children can acquire through experiences with rich oral and written language. While vocabulary at this level comprises that largest number of words, it involves the least amount of effort and time on part of the learner or the teacher.

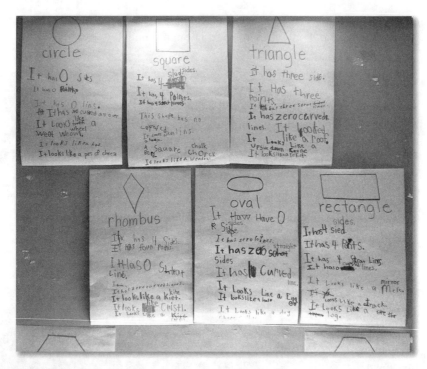

Geometric shapes and vocabulary

Next we discuss ways in which teachers immerse children in words by creating language-rich environments. Within these environments we look at how teachers make use of read-alouds, wide-reading programs, and word walls to support vocabulary development. We also look at the use of graphic organizers and the study of word parts as aids in studying vocabulary.

Language-Rich Classroom Environments

By the time children begin kindergarten they have developed a large oral language vocabulary. Classroom teachers, aware of these early vocabulary acquisition strategies, continue to support young learners through **language-rich classroom environments.** A language rich-classroom environment is a setting rich in oral and written language. Stahl and Nagy (2006) consider a language-rich environment to be "the crucial channel of vocabulary growth" (p. 49). To maximize vocabulary learning in these settings, teachers capitalize on books. Books, these authors remind us, are "where the words are" (p. 126) and provide the most powerful source of new vocabulary. Written language not only has more varied vocabulary but it also contains more technical terms. Children are likely to encounter the word *rain* in daily conversation. Words such as *precipitation* or *condensation,* on the other hand, are more likely to be encountered in academic texts. To support vocabulary development in language-rich classrooms, teachers maximize opportunities for students to engage with books.

Read-Alouds

When teachers engage in **read-alouds,** they orally read books that children can't yet read on their own. Read-alouds provide children with the opportunity to acquire words that are outside their current vocabulary (Cunningham, 2005). Certain conditions must exist for read-alouds to benefit students' vocabulary development. That is, rather than "being talked at or read to," children benefit from "being talked with or read with" (Blachowicz & Fisher, 2009, p. 23). Beck et al. (2002) refer to this type of interaction as "Text Talk," and suggest that teachers enhance vocabulary development by teaching approximately three words each time they read aloud to students. While the children are unfamiliar with the vocabulary, they should be familiar with the concept behind the words. Teachers begin by discussing the target words within the context of a story. To enhance vocabulary development they do the following:

- Ask students to repeat the word
- Explain the meaning of the word
- Provide examples of other contexts for using the word
- Have children provide their own examples using the new word

Having students see how the word is used in other contexts is key to this practice. Children, these experts argue, tend to limit the use of a word to the context in which they first encounter it and need multiple experiences using a word to make the new vocabulary item their own.

Though teachers are aware of the merit of reading aloud with younger children, excellent reading teachers also understand that this practice is effective when used with older students, particularly if they are struggling readers. This type of scaffolding is crucial since texts are likely to be more complex than what struggling readers can read by themselves. As children become more proficient readers, however, they are better able to comprehend text when reading on their own.

Wide Reading Programs

Wide reading programs provide the best avenue for students to develop vocabulary. *Wide reading* refers to the variety of programs that provide fixed times during the school day for children to engage in reading self-selected materials. SSR (sustained silent reading) or DEAR (Drop Everything and Read) are acronyms for the wide reading programs we most often see implemented in schools. During SSR or DEAR time, students, classroom teachers—and in some buildings, all school personnel—read silently for 10 to 20 minutes every day. According to Stahl and Nagy (2006), 25 minutes of daily reading can lead to the acquisition of more than 2,000 words per year. Other researchers report similar findings in terms of the positive effects that wide reading programs have on vocabulary development (Kelley & Clausen-Grace, 2006). Krashen's (2004, 2006) research has focused on the advantage of wide reading programs to support vocabulary development for English language learners (ELLs).

Common to this body of research is the understanding that most vocabulary is learned incidentally—Level I—through repeated encounters with words. Pilgreen (2000) identifies eight factors that are critical to the success of wide reading programs such as SSR and DEAR:

1. *Access:* Students must have access to a variety of books (including magazines and comic books).

2. *Appeal:* Reading materials must be interesting to the students.

3. *Conducive environment:* The environment where children read must be comfortable and inviting to participate in quiet activity (e.g., have beanbag chairs, rugs).

4. *Encouragement:* Teachers must model reading and encourage children to read and discuss what they read.

5. *Staff training:* School staff must be trained in ways to develop effective SSR programs; staff's shared philosophy and buy-in is critical to the program's success.

6. *Nonaccountability:* Children should not be forced to take tests after reading.

7. *Follow-up activities:* Children should engage in follow-up discussions that will continue to foster the enjoyment of reading.

8. *Distributed time to read:* Children should have short periods of time to engage in sustained reading (2 times a week is minimum).

Word Walls

Math word wall

An instructional element often found in language-rich classrooms is the word wall. **Word walls** display a collection words used for reading and writing instruction and provide children with one more opportunity to actively engage in vocabulary development. Words selected for display can focus on high-utility vocabulary. Joey Mantecon, a first-grade teacher at Alice Carlson in the Fort Worth Independent School District, uses word walls to support his students in acquiring math-related vocabulary. This word wall highlights math vocabulary that the children will need consistently throughout the year. Allen (2007) emphasizes the need for words walls to become a "living part of the classroom" and stresses the need for children's participation in their development: "I have found few Word Walls that are successful if they are prepared in the absence of teaching and learning" (p. 120). In Joey's classroom, as we can see from the hand-written word entries, children actively participate in adding new words to the math word wall.

Graphic Representations

As students develop the background to understand new concepts, teachers can support them in further extending their knowledge of the new vocabulary through the use of **graphic organizers**. Graphic organizers provide a **nonlinguistic representation** of words. The construction of these images allows readers to create a personal connection for learning new concepts (Blachowicz & Fisher, 2009; Marzano, 2004; Stahl & Nagy, 2006).

One strategy commonly used to help students further define new words and examine their characteristics is the **word map**. Though there are a number of variations for this graphic organizer, to create a word map the student writes the word in a box at the center of the paper. The vocabulary word is then defined in the student's own words. Some teachers also ask that students provide examples and non-examples of the word as well as an illustration. Word maps, Stahl and Nagy (2006) advise us, work better when dealing with abstract words.

Word Parts

While it is not uncommon to see students engaged in the study of *morphemes* or word parts (i.e., learning prefixes, suffixes, and root words), researchers caution classroom teachers against too broad a use of this strategy (Freeman & Freeman, 2004a, 2004b; Stahl & Nagy, 2006). Prefixes, suffixes, and root words are taught thinking that they can support children in determining word meaning. Even though 60% of English words have Latin or Greek roots, it is easier for children to learn the meaning of the whole word than to have to have them learn the meanings of the word's parts (Freeman & Freeman, 2004a, 2004b). Rather than placing emphasis on the study of word parts, these experts suggest that teachers support students in learning how these parts function. Older students, for example, can engage in an investigation of the English language and examine how prefixes or suffixes affect word meaning. Once students understand how prefixes, suffixes, and root words function, teachers can highlight word parts as they examine words within the context of vocabulary instruction.

Working With English Language Learners

Given the growing number of English language learners (ELLs) in today's classrooms, teachers are particularly aware of ways they can support vocabulary development for these students. While teachers working with ELLs take advantage of the instructional practices previously discussed in this chapter, they make sure to magnify vocabulary in other ways. To contextualize learning, teachers use **realia**—a term employed in ELL settings to refer to the objects a classroom teacher uses to represent real-life objects and help students better understand the vocabulary terms being targeted (Blachowicz & Fisher, 2000; Rule & Barrera, 2003). When presenting vocabulary on clothing, for example, teachers often bring articles of clothing. An additional point to consider in a discussion on word meaning and ELLs is that, when developing everyday vocabulary, these children can draw from concepts they know in their first language to acquire vocabulary in their second language. For example, Spanish speakers, familiar with the Spanish words *caballo* and *vaca,* can easily acquire the English words *horse* and *cow.*

The development of academic vocabulary, challenging for all students, is particularly difficult for ELLs. **Thematic units** of study allow ELLs to have repeated encounters with academic concepts and vocabulary to develop the academic language that they will need to succeed in school (Carrasquillo, Kucer, & Abrams, 2004; Echevarría, Vogt, & Short, 2008; Kucer, Silva, & Delgado-Larocco, 1995; Mercuri, Freeman, & Freeman, 2002). Through engagements in thematic units students have direct experiences with new ideas while developing the vocabulary to express these new concepts. For the past 3 years, we have had the opportunity to participate in a summer program where the curriculum has focused on a thematic science unit on erosion. To develop concepts such as *alluvial fan, gully,* and *sediment,* the teachers engage students in hands-on experiments, as well as in the creation of models and diagrams. Throughout these experiences, students naturally begin to make use of the academic vocabulary related to the theme. Through the thematic units, children are also likely be exposed to a variety of resources—trade books, videos, Web sites, and interactive technology—to reinforce the conceptual development of the vocabulary linked to the unit. To support them to "own" the words, students are encouraged to use the new vocabulary items in their journals, research reports, and during class discussions. These types of experiences ensure that children acquire a deep understanding of the vocabulary being learned.

Word walls were used with children participating in the summer program as they encountered new erosion concepts and academic language. As reflected in this word wall, children were often engaged in discussions that compared everyday words with their more academic counterparts. Teachers often made reference to the word wall as they encouraged children to use the academic language during classroom discussions and in their writing.

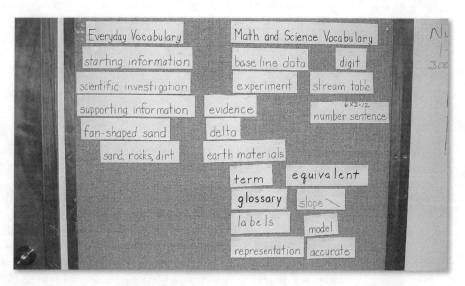

Everyday and academic English word wall

In this classroom, the word wall was a key component of the vocabulary instruction that took place in math and science.

One area that seems promising in terms of vocabulary development is using **cognates** with ELLs whose first language is Spanish (Bravo, Hiebert, & Pearson, 2003; Freeman & Freeman, 2004b; Jiménez, García, & Pearson, 1996). Cognates are words that have the same linguistic root and are similar in spelling and meaning (Spanish *precipitación* and English *precipitation*). Research on cognates has shown that (a) Spanish and English share a large number of cognates and (b) that bilingual readers use cognates to determine word meaning when reading. Bravo et al. (2003) examined science vocabulary cognates and found that that three out of every four words of the text they analyzed shared a cognate. Different from English, one out of every three of the cognate words they found is a word that is commonly used in everyday Spanish. These findings are particularly important in terms of the development of English academic vocabulary for Spanish speaking ELLs. Children participating in the summer camp we describe in this section quickly became adept at recognizing such cognates. In this classroom, as children identified cognates related to the unit on erosion, they were invited to add a green dot sticker to the words on the word wall.

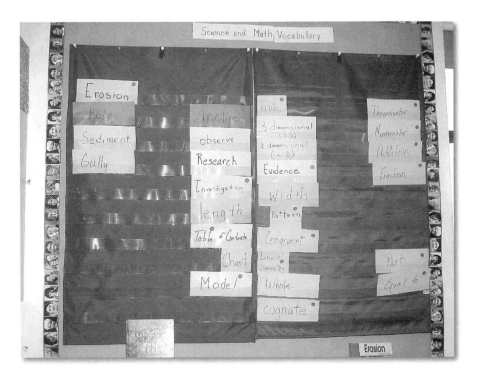

Wall cognates

Inside the Classroom:
Chinn Elementary School, Parkhill, Missouri

Patience Sowa

Mrs. Kasper teaches kindergarten through fifth-grade ELLs at various levels of English language proficiency at Chinn Elementary School in the Park Hill School District in Kansas City, Missouri. Because she is an English as a second language (ESL) "pullout" teacher, students come to Mrs. Kasper's classroom for 30 minutes of instruction on a daily basis. While some of her ELLs are newcomers to the United States and her school, others have been at Chinn Elementary since kindergarten and receive language support before they are fully immersed into mainstream classes. Mrs. Kasper's students also work with her at the end of the school day when they come back to her classroom for help with homework or reading.

Mrs. Kasper has taught ELLs for 15 years in the Park Hill School District. She is certified in high school English and has an endorsement in ESL. In addition, Mrs. Kasper is a National Board Certified Teacher. To achieve this recognition for her teaching excellence, Mrs. Kasper has undergone a rigorous evaluation process based on the National Board for Professional Teaching Standards.

Mrs. Kasper's classroom is small, but colorfully decorated. On the board she has a word wall for each grade she teaches. Her room has two computers and a television. On the right side of the room, by the door, is a world map. Around the map are pictures of her ELLs with arrows pointing to their country of origin—Micronesia, Paraguay, Cote d'Ivoire, Mexico, Haiti, Egypt, and Ethiopia. Underneath each picture is a description of the child's place of origin and the language spoken at home.

Mrs. Kasper's Classroom

Mrs. Kasper uses a content-based language approach to make sure that her ELLs are developing academic English and are keeping up with topics they are learning in their general education classroom. Although Mrs. Kasper develops her own curriculum to teach her ELL students, she also provides support to their classroom teachers and meets with them to keep informed about what her students are learning in their classrooms. Mrs. Kasper teaches her students vocabulary through thematic units in which reading fiction and nonfiction books is an integral component of each thematic unit. Integrating the four skills of reading, writing, listening, and speaking, Mrs. Kasper uses **visuals** and *graphic organizers*. She also uses strategies to contextualize key vocabulary, and recycles information to help her students learn and retain vocabulary.

Using Literature

It's noon, and Mrs. Kasper's fourth graders gather to continue their reading of *The Hundred Penny Box* (Mathis, 1986). First, Mrs. Kasper asks them to recap the story, and she guides the process through questioning the students about the characters in the story and their relationships. Mrs. Kasper calls on Lamine:

> "Why is Aunt Dew living with Michael, John, and Ruth?" she asks.
> "Because she took care of John," Lamine replies.
> "Exactly," said Mrs. Kasper, "because John's parents had drowned."
> "What can you tell me about Ruth and Aunt Dew, Sonya?"
> "They don't like each other," she answers.
> "How do we know this," Mrs. Kasper asks. "How do we know that they do not get along?"
> "Because she didn't say anything about the ice cream," Nii Ablade says.
> "She wants to throw away the hundred penny box," Julia interjects.

Mrs. Kasper continues to question the students, asking them more in-depth questions about Aunt Dew and her relationship with John, Michael, and Ruth. She asks them to examine the big idea posters they had developed after their previous readings and has them reexamine key vocabulary—*furnace, comfortable,* and *precious*—from these readings. Then she asks each child to read aloud. She reminds them to raise a hand, or a finger, if they do not understand a word or sentence while they are reading.

Sonya starts to read and stumbles over the passage: "'You John's baby,' she said, still staring at him. 'Look like John just spit you out'" (Mathis, 1986, p. 21).

"Hold, on, hold on," Mrs. Kasper says, stopping Sonya. "Why does Aunt Dew talk that way? What does she mean?" Mrs. Kasper and the children then have a conversation about dialects and accents. In the story, Aunt Dew has come from Atlanta to stay with Michael's family. Since the children are doing U.S. geography in their regular class, she asks them where Atlanta is and imitates a southern accent. She explains the difference between an accent and a dialect: "An accent is the way you sound or say words. A dialect is different, the grammar may not be the same as what we learn in school. What would we say in school instead of 'You John's baby?'" Julia hesitates and then raises her hand, "We would say 'You are John's baby?'" "Close," Mrs. Kasper says, "think about it, how would we ask a question?" "Oh," Julia says, "Are you John's baby?" "Excellent," Mrs. Kasper says, "now what does Aunt Dew mean when she says 'Look like John just spit you out?'"

Nii Ablade raises his hand, "He looks like John." "Great," Mrs. Kasper says, and the class continues to read the chapter and discuss it.

Visuals

The fourth graders take turns reading the chapter in *The Hundred Penny Box* (Mathis, 1986). As students read, Mrs. Kasper asks them questions: "So what do you think Michael is trying to get Aunt Dew to do?" she asks.

"He is trying to get her to hide the box," Lamine says.

Mrs. Kasper then asks the students to pair up and to draw a poster containing the big ideas in the chapter. She asks them first to discuss what they are going to draw and then take turns drawing the poster. "Only pictures?" Nii Ablade asks. "No," Mrs. Kasper answers, "you can add speech bubbles if you want, like in comics." She demonstrates how to do this on the board. "Also, make sure you label your characters and the objects in your pictures," Mrs. Kasper adds. Two of the girls, Sonya and Julia, draw a picture of Aunt Dew in her rocking chair telling Michael stories. Nii Ablade and Lamine draw a picture of Michael and Aunt Dew in her rocking chair, and Paulo and Pierre draw a picture of Michael's mother and the furnace. As they draw their pictures, Mrs. Kasper asks them to explain what they are drawing and encourages them to add more details to the pictures. "What else could you add to the picture?" she says to Pierre. He hesitatingly whispers, "box," and then starts to draw one. The children describe their posters, and Mrs. Kasper wraps up the class by asking them to predict what they think will happen to the hundred penny box.

The fifth-grade ELLs are reading *The Lightening Thief* (Riordan, 2005). To teach vocabulary, Mrs. Kasper uses nonlinguistic representations and graphic organizers to help them understand and retain the meanings of words. She constantly models how students can use these strategies to help them comprehend text.

The fifth graders are on Chapter 6. Mrs. Kasper assigns them chapters to read at home, and they discuss each chapter in class. After a brief discussion about the big ideas in the chapter, Mrs. Kasper asks the students to try to determine the meanings of seven words: *labyrinth, gladiator, sauntering, hoard, aura, brandished,* and *siblings.* On the board, she draws a graphic organizer to demonstrate what the students need to do (see Figure 5.2).

Mrs. Kasper asks the students to write down each of the seven vocabulary words in individual boxes. Next to each word the students write the numbers 1, 2, 3, and 4. Using these numbers, the students are to rate their understanding of the words. The number 1 represents that students do not understand the word at all, and the number 4 represents that they fully understand the word. She also asks them to go back to the book and write down the page numbers where they find the vocabulary words. She then asks the students write an explanation of the vocabulary item in their own words and to draw a picture to represent the word.

"Remember to look at the words and sentences around the word . . . look at them in context, to see if you can get a better understanding of the word," Mrs. Kasper tells them.

Then Mrs. Kasper and her students look for the words together. Mrs. Kasper asks Ricardo to read the page of dialogue that contains the word *labyrinth.*

"So what is a labyrinth?" she asks. "How can the words and sentences around this word help you know what it means?"

"A dungeon?" Tokozani asks.

"It's a place where you get killed," Oksana says.

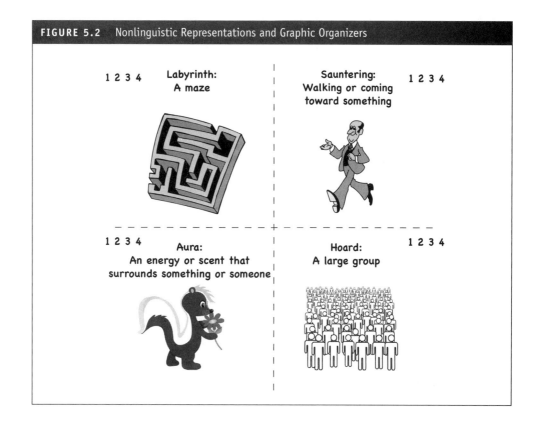

FIGURE 5.2   Nonlinguistic Representations and Graphic Organizers

"I think there was one in *Harry Potter,*" Ricardo says. "It's a winding place where you can get lost," he adds.

"Yes," Mrs. Kasper says, "very good, and another word for it, a synonym, is *maze.*"

Mrs. Kasper asks them to draw a labyrinth in their notebooks. The class moves on to *sauntering.* "What does *sauntering* mean?"

"Coming toward you," Oksana says.

"Good," says Mrs. Kasper, "it says the mean girl Clarisse is walking toward them. Does this mean she is walking fast or slowly?"

"She is walking slowly," Ricardo answers.

"Do you think she is going to do something nice," Mrs. Kasper asks?

"I think she is not walking in a nice manner," Rosa says. "She has a bad plan for him," she adds.

"Tell me some of the words that help you know this," Mrs. Kasper says.

"Big ugly and mean," Tokozani says.

"Great job," Mrs. Kasper says.

Mrs. Kasper asks for a volunteer to demonstrate what sauntering might look like. Rosa raises her hand and quickly gets up to saunter. "Very good," Mrs. Kasper says. "Go ahead and draw a picture of Clarisse sauntering in your graphic organizer, if you haven't already done so." Mrs. Kasper continues in this way with the rest of the words, and then facilitates a discussion of Chapter 7.

Recycling Words and Nonlinguistic Representations

The Chinn Elementary kindergartners file excitedly into Mrs. Kasper's classroom. They are engaged in a unit on farms in their homeroom classrooms. They have also visited a petting zoo. Mrs. Kasper is working on reinforcing and recycling the vocabulary words they have been learning during the unit.

Mrs. Kasper has a cardboard farm and sets it up in front of the class. The farm has a barn and animals in a corral. Mrs. Kasper asks the children questions about what they have been learning. "So who can tell me what we have been learning in class?" "The farm and animals," most of the children answer. She asks them to name the animals on the cardboard farm. The children name each animal as she points to its picture. She also asks the children for information about who owns the animals on the farm and where the animals are kept.

Mrs. Kasper then asks the children to tell her the sounds each animal makes. When they are not sure about the sounds horses make, Mrs. Kasper demonstrates and tells them that horses neigh. Then she sings a song: "Farmer Brown has one cow, one cow, one cow. Farmer Brown has one cow, moo, moo, moo." She sings the song using other animals—a horse, a chicken, a goat, a sheep, and a goose—and then asks the children to sing along with her. The children enjoy making the sounds the animals make. When Mrs. Kasper gets to the goose she tells the children that more than one goose are called geese. She points to a gosling.

"This is a gosling. What's a gosling?" she asks.

"A baby goose," Desta answers.

"Good," Mrs. Kasper says. "Can anyone remember what a baby cow is called?"

"Calf," Sai says.

"What about a baby goat?" Mrs. Kasper asks. "Does anyone know what they call baby goats?"

The class is silent. "Baby goats are called kids," she tells the class. "Oh, like children," Miguel says. "That's right, Miguel. We call boys and girls kids." She has the children repeat the words *gosling, calf,* and *kid* after her, and they sing the song through one more time. This last time, Mrs. Kasper stops singing after the chicken and lets the children sing the last three verses on their own, which they do loudly and excitedly.

Mrs. Kasper then takes out a big book, *Silly Little Goose* (Tafuri, 2001). She tells the class, "We are going to do a picture walk. Remember when we do a picture walk we do not read all the words. Why do we do picture walks?" Mrs. Kasper asks the class. Afi raises his hand. "We learn about the book," he says. "Very good," Mrs. Kasper says. "A picture walk helps us learn about the book."

Silly Little Goose is a book about a goose on a farm trying to find a place to nest. The goose looks for a place in the pig's sty, the cat's bed, the sheep's fold, and the chicken coop, until she finally finds a place of her own. Mrs. Kasper goes through each page, asking questions, pointing to the farm animals, and asking the children to describe the pictures and to predict what they think might happen next. When the goose finally finds a place, it has goslings. "What do we call her babies?" Mrs. Kasper asks. "Geese," Ali says. "No, goslings!" Afi and Desta say together.

Mrs. Kasper reads the story to the children, and then the class does an echo read. Mrs. Kasper reads the book a sentence at a time, tracking or pointing to the words as she and then the children read. After the echo read, Mrs. Kasper asks the children to draw a picture in their literature journals of the silliest place that the goose visits. To remind them of what they just read, she asks each child to name a place the goose visited. "Remember to label your pictures," she says, "and do your best drawing." The children work until the bell rings.

Questions for Discussion

1. What did you find most interesting about this vignette?

2. In what ways does the above vignette demonstrate examples of effective vocabulary instruction?

3. How does Mrs. Kasper integrate the four skills of reading, writing, listening, and speaking along with vocabulary instruction in each of her grade levels?

4. How does Mrs. Kasper use nonlinguistic representations in her instruction? How might you use nonlinguistic representations in your own teaching situation?

5. Discuss Mrs. Kasper's use of fiction with her ELLs. How can you use fiction and nonfiction books in your teaching situation to support vocabulary development?

Summary of Strategies Used

Mrs. Kasper understands that vocabulary development is a critical component of an effective literacy program for ELLs. Rather than leaving vocabulary development to chance, her students have many opportunities to gain knowledge of new words while developing strategies that they can use when encountering unknown words in independent reading. Mrs. Kasper's teaching, without doubt, reflects the first of the qualities identified by the International Reading Association (IRA; 2000) in its position statement on excellent reading teachers. As a teacher who works with ELLs, Mrs. Kasper's practices reflect her belief that *all* children can learn to read and write. In addition, in this vignette we also observe how an excellent reading teacher provides students with a number of strategies to help them learn and retain vocabulary by using a variety of materials for reading instruction. While the instructional strategies that we observe in Mrs. Kasper's classroom can be used with all students, in this vignette we are particularly aware of how Mrs. Kasper tailors instruction to the individual needs of her students, who vary in terms of their levels of language acquisition and grades.

Case for Exploration: Chinn Elementary School, Parkhill, Missouri

Patience Sowa

Pierre is in Mrs. Kasper's fourth-grade class. He is a newcomer who started attending Chinn Elementary in the middle of the second semester. Pierre is from a war-torn country. Mrs. Kasper is not too sure how much formal schooling he has had. He seems to be somewhat literate in French. He can sound out words and listens to read-alouds. Pierre also uses stock phrases, but is reluctant to speak or read. More important for Mrs. Kasper, he now seems to be more at ease in school. "He was clearly not comfortable in school. Once he tried to get out of class through the window," Mrs. Kasper said. Sometimes he also refused to do his work in his regular classroom.

Mrs. Kasper meets with Pierre twice a day. She meets with him both individually and with the fourth grade. In her meetings with Pierre, Mrs. Kasper has worked on school vocabulary, and is now working on home vocabulary. He is making progress slowly. Mrs. Kasper continues to review school vocabulary, especially since many of these words are words he hears in school. She reinforces the vocabulary through books, computer software, and writing. Pierre loves using the computer, so Mrs. Kasper makes it a point to use various software programs to help him learn new vocabulary. Today, after Pierre uses a computer software program to review classroom vocabulary, Mrs. Kasper conducts a brief information gap activity to get Pierre to use the vocabulary words orally. As they pick up vocabulary picture cards, they take turns asking and answering questions about the school vocabulary he is learning—for example:

"Do you have the glue?"

"Yes, I have the glue."

She then gives him a handout with vocabulary words and has him circle each word she calls out. Mrs. Kasper then moves on to working with Pierre on household vocabulary. When she tries to get him to read some of the words aloud, he sounds them out and then whispers them. Mrs. Kasper tries to get him to speak a little louder, but can still barely hear him. The same thing happens when Mrs. Kasper asks him to read sentences and then put the corresponding pictures next to the sentences.

When he is with the fourth-grade ELLs, Pierre is mostly silent. Mrs. Kasper does not push him to read, but does have him draw visual representations of what they are reading, either alone or with a partner to assess how much he understands. She chose *The Hundred Penny Box* (Mathis, 1986) to help teach Pierre about American money, and to help him and his classmates make connections with their own backgrounds. To connect with regular classroom instruction, she also has the fourth graders write timelines for the story and of their own lives. This way she also reviews birthdays, the months of the year, and numbers. By working closely with Pierre, Mrs. Kasper finds some of Pierre's strengths. He likes geography, and knows the capitals of all the countries in the world. He can also point to U.S. states on a map, when Mrs. Kasper calls them out. When they paint their hundred penny boxes in Mrs. Kasper's class, he paints the box in the colors of his country's flag.

Mrs. Kasper knows that ELLs have "a silent period" where they do not produce oral language. She therefore makes sure that she is uses simple language, and that her classroom climate is free of anxiety. She also reads many fiction and nonfiction books to her students and encourages them to do so on their own. Mrs. Kasper's dilemma is how best to encourage Pierre to read more, and to draw him out without frustrating him. He does not read the easy fiction books targeted toward ELLs, which she knows he can read, when they are assigned as homework. He frequently does not participate in silent reading. Mrs. Kasper knows all language learning takes time, and that ELLs make better progress when they are given enough time to process the language.

Questions for Discussion

1. What strategies do you think Mrs. Kasper might use to encourage Pierre to engage in reading to support vocabulary development?

2. How might Mrs. Kasper use Pierre's enthusiasm for geography and computers to encourage vocabulary development?

3. What other strategies do you think Mrs. Kasper might use to increase vocabulary learning for Pierre?

Concluding Thoughts

Vocabulary development is crucial for all students, but especially for ELLs, who need academic language to be successful in school. In her instruction, Mrs. Kasper uses a variety of strategies to help her students learn as well as internalize the new words they are learning. Mrs. Kasper capitalizes on the use of books to support vocabulary acquisition. Through the development of thematic units of instruction, she creates opportunities for students both to encounter words and to recycle these words in a variety of contexts. In addition she uses nonlinguistic representations. All the strategies Mrs. Kasper uses are powerful ways of building background and helping children learn new vocabulary.

TERMS TO KNOW

Cognates	Visuals
Graphic organizers	Wide reading programs
Language-rich classroom environments	Word map
Nonlinguistic representation	Word meaning
Read-alouds	Word recognition
Realia	Word utility
Thematic units	Word walls

RESEARCH THAT WORKS

Allen, J. (2007). *Inside words: Tools for teaching academic vocabulary grades 4–12.* Portland, ME: Stenhouse.

Beck, I. L., McKeown, M. G., & Kucan, L. (2002). *Bringing words to life: Robust vocabulary instruction.* New York: Guilford.

Blachowicz, C. L. Z., & Fisher, P. (2009). *Teaching vocabulary in all classrooms* (4th ed.). Upper Saddle River, NJ: Pearson.

Krashen, S. D. (2004). *The power of reading* (2nd ed.). Portsmouth, NH: Heinemann.

Stahl, S. A., & Nagy, E. (2006). *Teaching word meanings.* Mahwah, NJ: Lawrence Erlbaum.

WEB SITES

Education World Word: **http://www.education-world.com/a_lesson/lesson/lesson328.shtml** provides suggestions for using word walls to develop vocabulary.

Read Write Think: **http://www.readwritethink.org/index.asp** is a Web site sponsored by the National Council of Teachers of English and the International Reading Association that offers teachers a variety of vocabulary resources including vocabulary lesson ideas and graphic organizers. Research and journal articles published by these two associations back up the resources. The Web site's search engine allows teachers to search for information by subject, grade level, and resource type.

Scholastic: **http://content.scholastic.com/browse/article.jsp?id = 4503** offers general resources for vocabulary development and includes a video demonstration of a teacher using a word map.

Visual Thesaurus: **http://www.visualthesaurus.com** is a commercial site that displays dictionary words through concept maps. A trial version permits users to conduct a limited number of searches.

CHAPTER 6

Comprehending Text

Prior to reading, try to answer the following questions:

1. How would you define *reading comprehension*?

2. What does it mean to be a *strategic reader*?

3. What is the role of background knowledge in comprehension?

Reading Research to Know

While teachers, researchers and educators continue to engage in debates regarding best practices to support reading instruction, there is consensus as to what is involved in the **reading comprehension** process. Block, Gambrell, and Pressley (2002) encapsulate this understanding in the following statement: "In sum, reading comprehension is the process of meaning making" (p. 5). Experts further discuss comprehension as a process that involves the transaction between two elements: the reader and the text. The term *transaction,* first used by Rosenblatt (1978), refers to the symbiotic relationship where reader and text are interdependent; each is not only conditioned by, but also conditions the other. Consequently, meaning does not lie entirely in the text or in the reader; instead, meaning is constructed each time the reader and the text come together. The reader, Rosenblatt reminds us, is not a "blank tape registering a ready made message" (p. 10). Readers actively participate in the process of reading comprehension.

The International Reading Association (IRA; 2000) recognizes the ability to coach reading comprehension as a critical quality shared by excellent reading teachers. When coaching, teachers demonstrate a range of comprehension strategies and provide strategic support to students based on their reading needs. In this chapter we look at how excellent reading teachers coach students as they make meaning out of text. We begin our discussion by examining (a) knowledge of language systems, (b) knowledge of reading strategies, and (c) background knowledge, and how these affect reading comprehension.

Language Systems

Readers do not simply string words together to comprehend text. Words in isolation have a range of potential meanings; rather it is the context in which a word appears that supports the reader in actualizing its meaning. While readers are generally unaware that text comprehension requires that they use what they know about language, excellent reading teachers understand that readers must draw information from the same systems of language that are reflected in the text. In this section, we discuss how excellent reading teachers focus on pragmatics, semantics, syntax, and graphophonics in order to support readers in comprehending text (Freeman & Freeman, 2004b; Kucer, 2009; Kucer & Silva, 2006).

The **pragmatic system of language** governs the various uses of language in relation to the contexts in which they occur. In order to become effective comprehenders of text, readers must learn how authors use language to fulfill different functions when composing the text. Young children demonstrate their awareness of these subtle rules when early in their reading experience they recognize that a *shopping list* looks different from a *menu* or a *story*.

Excellent reading teachers know that when students are aware of the author's purpose and text functions, they are more likely to take a stance that best supports comprehension. Consequently, these teachers provide students with print-rich environments where they have many opportunities to come across texts that serve a variety of literacy functions. In addition to fiction, nonfiction, and reference materials, children encounter other genres—biographies, fantasy, poetry, fables, myths, fairy tales—as well as newspapers, cookbooks, brochures, directions, and other print materials. Key here is that teachers support comprehension by helping students understand that how students interact with text will differ depending on the function of the text. Another way classroom teachers demonstrate this is by inviting children to list different purposes they have for reading (e.g., enjoyment, finding information, complete a task, etc.) and recording their responses on a chart (Harvey & Goudvis, 2007). Once the children have developed a list, the teacher and students discuss ways in which purpose affects book selection and ways in which they approach the reading.

The **semantic system of language** refers to word meaning. Readers make use of the context—the words, phrases, sentences, or passages—in which a word appears to predict its meaning. For example, when encountering the word *bank*, a reader uses **semantic context clues**—the information that precedes and follows it—in order to identify whether the text is making reference to a building, a business transaction, or a steep side along a river. Teachers use a number of strategies to support students in using contextual analysis to determine word meaning. Often, when coaching readers, teachers facilitate the effective use of semantic cues by teaching **strategies-on-the-run**. That is, teachers support readers in applying strategies through the use of questions that prompt them to make effective use of different information sources while reading. For example, while observing a student lose meaning due to semantic miscues—such as substituting *house* for *horse*—a teacher can prompt the child to focus on semantic cues by asking, "Does this make sense?" (Fountas & Pinell, 1996, 2006).

In addition to on-the-run strategies, teachers can plan and present strategy lessons to help students specifically focus on the use of semantic cues. An example of such a strategy is *Predicting Word Meanings* (Kucer & Silva, 2006). To prepare for this strategy lesson the teacher selects a short passage—one that students can easily read in one sitting—and underlines some of the words that the students might not know. Prior to reading the text, the teacher lists the words on the board and has the students predict their meaning and records their predictions. The students then read the passage and return to the list of words and record their postreading predictions using the text as a guide. Key to this strategy is its closure when students are asked to reflect and discuss how they used the context to generate their postreading predictions. This strategy is particularly useful when working with struggling readers who have a difficult time making use of their background knowledge to predict word meaning based on the word's context.

To comprehend, readers also draw on what they know about the **syntactic system of language**—how words are arranged in a sentence. When encountering the sentence "Please open the _____," a reader is likely to predict that a noun such as *door, book,* or *refrigerator* will follow the word *the.* Readers, though able to predict the noun that follows *the* in the previous sentence, might not be able to articulate that this type of prediction requires that they understand how articles and nouns work in English. English native speakers can make use of this unconscious knowledge of the language to know when something "sounds right" and often self-correct when it does not. To support readers in making sense of text, teachers can also prompt readers to focus on syntactic cues through the use of on-the-run strategies. In this case, the prompt used is "Does that sound right?" (Fountas & Pinell, 1996, 2006).

A strategy lesson such as *selected deletion/multiple known concepts* (Kucer & Silva, 2006) exemplifies the type of lesson teachers can use to help students focus on syntactic cues in order to support comprehension. For this strategy lesson, teachers select a short passage that is unfamiliar, yet easy for the student to handle. Prior to presenting the material, the teacher replaces selected words with a line of standard length. Please refer to Table 6.1 for sample materials. The deleted words should allow the reader to make use of syntactic context to predict what word should go in the blank. It is also helpful to number each blank for easy reference during the lesson. The students peruse the entire text before being asked to read it aloud together. When students encounter a blank, they are asked to predict what word might go in it. After reading the text, the students discuss the entire range of predictions for each blank and list them on the board. As predictions are listed, the teachers asks students to evaluate them in terms of whether they *sound like language* or *sound right.* The students then reread the passage, inserting their favorite predictions for each blank. As the lesson is brought to a close, it is important that the teacher highlight how students, similar to what they did with the blanks, can use this strategy when encountering text containing words they do not know or recognize.

TABLE 6.1 Sample Materials for Selected Deletion/Multiple Known Concepts Strategy Lesson

Cinderella

Many years ago, in a far away land, there lived a poor farmer and his good wife. Their only child was a beautiful daughter. One day the wife became ill and died. The farmer was heartbroken. Time passed and the (1) _____ decided to take a second wife. She had two ugly daughters who grew envious of the farmer's (2) _____ daughter. Soon the farmer's daughter was doing the (3) _____ difficult chores in the house. (4) _____ had to get up before sunrise to cook, wash, and clean. Because she was always covered with ashes, (5) _____ ugly stepsisters named her Cinderella.

Readers draw from their understanding of **graphophonemic system of language** to comprehend text. This knowledge allows readers to distinguish letter–sound patterns such as *name* and *same*. In English this involves understanding the relation between letters (graphemes) and sound (phonemes). Teachers typically support young readers in developing knowledge of graphophonics through a variety of reading and writing activities that, while focusing on comprehension, allow children to explore letters and sounds. Alphabet books, poetry, songs, rhymes, alliteration, and name games are often used with young children. Often these books are available as **big books** or enlarged editions of the book that students can read together when participating in large-group activities. A teacher reading the big book edition of *Brown Bear, Brown Bear, What Do You See?* (Martin, 2008) might have students point to all of the words that begin with the letter *b* and identify its sound /b/. As interactive whiteboards become more readily available in classrooms, teachers can take advantage of their interactive nature to highlight sounds and letters during reading lessons. Older children might engage in strategy lessons that allow them to examine letter–sound generalizations (when *c* is followed by *e* or *i* the sound is /s/, but when followed by *a, o,* or *u* it is /k/).

Strategic Reading

In addition to making use of language cues to construct meaning, readers also draw on a number of **cognitive strategies** to process text. These strategies refer to the mental operations readers engage in while transacting with print (Block & Pressley, 2003; Harvey & Goudvis, 2007; Keene & Zimmerman, 2007; Kucer, 2009; McGregor, 2007; Tompkins, 2009; Weaver, 2002). While experts differ in terms of the labels they assign to these cognitive strategies, they generally agree that in order to comprehend text, readers make predictions about what is being read, connect to the text, ask questions, draw inferences, synthesize information, and monitor meaning (see Table 6.2). In their synthesis of research on reading comprehension, the experts commissioned by the U.S. Department of Education Office

TABLE 6.2 Reading Strategies	
Cognitive Strategy	
Predict	Readers anticipate meaning based on their background knowledge and what has been previously read.
Connect	Readers make use of background knowledge and linguistic knowledge to generate meaning. Readers also make links to previously read texts.
Question	Readers generate questions to set purpose for reading and clarify meaning.
Inference	Readers go beyond the information given in the text and draw conclusions about the text.
Synthesize	Readers draw major ideas from the text.
Monitor	Readers check for understanding and assess whether text makes sense.

of Educational Research and Improvement (RAND Reading Study Group, 2002) concluded that effective comprehension instruction must (a) support all readers in developing a repertoire of comprehension strategies, and (b) provide explicit demonstration on the use of these strategies, for low-proficiency readers in particular.

To support all readers in developing a repertoire of strategies, effective reading teachers structure instruction so that strategy lessons move from lessons where the teacher provides the most support to lessons where the students use comprehension strategies independently. This **gradual release of responsibility**, first discussed by Pearson and Gallagher in 1983, is based on the notion that when engaged in comprehension instruction, teachers initially take the majority of the responsibility for the reading task. As students become more proficient in using comprehension strategies they assume more control of the task, eventually reading on their own by using all of the comprehension strategies they have learned. Building on Vygotsky's (1978) **zone of proximal development** notion, developing as a strategic reader involves an adult or more knowledgeable peer capable of scaffolding an internal process by making it more *visible* to the less proficient reader. An instructional framework where the teacher gradually releases responsibility begins with teacher demonstrations, is followed by shared and guided reading, and culminates with independent application of comprehension strategies through self-selected reading (Cappellini, 2005; Carrasquillo, Kucer, & Abrams, 2004; Fisher, Rothenberg, & Frey, 2007; Freeman & Freeman, 2006; Kendall & Khuon, 2005; Smolkin & Donovan, 2001).

Teachers regularly make use of **think-alouds** to allow students to *see* what they do as they read. In a think-aloud, while reading a text out loud to the students, teachers demonstrate the strategies that they use by periodically stopping and voicing what is going on in their mind. Referring to these as "inner conversations," Harvey and Goudvis (2007) recommend that teachers "share the many thoughts, reactions, connections, confusions, questions" (p. 46) that arise as they engage with text. This process makes an internal process explicit to less-experienced readers. Tovani (2005) recommends that teachers reflect on their own reading practices and identify those strategies that they use as they read text that may have been difficult for them to read in college, such as a theoretical article. These insights, she argues, are useful in helping students do the same with their own text. Teachers regularly make use of think-alouds to highlight for students how to make use of the various language systems to comprehend text. Teachers, for example, might note that when they come to a word that they do not understand they stop reading, look at the pictures or other illustrations on the page, make a guess as to what the word might mean, and continue reading to see if the guess makes sense. As the class identifies solutions to breakdowns in comprehension, these can be recorded on a *Reading Wall Chart* (Kucer, Silva, & Delgado-Larocco, 1995) that can be posted for readers to refer to when working their way through text. Struggling readers, in particular, benefit from these explicit strategy demonstrations.

During the **shared reading** (Allen, 2002; Holdaway, 1979) phase of instruction, students begin to take responsibility for the reading task. At this point, the teacher introduces students to a short text—material that can be read in one sitting—that is of interest to the class. Big books work well for shared reading. Students follow along as the teacher reads, and when appropriate, the teacher stops the reading and involves the students in discussing what is being read as well as the various strategies being used to comprehend the text.

Through **guided reading** (Fountas & Pinell, 2006; Witherell, 2007), students assume more of the responsibility for the reading task. Guided reading provides students with the opportunity to read texts by themselves while receiving support from the teacher in using previously taught strategies. Texts for guided reading are selected based on their level of difficulty. A suitable book should be challenging, yet one that can be read independently. Generally this means that the child is able to read 90 out of 100 words of text without difficulty. These books are often referred to as **leveled texts**. Working with small groups, the teacher introduces a text and asks students to read individually. As all group members engage in reading, the teacher focuses on individual students and monitors their reading. At this point teachers are particularly focused on whether readers are using semantic, syntactic, and graphophonic cues effectively. Based on their observations, this is also the point where teachers most often make use of teaching strategies-on-the-run to help problem solve reading difficulties. After the text is read, students discuss the meaning of the story and the teacher validates the students for their use of comprehension strategies. A guided reading lesson concludes as the students discuss any problems they encountered while reading the text and summarize the strategies they used to overcome these problems.

The last phase of the gradual release of responsibility model involves **independent reading**. Usually known as sustained silent reading (SSR) or Drop Everything and Read (DEAR) time, this instructional component involves students in self-selecting the materials they want to read on their own. During SSR or DEAR time, students read silently for 10 to 30 minutes every day. During independent reading, students apply reading strategies they

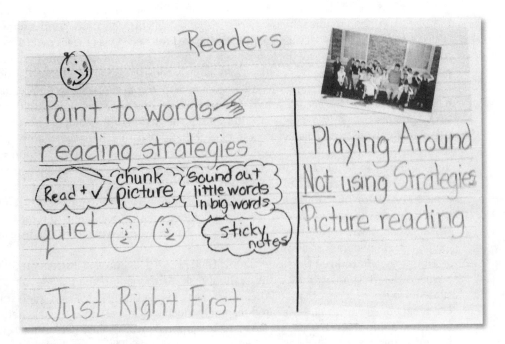

Strategies good readers use

have learned in the previous phases of the instructional cycle. Critical to the success of independent reading programs is students' access to a wide range of reading materials.

Background Knowledge

A third type of knowledge from which readers draw that is critical to the comprehension process is background knowledge. According to Rosenblatt (1987), texts are not just the ink marks on the page; they act as the blueprints that guide readers in constructing meaning. That is, meaning is not in the text; texts only offer meaning potential to the reader.

A large body of research has examined the relationship between the reader's background knowledge and his or her ability to comprehend text. Researchers consistently find that **schemata,** the mental structures representing the reader's knowledge of the world, significantly affect comprehension. Readers who were familiar with the topics being read were most able to recall the text being read (Marr & Gormley, 1982; Stevens, 1982; Tierney & Pearson, 1994).

Teachers rely on a variety of instructional strategies to support students in activating or building knowledge in order to support comprehension. Some of these activities take place prior to the students' engagement with a particular text, others take place over a longer period of time. Prior to reading a text, teachers often activate prior knowledge by having the students reflect and engage in a discussion related to the topic they will be reading about. Table 6.3 highlights pre-reading strategies commonly used in the classroom.

TABLE 6.3 Activating Prior Knowledge: Pre-Reading Strategies	
Activity	*Purpose*
Informal discussion	Teachers and students engage in informal talks about the reading topic.
Advance organizers	Advance organizers are organizational frameworks teachers use to support students in recalling previous knowledge before reading new texts. Sample advance organizers include the following: KWL Concept maps Story maps Venn diagrams Please refer to the "Web Sites" section of this chapter for links to examples and other graphic organizers.
Book walks	Teachers "walk" students through a book by encouraging them to predict the text's meaning based on pictures, titles, subtitles, or other graphic organizers. Teachers informally discuss vocabulary that the students might encounter during the book walk. In addition, the teacher might highlight text structures (chronological sequence, comparison/contrast, description, point of view, problem/solution, cause/effect).

Working With English Language Learners

Like their native English counterparts, English language learners (ELLs) draw on their understandings of language systems, their knowledge of reading strategies, and their background knowledge in order to comprehend text. Effective reading teachers, however, understand that while differences in English language proficiency affect reading comprehension, background knowledge plays a key role in processing text (Anderson, 1994; Carrell, 1987; García, 1991; Hacquebord, 1994; Malik, 1990).

To comprehend text, readers actively construct schemata or mental structures to represent their understanding of the world. Drawing from their work with ELLs, Carrell and Eisterhold (1988) further differentiate between two types of schemata: content and formal. Content schemata refers to the reader's knowledge structures regarding the content of the text. Readers who are culturally familiar with the text can recall more information about the reading. Steffensen, Joag-Dev, and Anderson's (1979) seminal research provided strong evidence for the role of content schemata in reading comprehension. In their study, U.S. and Indian adults were asked to read passages describing either an American or an Indian wedding. Results indicated that when the reading material matched the reader's cultural background, the text was easier to read and reading comprehension was higher. When reading about an Indian wedding, for example, Indian students in the study read faster and could recall many more details than when reading about American weddings.

Formal schemata, on the other hand, refer to the reader's background knowledge of organizational structures of different types of texts. Early research in the effects of formal schemata on comprehension noted that background knowledge in discipline-specific content affected the reading comprehension of second language learners (Alderson & Urquhart, 1988). More recently, researchers have closely examined the distinctive features of academic texts and argue that in order to comprehend these texts, readers in general, and ELLs in particular, must understand the role of text types, genres, and structure in conveying meaning (Schleppegrell & Colombi, 2002). For example, to comprehend expository text—the type of text associated with academic content areas such as social studies or science—readers must be able to recognize a variety of text structures, such as cause/effect or compare/contrast. Readers must also be able to understand that signal words such as *therefore* and *in order to* indicate cause/effect; whereas signal words such as *on the contrary* or *on the other hand* indicate compare/contrast.

Teachers working with ELLs also understand that they must provide additional scaffolds to support children in developing aspects of language that they will need to know to comprehend text. Excellent reading teachers know that to draw on semantics and syntactic cues to comprehend text, ELLs need to learn how these language systems operate in English. ELLs, for example, may not have enough knowledge of English syntax to know whether something "sounds right" or not. This is particularly the case if the students are in the beginning stages of language acquisition. More proficient students might encounter difficulties in those instances where their primary language and English do not share the same features—for example, languages that do not have markers for possessive forms (the boy's toy), or have different ways of noting possessive forms than the way we note possessives in English. Further reading experiences with books that contain repeated, predictable language patterns are particularly appropriate for this group. Through read-alouds and shared reading, teachers help ELLs learn new word meanings and language patterns.

Though reading instruction over the past decade has focused on systematic and explicit instruction of phonemic awareness and phonics, there is no clear evidence that such narrowly focused programs support ELLs. This view was expressed by the National Literacy Panel on Language-Minority Children and Youth (Shanahan & Beck, 2006) that, after reviewing the five research studies available in this area, arrived at the following recommendation: "Clearly, five small studies of phonological awareness and phonics are far from sufficient to allow a determination of the most useful instructional methods for meeting the early literacy needs of English-language learners" (p. 427). While effective reading teachers support ELLs in using graphophonic cues, they do so through activities that make English comprehensible. ELLs, unlike their native English counterparts, need to develop knowledge of words and their meaning along with the ability to associate letters and sounds related to these words. Big books, alphabet books, poetry, songs, rhymes, alliteration, and name games are also used with ELLs because they provide other contextual cues to develop word meaning along with knowledge about letters and sounds.

In our discussion of comprehension strategies we also note that experts document that ELLs, like their monolingual counterparts, employ similar strategies when dealing with text (Dressler & Kamil, 2006). Jiménez, Garcia, and Pearson (1996) examined the reading strategies used by bilingual readers and concluded that while bilingual children make use of unique strategies involving their ability to draw from both languages, they also use those strategies most commonly used by monolingual readers: use of prior knowledge, inferencing and drawing conclusions, questioning, using context, and monitoring meaning. Unique to bilingual readers was their ability to use cognates—words with a common origin, such as English *thermal energy* and Spanish *energía térmica* (p. 103)—and translating. These students were also able to transfer information that they knew in one language to reading in the second language and were aware that they could use the same basic reading strategies in both languages. Monolingual English readers, unlike bilingual readers, could focus more on monitoring comprehension because they did not struggle with unknown vocabulary and could more often make use of their prior knowledge. The teaching of comprehension strategies with ELLs is widely supported by educators in the field (Cappellini, 2005; Carrasquillo et al., 2004; Fisher et al., 2007; Freeman & Freeman, 2006; Kendall & Khuon, 2005; Smolkin & Donovan, 2001).

Inside the Classroom:
Baggaley Elementary School, Latrobe, Pennsylvania

Donna Witherspoon and Julie Ankrum

Baggaley Elementary School sits amid the rolling farm fields and small communities of southwestern Pennsylvania, in the foothills of the Laurel Mountains. As part of the Greater Latrobe School District, Baggaley is a rural school with 700 students in Grades K through 6. This vignette features teacher Mrs. Weatherton and her fifth-grade students. Mrs. Weatherton and her colleague, Mrs. Allison Kesslar, developed the strategies described in the vignette.

It is the middle of April in Mrs. Weatherton's fifth-grade classroom, and the students are engaged in a whole-class discussion of Chapters 9 and 10, the latest installment of the novel they are reading, *Walk Two Moons* (Creech, 1994). Student desks are arranged in a large, center-facing square, allowing students to interact with one another. Each student has a copy of the novel and a set of index cards marked with symbols. Johnny begins by holding up an index card with a question mark on it.

Johnny:	I have a question. I wanted to discuss why Mary Lou's parents don't care as much as Phoebe's parents.
Morgan:	Maybe they care but there are just too many kids.
Kelly:	I agree. It would really be hard to raise that many kids.
Mrs. Weatherton:	Well, let's take a look. On page 46, how did the author describe the house? *[Students locate the page.]*
Castle:	" . . . complete pandemonium."
Mrs. Weatherton:	What do you think that means?
Johnny:	It's easy to tell. The book says: *[reading from the text]*

> There were footballs and basketballs lying all over the place, and boys sliding down the banister and leaping over tables and talking with their mouths full and interrupting everyone with endless questions. (Creech, 1994, p. 46)

Mrs. Weatherton:	Good, you found some **context clues** that help us to understand what the author means by "complete pandemonium." We know that often we can find clues to the meaning of unknown words by reading what comes before and after them in the text. That's a strategy we've learned.
Castle:	Maybe mom was on top of the garage to escape all the jumping around. I think they had a few basic rules to follow but not too many.
Morgan:	I agree with Castle. The parents had some rules but pretty much it was just do whatever you want. But why was Mr. Finney in the bathtub with his clothes on?
Casey:	That was my question, too. Was there water in the tub? *[laughter]*
Johnny:	Yeah, I was wondering that, too. Maybe he just wanted to get away. I guess it's really hard to tell.

The students continue to explore the text, with individual students initiating points of discussion. Students have marked sections of the text by flagging them with mini sticky notes on which they've written symbols to signify personal connections, questions, and predictions that they formed as they read. They use bookmarks that have keys to the meaning of the symbols and to which the mini sticky note pads have been attached (see Figure 6.1.) The bookmarks also have symbols for coding places in the text where students find new or interesting vocabulary words or examples of similes that they

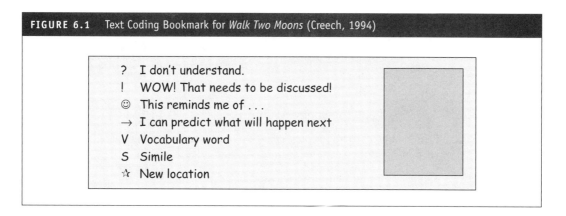

FIGURE 6.1   Text Coding Bookmark for *Walk Two Moons* (Creech, 1994)

> ?   I don't understand.
> !   WOW! That needs to be discussed!
> ☺   This reminds me of . . .
> →   I can predict what will happen next
> V   Vocabulary word
> S   Simile
> ☆   New location

encounter while reading. Mrs. Weatherton has students use this strategy of "coding text" (Harvey & Goudvis, 2007) to encourage them to be thinking readers; it also acts as a catalyst for group discussions. For *Walk Two Moons,* she has included a symbol for "new location" because the plot for this novel involves a physical journey across several states as the main character, Salamanca, travels from Ohio to Idaho with her grandparents.

On this day, the whole-class discussion is followed by small, breakout group discussions. Breakout groups are comprised of four or five students of mixed abilities. As students transition to small groups, Mrs. Weatherton reminds them that the expectations for participation in breakout groups are that everyone participates equally and takes "five or more" turns to share thoughts and ideas. In one breakout group, Daniel begins the conversation by directing group members to page 55. He reads his selected section of text aloud:

> There's a part of the city where no cars can go, and thousands of people stroll around eating ice cream. We went into Ella's Kosher Deli and Ice Cream Parlor and ate pastrami sandwiches and kosher dill pickles, followed by raspberry ice cream. (Creech, 1994, p. 55)

Daniel: This part reminds me of the time we went to the Outer Banks. We went to an island on a ferry. There wasn't too much to do there so we just walked around eating ice cream all day *[laughing].*

Morgan: I have two thoughts. It reminds me of going to Florida. My second is that every Saturday, me and my grandpa eat lunch at The Pond Restaurant and every time we go I order a plate of kosher dill pickles!

Alexis: A whole plate of pickles?

Alex: I want to talk about page 58. *[reading from the text]*

> I looked closer. The woman in the center was hopping up and down. On her feet were flat, white shoes. In the space between drum beats, I heard her say, "Huzza, huzza." (Creech, 1994, p. 58)

Alex: This makes me think about my grandma. My grandma is very old and she loves to get attention. She likes to interrupt everyone. She gets in the middle of everything and she dances around—it doesn't matter what the beat is.

Alexis: Is it embarrassing?

Alex: Sometimes, and sometimes it's funny.

Miranda: I have a question about page 55 at the bottom. *[Group members locate the page.]* Why doesn't Sal want to send postcards?

Morgan: Maybe they remind her of her mother because her mother sent her postcards.

Daniel: And maybe she just doesn't want to waste the time, you know, it takes some time to write out postcards and send them.

Alexis: Yeah, I think she just wants to get to her mom.

Alex: I think she's sad.

Miranda: Okay, those are pretty good reasons. I get it now.

Small-group discussion of *Walk Two Moons*

While her students continue their discussions, Mrs. Weatherton circulates the room, primarily listening and observing. Mrs. Weatherton's reading goals for students are that they love reading, choose to read in and outside of school, and constantly go deeper with comprehension. From the beginning of the year she has provided a series of instructional experiences that move students toward these goals. She begins the year by selecting a high-interest, lower readability novel as a whole-class experience. This year she used *Shiloh* (Naylor, 2000). Mrs. Weatherton set the expectation early on for active thinking and sharing by modeling and providing guided practice for students in previewing, predicting, reading, and discussing each section of *Shiloh* as it was read.

Mrs. Weatherton is deliberate in choosing realistic fiction for the first whole-class novel because she has noted that her students relate to the characters and situations in this genre, which helps them to begin making personal connections to what they are reading. She has found that survival stories, where the main characters are about the same age as her students, encourage them to think about how they would react in similar situations. Mrs. Weatherton believes that this personal involvement fosters interest and enthusiasm, especially among those students who come to her as reluctant readers.

During the year, Mrs. Weatherton alternates whole-class novels with literature circle (see Table 6.4). In **literature circles,** small groups of students read and discuss books that they self-select from **text sets** that she provides. A text set (Kucer & Silva, 2006) is a grouping of two or more books that are linked by a topic or concept, but vary in terms of author, point of view, organizational structure, genre, or text type. When reading a text set—where each book is intertextually linked to other books—readers can focus on a range of related meanings and make use of their experiences with one text to comprehend other texts (Hartman, 1995).

TABLE 6.4 Examples of Whole-Class Novels and Text Sets

Whole-Class Novels	Text Set: Fiction	Text Set: Biography	Text Set: Informational
Shiloh (Naylor, 2000) *Sign of the Beaver* (Speare, 1983) *The Westing Game* (Raskin, 1978) *Island of the Blue Dolphin* (O'Dell, 1960) *Walk Two Moons* (Creech, 1994)	*Shadow of a Bull* (Wojciechowska, 1964) *Indian in the Cupboard* (Banks, 1980) *Dear Mr. Henshaw* (Cleary, 1983) *Night of the Twisters* (Ruckman, 1984) *Maniac McGee* (Spinelli, 1990) *Sounder* (Armstrong, 1969)	Who Was Series: *Who Was Wolfgang Amadeus Mozart?* (McDonough, 2003) *Who Was Helen Keller?* (Thompson, 2003) *Who Was Harry Houdini?* (Sutherland, 2003) *Who Was Ferdinand Magellan?* (Kramer, 2003) *Who Was Thomas Jefferson?* (Fradin, 2003)	Historic Flights: *Inside the Hindenburg* (Majoor, 2000) *First Flight* (Shea, 1997) *To Space and Back* (Ride, 1986) *Moonwalk* (Donnelly, 1989)

Compared to a classroom where the teacher has all students read the same text at the same time—a one-size-fits-all approach—Mrs. Weatherton uses text sets to support students who differ in terms of background knowledge and literacy abilities.

Again, because students choose the book they want to read and discuss, literature circle groups are heterogeneous. Mrs. Weatherton has adapted the cooperative learning strategy called fishbowl as a way for students to understand and internalize expectations for literature circle discussions. During fishbowl, one group of students models a complete literature circle discussion while the rest of the class looks on. Following each fishbowl demonstration, Mrs. Weatherton and her students critique the discussion. Mrs. Weatherton believes that this modeling and debriefing process is critical in helping students understand and carry out effective and inclusive conversations about texts. She guides students to focus especially on those aspects of discussion that deepen the meaning of what's been read. Mrs. Weatherton believes that the time spent on these modeled discussions at the beginning of the year allows students to function very independently later on.

As with prevalent literature circle models (Daniels, 1994), Mrs. Weatherton assigns roles to individual students to structure discussions. Every student, however, is assigned the role of "Questioner." Students learn the difference between "right there" questions to which answers can be found in the text and "author and me" questions that require higher-level thinking skills (Raphael, Highfield, & Au, 2006). At first, Mrs. Weatherton structures this process by providing each student with a notebook ring of cards on which the following question starters are written:

How did . . . ?
What would happen if . . . ?
What caused . . . ?
What might . . . ?
How would you feel if you . . . ?
Why did . . . ?
Why do you think . . . ?
Why is . . . ?
What if . . . ?
Who do you think . . . ?

Each student in the group selects two starters to use in formulating his or her questions about the section of text read. Mrs. Weatherton believes that this structure provides appropriate support for all of her students, but especially those who initially have difficulty moving beyond the literal level of thinking about text meaning.

A district-developed curriculum map that is tied to Pennsylvania state standards for language arts serves as a guide for the specific skills and strategies that Mrs. Weatherton includes in her daily language arts instruction. She believes that the context in which students develop these skills and strategies needs to be interesting, relevant, compelling literature. She also believes that the social construction of comprehension through meaningful, student-led discourse provides all of her students with a supportive structure for developing deep understandings of the texts they read.

Questions for Discussion

1. What did you find most interesting about this vignette?
2. In what ways does Mrs. Weatherton scaffold student-led discussions of text?
3. How does focused discourse help students to construct meaning?
4. How do personal connections to text help deepen understanding and enrich reading experiences?
5. How are less-able readers supported in this learning environment?
6. How might the processes in Mrs. Weatherton's fifth grade be adapted for older students? Younger students?

Summary of Strategies Used

Mrs. Weatherton's approach to comprehension instruction reflects three of the qualities identified by the IRA (2000) as distinguishing excellent classroom reading teachers. In the vignette we see how Mrs. Weatherton supports her students by offering a variety of reading materials. Students in her classroom make use of text sets that include narratives as well as expository texts. In her classroom we also recognize grouping strategies to tailor instruction to individual students. While at times she uses whole classroom instruction, she also knows that for students to participate equally in discussion, she must break her class into smaller groups of students with diverse reading abilities. Lastly, we see various examples of strategic teaching and coaching in her classroom. Mrs. Weatherton's students feel at ease demonstrating their own use of strategies by flagging text with sticky notes to signify how they connect, question, and predict text as they engage in reading. Mrs. Weatherton has students first observe how she uses these strategies through think-alouds. She then coaches students to use these strategies on their own.

Case for Exploration: Morningside Elementary School, Pennsylvania

Donna Witherspoon and Julie Ankrum

Ms. Bruster has been teaching second grade at Morningside Elementary School for the past 9 years. Although her educational background is in elementary math education, Ms. Bruster is known throughout her rural school district as an exemplary teacher of literacy. Her expertise has developed through participation in many literacy professional development opportunities provided through the district's literacy initiative. In addition to participating in study groups, workshops, and inservices, Ms. Bruster interacted with a literacy coach to hone her skills. As a result of this extended study, Ms. Bruster has become a master at teaching young readers to comprehend text.

Comprehension instruction is not an add-on at Morningside Elementary School; it is a vital part of the reading curriculum, beginning in kindergarten and continuing through sixth grade. Each fall the children entering Ms. Bruster's second-grade classroom come to her with a wide range of abilities; she considers it her mission to teach every child how to comprehend the print in front of them. She explains, "The goal is to make a lifelong reader. You have to make sure they can be independent problem-solvers, independent thinkers, and love to read."

Earlier in the year, Ms. Bruster discovered that although Wade could fluently read grade-level texts, he struggled to understand the author's message. Sara struggled to decode unknown words, which adversely affected her comprehension. These students, along with others in the class, quickly became a priority for Ms. Bruster. During independent work time, she conducts mini comprehension lessons for these students. For example, in her last meeting with Wade, Ms. Bruster coached him to reread a short text with phrased fluency. When Ms. Bruster last met with Sara, she modeled how to use known chunks to decode unknown words.

Wade, Sara, and all of the other students have been taught to select *just-right* books, that is, books that they can read with a high level of accuracy and comprehension. This is important so that students can practice the comprehension strategies that have been taught during previous whole-class and small-group lessons. While the students read their self-selected books, Ms. Bruster informally assesses and teaches two or three children per day through an individual reading conference. The focus of these meetings is varied: general enjoyment of reading, decoding strategies, text selection, author's style and craft, and the use of comprehension strategies have all been covered in these conferences. The following is an excerpt from one such conference between Mrs. Bruster (T) and one of her students (S):

T: Tell me what made you pick that book (*Caught in the Web [From the Files of Madison Finn]*, by Dower, 2001).

S: Well, I looked at it and it looked really interesting. I saw the other one. I looked at it and I read a page and I really liked it and the title and the front page looked really fun and . . .

T: So you liked the cover and then you also previewed a little bit of it.

S: And I read the back. So, the back said a lot.

T: OK, so you used the summary on the back to help? And then when you read the page in the book, what were you looking for when you read the page?

S: Um . . . if it was like not so it was like really boring. Me and my mom don't like books when they say "she said" and "he said" on the phone. Instead of the names, they go "he said" and "she said," when there's like five people gabbing on the phone. We read a mystery book that was like that and we had to stop because it was too confusing.

T: OK, so you knew what would make a book too hard for you.

S: Because right here it says "dad said" instead of "he said."

T: OK, and we talked about that when we were learning about conversation. That can be tricky. So, I know you're just getting started but tell me, just by looking at it, is it hard? Is it just right? Is it easy? What do you think it . . .

S: Um . . . I think it's just right.

Ms. Bruster uses these conversations to hone in on the comprehension strategies that are most appropriate to the individual.

Ms. Bruster's reading block is devoted to small-group reading instruction. This is another time devoted to **differentiated reading instruction** to meet the needs of all of the learners in her class. The students are grouped homogeneously based on reading strengths and needs; however, group membership changes often throughout the year. Ms. Bruster meets with five to seven different groups throughout the course of the week; the number of meetings varies by group ability.

Although both Sara and Wade struggle to read grade-level texts, they are not placed in the same small group because their needs are so different. Sara struggles to decode unknown words, so she is assigned to Group 5, where the dual focus of all lessons is decoding skills and comprehension strategies. Wade is a fluent reader and a strong decoder who struggles to comprehend as he reads. Therefore, he works with Group 4, where the focus is on practicing comprehension strategies that were modeled in the day's shared reading lesson. Table 6.5 provides a description of the focus of each of Ms. Bruster's groups as observed in mid-May.

TABLE 6.5	Small-Group Lesson Focus		
Group Number	Class Rank	Reading Level	Instructional Focus
1	Highest	Q (Grade 4)	Comprehension Making connections Main idea
2	Highest	Q (Grade 4)	Comprehension Questioning Character traits
3	Average	N (Grade 3)	Comprehension Character traits Predictions Making connections Word study Vocabulary
4	2nd Lowest	M (End of Grade 2)	Comprehension Making connections Main idea
5	Lowest	L/M (End of Grade 2)	Comprehension Making connections Character traits Word study Decoding Vocabulary

While Ms. Bruster meets with a small group of students, the rest of the children are actively engaged in literacy centers. Students work in small (four to six children) heterogeneous groups to practice and extend the strategies that have been taught during whole-group and small-group instruction. The theme this week is centered on a science unit about life under the sea; the literacy centers revolve around this theme. Table 6.6 provides a brief description of the literacy centers used in Ms. Bruster's classroom this week.

TABLE 6.6 Literacy Centers		
Literacy Center	*Activity*	*Instructional Focus*
Research center	Students research facts about sea creatures using informational books from the library. Students record interesting facts.	Locating details in expository text
Book browse and Trio talk	Students work in groups of three to browse books about sea life. Students use role cards to take turns reading, questioning, and summarizing.	Comprehension strategies applied to expository text Cooperative learning
Writing center	Students write a fictional story applying facts learned about the ocean.	Writing process
Readers Theatre	Students practice reading a short fictional text starring sea creatures.	Fluency: expression, phrasing, and rate
Computer center	Students practice reading expository text and answering comprehension questions with interactive computer games.	Silent reading comprehension

Ms. Bruster organizes a variety of instructional components each day in order to teach her second graders how to read. Comprehension instruction is a complex endeavor; it is necessary to echo the lessons throughout the day to ensure understanding. Ms. Bruster introduces strategies to the whole group through shared reading experiences. This is when she models and explicitly teaches the children how to apply specific skills and strategies. Small-group instruction is the venue through which she tailors the instruction to meet the needs of the learners. She reteaches, deepens understanding, or introduces new concepts, all based on the needs of group members. Finally, Ms. Bruster employs individualized instruction to focus on needed skills and strategies for each child in her classroom.

Questions for Discussion

1. How does Ms. Bruster support readers at various proficiency levels to develop comprehension strategies?

2. Why would Ms. Bruster change group membership during small-group instruction?

3. Discuss other strategies you have observed teachers use to differentiate reading comprehension instruction.

Concluding Thoughts

Excellent reading teachers, as noted in IRA's (2000) position statement, recognize the importance of coaching students in developing reading comprehension strategies. In this chapter we discussed how readers draw from what they know about language systems, use a variety of reading strategies, and make use of background knowledge to comprehend text. In Mrs. Weatherton's classroom, we had the opportunity to see how teachers scaffold instruction by initially modeling how to use comprehension strategies and then guiding students through small- and large-group discussion activities that allow them to deepen their understanding of a variety of texts.

TERMS TO KNOW

Big books	Pragmatics
Cognitive strategies	Reading comprehension
Context clues	Schemata
Differentiated reading instruction	Semantic context clues
Gradual release of responsibility	Semantic system of language
Graphophonemic system of language	Shared reading
Guided reading	Strategies-on-the-run
Independent reading	Syntactic system of language
Leveled texts	Text sets
Literature circles	Think-alouds
Pragmatic system of language	Zone of proximal development

RESEARCH THAT WORKS

Cappellini, M. (2005). *Balancing reading & language learning*. Portland, ME/Newark, DE: Stenhouse/ International Reading Association.

Harvey, S., & Goudvis, A. (2007). *Strategies that work: Teaching comprehension to enhance understanding* (2nd ed.). Portland, ME: Stenhouse.

Keene, E. O., & Zimmerman, S. (2007). *Mosaic of thought*. (2nd ed.). Portsmouth, NH: Heinemann.

Kendall, J., & Khuon, O. (2005). *Making sense: Small-group comprehension lessons for English language learners*. Portland, ME: Stenhouse.

McGregor, T. (2007). *Comprehension connections*. Portsmouth, NH: Heinemann.

WEB SITES

Comprehension Lessons: **http://www.readinglady.com/index.php?module = pagemaster& PAGE_user_op = view_page&PAGE_id = 2&MMN_position = 4:4** offers comprehension lessons based on *Mosaic of Thought* by Ellin Keene and Susan Zimmerman and *Strategies That*

Work by Stephanie Harvey and Anne Goudvis (see references in "Research That Works" section of this chapter).

Engaging With Literature: **http://www.learner.org/resources/series183.html** provides video workshops to support teachers in engaging readers make meaning when reading literature.

Reading Comprehension: **http://www.literacy.uconn.edu/compre.htm#strategy** is a link to The Literacy Web at the University of Connecticut site that offers a variety of links to general discussions on comprehension as well as teacher support for developing comprehension strategies.

Reading Rockets: **http://www.readingrockets.org/teaching/reading101/comprehension** is a site sponsored by the U.S. Department of Education and Public Broadcasting Service (PBS) to support reading development.

Strategies for Helping Readers: **http://www.thinkport.org/career/strategies/reading/default.tp** is a site that provides teachers information regarding comprehension strategies. Videos demonstrate strategies; teachers' video demonstrations of comprehension strategies.

CHAPTER 7

Writing Development

Prior to reading, try to answer the following questions:

1. How do children learn to write?

2. What does it mean to be an effective writer?

3. What are some strategies for teaching the writing process?

Reading Research to Know

In the popular children's book, *Anastasia Krupnik,* Lois Lowry (1979) captures a child's love for writing. Anastasia, the fourth-grade main character, spends days reflecting on how to best use words as images—so that readers can feel and understand the poem she is writing. She uses poetic devices, such as onomatopoeia and metaphor, to bring her poem to life; however, Anastasia's teacher, Mrs. Wesvessel, is a traditional teacher of writing and wants children to write only poems that have rhyme and use capital letters. As she hears Anastasia reading her poem, she replies, "Well. Anastasia, when we talked about poetry in this class we simply were not talking about worms and snails crawling on a piece of paper. I'm afraid I will have to give you an F" (p. 13). Hearing Mrs. Wesvessel's discouragement—and harsh criticism—breaks Anastasia's spirit and love of words. Since the publication of Lowry's book in the late 1970s, the teaching of writing has changed, and many teachers today seek to create a community of writers within their classroom. In progressive writing classrooms, teachers teach structured writing mini lessons, conference with students about their writing, and use rubrics and ongoing conferences to provide writers feedback throughout the writing process. Classrooms like Mrs. Wesvessel's are no longer the norm, nor are teachers like Mrs. Wesvessel viewed as effective teachers. In this chapter, we examine research to support ways that teachers can create a community, while at the same time prepare students to progress as writers and view themselves as writers.

Learning to Write

Young children learn to write early in life. At even 18 months old or younger, children begin making marks on paper, and they also make marks on walls, books, and clothes. When they make these marks, children look for others to also make sense of their work (Smith & Elley, 1997; Tolchinsky, 2006). These early stages of writing are described by researchers as *emergent writing,* which involves nonlinear scribbles and linear scribes; as children age and develop, they begin to write using letter-like forms. Researchers describe numerous developmental stages of writing in the early years, and most of these researchers agree that these stages are not necessarily sequential (Dyson, 1993; Dyson & Freedman, 1990; Morrow, 2009; Soderman & Farrell, 2008; Sulzby, Barnhart, & Hieshima, 1989; Temple, Nathan, Burris, & Temple, 1988; Tompkins, 2007). Three broad stages of writing development are described below.

Emergent writing is a term used to describe scribbling, one-letter writing, and invented spelling that children use without necessarily including spacing between words (Tompkins, 2007). Young children use drawing as a way to communicate and write, and they view their drawings as a way to communicate an important message, as seen in the 2-year-old's drawing in Figure 7.1. Reading and writing are an integral part of Caroline's life at her preschool

FIGURE 7.1   Emergent Writing Example

and at home. She attends a preschool that values the importance of reading aloud to young children—and that reading and writing serve as an extension of the imagination. For example, role-playing and pretend play help children develop the language fluency and elaboration needed for narrative compositions (Lacina & Watson, 2002). At Caroline's preschool, students role-play the retelling of narrative stories in front of the class to help better comprehend the story and understand the structure of narrative texts. As Frank Smith (1997) says, we must encourage children of all ages to love writing for a lifetime, and we can do this by inviting them to join the "literacy club." Members of the literacy club are those parents and children who recognize the importance of reading and writing, and when children see their parents or caregivers involved in daily writing, children too will strive to be writers—even as emergent writers (Lacina & Watson, 2002). Even at an early age, Caroline desires to be a member of the literacy club. At age 2 she knows that print is a way to communicate with others. She makes random scribbles yet also finds meaning in the drawing. Caroline tells her mother what her drawing is about, and her mother records her words (see Figure 7.1).

As emergent writers develop, their scribbling becomes noticeably more sophisticated, and with this added sophistication, young children often use scribbles to represent writing. Often, children will scribble from left to right—just as if they are writing. As Caroline matures and becomes more aware of how authors write in a book, she also reexamines how she places words and pictures on a page. Figure 7.2 shows how Caroline begins to understand that words on a page are written to represent an idea—and pictures often tell the same story. At age 3, Caroline shows how she is playing with puppets, represented by the picture on the left of Figure 7.2—and the scribbles to the right of the drawing to represent a written description of how she enjoyed playing with the puppets at her preschool.

Beginning writing is a second stage of the development of young children's writing. Typically, beginning writing includes invented spelling with spacing, and the use of invented spelling while applying spelling and grammar rules learned in school. At age 4, Caroline understands spaces—and uses invented spelling, as seen in Figure 7.3. In this example, Caroline seems to grasp that words need to be separated with a space. She does not yet distinguish the rules for capital and lower case letters, but most important, she is communicating a message she feels is important.

Similarly, William, Caroline's 6-year-old cousin from Raleigh, North Carolina, learns to write at his traditional, private school by practicing writing sentences about holidays and special events. In this school example, he writes from left to right, includes capital letters for proper nouns, and includes periods and spacing to separate one sentence from the next. He still demonstrates invented spelling as he sounds out the spelling of words. However, his writer's "voice" does not come through in his in school writing as much as it does through his out-of-school writing at home (see Figure 7.4).

As William gets older and develops as a writer, his writing should become more fluent. **Fluent writing** is defined as having nearly conventional spelling (Tompkins, 2007). William is now in second grade; some of his most creative writing is written at home. The main characters in his story are his pet fish, and he designs his story in the format of a chapter book. William's mother frequently reads to him, and his love for reading, and his

FIGURE 7.2 Learning to Write

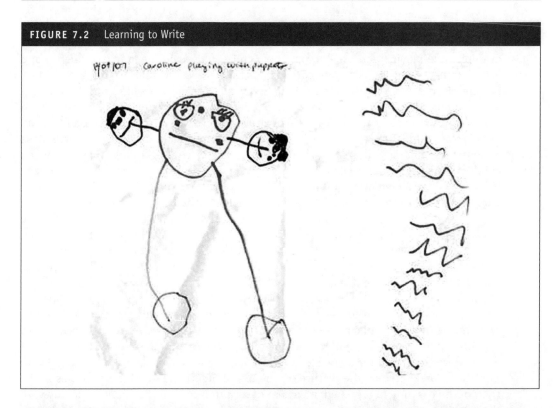

FIGURE 7.3 Beginning Writing

FIGURE 7.4 Beginning Writing

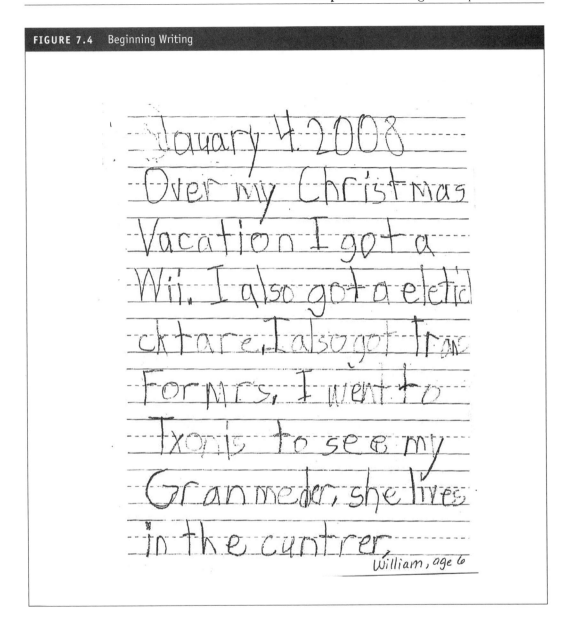

Jauary 4, 2008
Over my Christmas
Vacation I got a
Wii. I also got a eletic
cktare. I also got Tran
Formrs, I went to
Txoni to see my
Granmeder, she lives
in the cuntrer.

William, age 6

writer's voice, comes through in his writing at home. Examine Figure 7.5—and how William creatively writes a chapter book.

Although there are many examples of invented spelling and mechanical errors, William's content is more developed than examples of his school writing. William's focus in this example is on writing content—and telling a story—instead of focusing on the grammar/mechanics of writing, as emphasized in his school writing. As teachers

FIGURE 7.5   Fluent Writing

Finnster and Suckey vs. the King the Big Climintine

At First

Some bad fish were king of the good fish. The good fish were not happy. Finnster supper and suppers as supper suckey and angel and black and sordtail and bright. They were all friends and supper. That day Clmintine was the king of the old place called fishlin. The fish were very happy until Climintine was king.

Chapter 1 Life Is Supper

In old fishlin some fish were por. They wanted food. But they king wanted all of there monney the king was rich. The fish wanted monney. They were very por. They want monney bad! Finly Finnster had a idea. He told it to his teem. They were happy of o finnsters idea. Finnster supper the code to a power. The king herd them saying the code. He said it to. Now finnster herd the code. Now the king was mad that finnster herd it. Suckey get a sucking sucker out of your pocket. Sordtail get a firesord out of your pocket. Bright get two sunshines one for me and one for you. Angel get your invane shooter.

Chapter 2 There They Are

Out of your pocket. Finnster saw the King and the King saw him. The King sent his teem out of his home. They were very big. Finnster has not seen such big fish before. They were oscars finnster said to his teem they eat little fish. Crown was making robots at that time. The oscars looked mad. Finnster said ten fish and 10 meen oscars. Climintine swam away to check on crown. Then he herd something. It was bright with finnster eating a sunshine they got very bright. The king could not look. It was hot to. I get up to 108,015. The bad king did not give up. Climintine sent the monsters out to get them. They did what the king said. They were big and fat.

Chapter 3 Battles

They battled and battled so one could win. They did FS, B and N won. The good wins. The country fishlin was free! from the king they all went home but Climintine did not go hom. He was in jail. They slep. The next day they got up and eat.

The End

consider ways to include writing in the curriculum, they must think of ways to motivate and engage students, and even more important, how they can encourage children to view writing as important beyond the confines of the classroom. When

William Rhodes, age 7, Raleigh, North Carolina

students have a choice (Bright, 1995) of what to write, they are often more motivated and engaged during the writing process (Atwell, 1987; Routman, 1994; Wood & Dickinson, 2000).

Parents and teachers can encourage young and fluent writers to write by making writing fun and relevant to their lives. Activities at home to encourage writing include writing lists for the grocery store, letter writing with family members, and helping children write thank you notes for gifts they receive. In William's case, his mother encourages him to write notes to his cousins in Texas, and at 7 years old, he sends e-mail and video cam messages to his cousins. Similar to learning to read, when children see the adults in their lives reading and writing they understand that reading and writing are valued and important.

Word Recognition

There are numerous ways that teachers can scaffold writing for young children. For this chapter, we decided to focus on the strategies that we feel are the most helpful for

William composing, using his laptop computer

developing independent writers, and for scaffolding writing to develop independent writers. First, similar to learning to read, children need to recognize sight words when learning to write. These words help children develop **automaticity,** which is the ability to recall and recognize a word quickly and accurately (LaBerge & Samuels, 1974). Being able to recognize and spell **high-frequency words,** words that readers and writers read most often in books, helps them create a message more easily. Numerous researchers have analyzed and calculated lists of commonly used, or high-frequency, words. Dolch in 1936 prepared his well-known Dolch List of Basic Sight Words. A more recent list was created by Fry (2004; see word lists at http://www .literacyconnections.com/Dolch1.html). High-frequency words can be highlighted on **word walls,** which is space on a wall where words are organized alphabetically. As children learn new words, these words can be added to the class word wall. Word walls are helpful to young children as they write since they can refer to the word wall for the spelling of high-frequency words, and as a result, children can focus on the content of their writing instead of on spelling. Writing becomes more fluent for children with the use of these high-frequency words.

Modeled, shared, guided, and *interactive writing* are all types of writing in which the teacher serves as a guide, and gradually releases responsibility as children become independent writers. Table 7.1 highlights these types of writing. As you read the definitions and examples, glance at the figure to examine the types of writing in a reading/writing classroom.

First, **modeled writing** is a way for the teacher to show students what it means to be a fluent, active writer. The teacher models topics and demonstrates how to organize information, or how to proofread and edit one's writing. The teacher can model any aspect of content

TABLE 7.1   Reading/Writing Elements

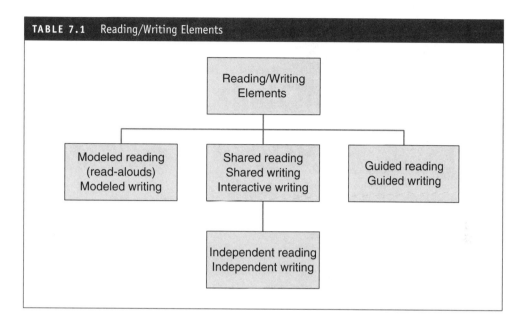

or convention development within any stage of the writing process. Graves (1994) explains that teachers often begin a modeled writing session by "thinking aloud" the process they are going through as they write. The teacher often says words and sentences slowly as she is writing, and she thinks-aloud this process of determining how to write. Teachers will sometimes ask students questions during the modeled writing session to involve them in the writing process and to include them in the decision making. Most commonly, teacher's model the following: topic selection, gathering/selecting information, new forms of writing, and how to include voice in writing. Modeled lessons introduce students to new forms of writing, and in the case of developing "voice" in writing, teachers can show how they developed their personal voice in a piece, which in turn helps students better understand the concept of developing a writer's voice.

Shared writing is when the children and teacher plan a text together. Typically, the children will tell the teacher what and how to write—as they compose a joint text. The purpose of such writing is for the teacher to model the thought process for writing. Unlike modeled writing, the children have more independence in this type of writing since they are more actively contributing to the composing of the text.

Guided writing is when the teacher works with a small group of children to provide explicit instruction based on the individual students' needs (Fountas & Pinnell, 2001). At other times, children may request help in this type of group; topics can be scheduled and students can sign up for guided writing groups when needed throughout the writing process. In guided writing, the teacher typically works with a group to help them with "crafting" their writing, which means incorporating ways to capture a reader's attention and interest in the text and ways to develop strategies and skills for writing.

Interactive writing involves the "sharing of the pen" between the children and teacher (Button, Johnson, & Furgerson, 1996; Tompkins, 2007). In this type of writing, the text is composed by a group of students, and the teacher assists the students as they work to write individual words on chart paper. As the children take turns writing words, writing punctuation, and developing their text, the teacher scaffolds instruction by helping them solve problems they encounter while composing. After composing the text, the teacher and students chorally read the text—and reread it many times. Table 7.2 highlights the types of writing found in many elementary schools across the country, while also noting the level of support provided by the teacher to her students.

TABLE 7.2	Reading/Writing and Level of Support	
Reading/ Writing Element	*Definition*	*Level of Support*
Reading aloud	The teacher reads a text out loud to children.	The teacher provides a high level of support, while encouraging children to respond to the story and pictures in the text.
Shared reading	Children read a text with the teacher. Typically, each child has their own copy of the text—and children often chorally read the text during re-readings.	There is a high level of teacher support; however, the students support one another as they find ways to read and make meaning of a text together.
Guided reading	Students are grouped in small, flexible groups—typically on the same reading level. The teacher selects and introduces a text, while children read the text.	There is some teacher support, but less support is needed than with reading-aloud and shared reading. Children problem solve as they are reading a new text—and they are mostly independent during guided reading.
Independent reading or sustained silent reading (SSR)	The children read silently to themselves or out loud to a partner.	Very little teacher support is needed—students are independent.
Interactive writing	Children "share the pen" with the teacher as they write. All children, and the teacher, participate in composing. Then, they read the text chorally.	There is a high level of teacher support. The students decide on the message—and then each word (word by word) is composed by the entire group.
Guided writing	The teacher works one on one with a small group or the whole class by providing mini lessons on how to develop their writing.	There is some teacher support, but not as supported as interactive writing. The teacher acts more as a guide than as the instructional leader.
Independent writing	Student write on their own, independently.	There is little teacher support.

SOURCE: Adapted from Fountas, I., & Pinnell, G. (2001). *Guiding Readers and Writers Grades 3–6: Teaching Comprehension, Genre, and Content Literacy.* Portsmouth, NH: Heinemann.

Independent writing is when children are able to move through the writing process while practicing the writing strategies and skills they have learned through shared, guided, and interactive writing. Independent writing is a key component in a **writing workshop,** which is an innovative community-based classroom, in which students write about their own lives and what is most important to them (Calkins, 1994; Fletcher & Portalupi, 2001; Graves, 1994; Tompkins, 2004, 2007). The writing workshop classroom is typically a time block that encompasses 60 minutes or more of independent writing, sharing of writing, writing mini lessons, and reading aloud to children in which teachers share good examples of ways that authors craft texts (Fountas & Pinnell, 2001; Tompkins, 2004). In a writing workshop, children move through the writing process as discussed below.

Writing Process

Teaching children to write means showing them that writing is a recursive process. For writers, composing does not necessarily include following each step of the writing process step by step. Traditionally, the **writing process** involves **setting a purpose for writing**, **drafting**, **revising**, **editing**, and **publishing.** Table 7.3 illustrates the recursive nature of writing. The first stage of the writing process, setting a purpose for writing, takes place during prewriting.

TABLE 7.3   Writing Process

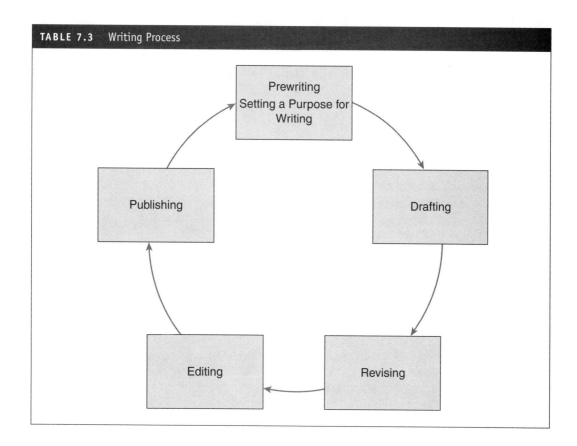

During prewriting, writers must choose a topic, determine who their audience is, and begin to organize their ideas for writing. Teachers guide students in selecting ways to prewrite by using graphic organizers as a way to organize their thoughts. For example, Read Write Think, a Web site developed by the International Reading Association and the National Council for Teachers of English, provides a plethora of online graphic organizers children can complete online as a form of prewriting (http://www.readwritethink .org/student_mat/index.asp). Similarly, using these online graphic organizers is an effective way to integrate technology into this stage of the writing process. The second stage of the writing process is the drafting stage. Although this is typically described as the second stage in the writing process, because of the recursive nature of writing, children will often draft at various times—such as after prewriting and then possibly again after revising and conferring with a teacher or peer about their writing. The third stage of the writing process is revising. During the revising stage, children share their writing with a writing group of their peers and/or with their teacher, and give and receive feedback on their peers' writing. Prior to this conference, children need to be prepared with strategies for conferencing with their peers. They need to learn specific ways to give positive feedback and to ask questions about what seems unclear or needs more explanation. Table 7.4 is a sample form that children can use to guide their peer conferences.

TABLE 7.4 Peer Content Conference			
Peer Reviewer	*What did you specifically like about the draft?*	*In what way has the author "crafted" writing?*	*What questions were you left wondering after reading the draft?*

Then each child reflects on the suggestions made by the writing group, and then makes substantive changes or revisions to his or her draft. During the editing stage, children may meet again with a peer to provide grammatical feedback on their peer's writing, or they may complete a self-assessment checklist. Self-assessment checklists enable children to become more independent writers, instead of relying on the teacher to provide all revision feedback. Table 7.5 shows

TABLE 7.5	Editing Checklist	
Me	*My Friend*	
		1. I have indented all paragraphs.
		2. I checked sentence capitalization.
		3. I underlined all words that may be misspelled.
		4. I checked punctuation marks (commas, periods, semicolons).
		5. I capitalized all proper nouns.

an example of an editing checklist children can use both independently and to provide feedback on a peer's draft.

Last, during the publishing stage of the writing process, children need time to celebrate and showcase their writing. This can be through reading their essay aloud to the entire class, or by inviting other classes and families to attend a publication celebration. In many classrooms today, publishing writing means typing a draft and illustrating the draft using technology. Teachers typically use class time for children to share their writing with an audience during this stage.

To teach children to understand this process, we use metaphors. For example, just like a sculptor, writers also must mold, develop, and revise before publishing their writing. By leading our students through a metaphorical activity using play dough, we find that students gain a hands-on experience with the writing process. We created a lesson appropriate for elementary students, adapting the concept of metaphorical writing from *Ideas Plus: 15* (NCTE, 1997). In NCTE's metaphorical lesson designed for middle/high school students, the teacher uses clay to illustrate a metaphor between what artists do when they sculpt and what writers do as they progress through the writing process. Our lesson is different from NCTE's because we note the various aspects of the writing process as distinct parts of the lesson, and we use a pace and language more appropriate for elementary school children. Using metaphors to show students how a writer is like a sculptor allows students to understand in a hands-on fashion the recursive nature of writing (see Table 7.6).

TABLE 7.6	Metaphors and the Writing Process
Excellent Reading Teachers (IRA)	Excellent reading teachers understand reading and writing development, and believe all children can learn to read and write.
Materials needed	Multiple colors of play dough, enough for each child to have 1 container; large picture of a sculptor; and a vase.
Introduction	*Teacher:* Today, we are going to discuss the steps a writer takes during the writing process. [Show a picture of a sculptor/sculpting and a writer/writing to the children.] Then, ask: "What do you know about the writing process? What do you know about a sculptor?" "What do you know about a writer?" "In what ways are these two artists similar?" Writers and artists must get a feel for their subject or topic before creating a project. Play with your play dough. Knead it slowly—and just like writers, sculptors must be familiar with their materials. [Show students what it means to knead, by modeling the process.]
Setting the purpose for writing	*Teacher:* Today you will create a very special project. You will put it on display for others at our school to see. We are going to create a vase. What do you know about vases? What is the most important function of a vase? Before you begin a writing or art project, you must know who your audience is. Why is this important? Your audience is all of the other students at our school—and other teachers. It is important to know who your audience is before you begin, because this tells you about who will be seeing your work. Just as writers must create publications based on who their audience is, sculptors must keep their audience in mind as they work.
Drafting	*Teacher:* You have had time to knead the dough and work with it. Now, mess up your vase—and start again, just as in drafting during the writing process. A writer creates several drafts. In prewriting, we get an idea of what we want to write about—and we go from there. As a sculptor, you will be re-sculpting your art work to re-think how to best create a vase. Start another design. Okay, now mush it up again. Let's start again. But before you do, think about the criteria for judging or evaluating your work. Writers often have a rubric to know how they will structure their writing. What type of criteria should we use to judge or evaluate your vase? [Write the criteria on the board.] Use these criteria as you design your vase. Now, you have a clear picture of what you are to design and how it will be evaluated. Just as when you write a narrative, you have a rubric that gives you a clear picture of the qualities of the narrative. Now, you are ready to begin working on your last draft. Let's take 5 minutes to create the draft.

Drafting	You have finished your first draft. A writer, like a sculptor, thinks about how the audience will respond to his or her work. The writer, like the sculptor, may stop at any point and get responses from other people. Ask your partner to look at your design and tell you the vase will be a useful vase.
	You have now gone through two stages of the writing process: (1) brainstorming, or rehearsal, in which you came up with ideas for your work, and (2) a first draft, in which you created your first work. What is the next step in the writing process? Yes, it is revision. What does the writer do during the revision process?
Revising	*Teacher:* Revision means to see your work again in a new way—and to think of how to create meaning in a way that your audience finds meaningful. Now, I want you to look at your vase from multiple points of view. This may help you see your vase in a different way. Based on looking from all vantage points at your vase, what do you want to change or revise?
	One of the ways you can revise is to look at your work from another point of view or have a friend read/review your work. Let's now let your classmates at your table look at it, and then listen to their ideas for improving the vase.
Editing	*Teacher:* What do you do during the editing stage of the writing process? That is right, you find ways to correct spelling or punctuation. Now is the time to "edit" your vases. You may want to exchange play dough to add new color to your vase, or you may want to think of a way to add intricate designs to your vase.
Publishing	*Teacher:* Now admire your work. A writer, like a sculptor, goes through a process that includes making numerous drafts and changes.
	Just as writers must think of a title for their work, now think of a name for your vase. Write the name on the card on your desk—and prop the card up next to your vase. Just as in a museum when you walk around admiring art, now is the time to admire the work of your friends. Just like sculptors, it is important for writers to share their work—and for others to appreciate and admire their work.
	Now let's walk around the room, admiring and celebrating our publication. Excellent work, sculptors and creators!
	[In closing, have students summarize what they learned about the similarities between a sculptor and a writer.]
	Teacher: How will this process be helpful to you when you work on a writing project?

SOURCE: Adapted from National Council for Teachers of English. (1997). *Ideas Plus: Book 15.* Urbana, IL; Author.

To begin the writing process, teachers often have students write in writer's notebooks about their lives. What constitutes a writer's notebook tends to vary from teacher to teacher and in various school districts. The next section of this chapter discusses in detail what a writer's notebook is, based on how notable writing teacher researchers describe such a notebook, and how it can be used during independent writing to begin the writing process.

Writer's Notebook

One of the best ways to begin teaching writing in school is to start with a **writer's notebook.** Young children can use this notebook to draw pictures, and older children can use it to record ideas for stories. Ralph Fletcher (1996) describes a writer's notebook as a place for children to write down their innermost thoughts, a place to write down ideas that they do not want to forget (see Table 7.7).

TABLE 7.7   A Writer's Notebook

What it is . . .

- It is uniquely yours
- A place where you can write your innermost thoughts
- A place to record your reactions—a place to write down what makes you angry, sad, happy—and things you just don't want to forget
- A place to record exactly what your grandmother whispered in your ear before she said goodbye for the last time

What it isn't . . .

- A daily journal or a diary
- A place to write down relationships and so forth
- A place to write linear sequences of events
- A place to record everything you do in a day. . .or a reading response journal
- A notebook gives you a place to live like a writer, not just in school during writing time, but wherever you are, at any time of the day!

SOURCE: (Fletcher, 1996).

We find that children best understand the purpose of a writer's notebook when their teacher models and shows examples of notebooks and—just as important—examples of her own writing (Lacina, Griffith, & Hagan, 2006). Numerous children's authors include main characters that keep a writer's notebook, such as *Amelia's Notebook* by Marissa Moss (1995), which includes a series of books written through Amelia's notebook. In the first book in this series, the main character, Amelia, keeps a notebook about her move to a new town. She draws pictures and doodles, while also noting ideas for stories. Seeing examples of children's notebooks is also a way for young writers to better understand how to keep their own writer's notebook. Figure 7.6 is an example from second grader in an east Texas elementary school. Students in this particular school begin keeping a notebook in kindergarten, and keep a notebook throughout their time in elementary school.

As you can see from the writing sample, when a notebook is used daily, students can convey important messages and develop their "voice" as a writer. This entry illustrates the student's personality and sense of humor. Readers smile and laugh while reading this example; however, it is clear the author is writing about a topic he dearly cares about. He has a passion for writing and expressing his feelings, and we also learn how devastating it can be for children to be grounded from an activity that they love, even if this is TV.

FIGURE 7.6   Writer's Notebook Example

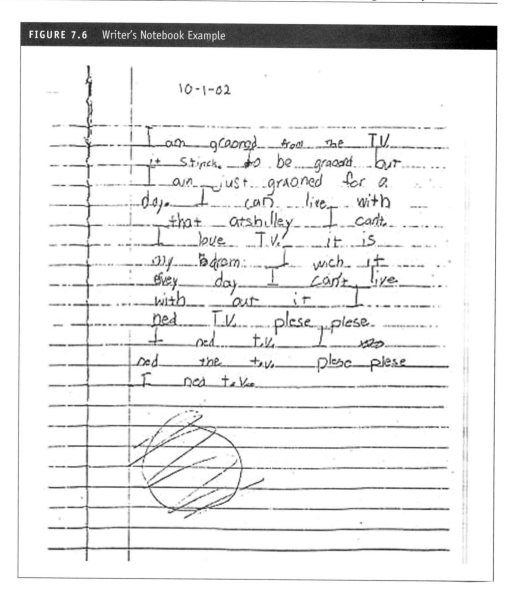

A writer's notebook is also a place to find a **seed idea**, which is an idea that a writer may want to expand to take through the writing process (Fletcher, 1996). Personal narrative writing is an effective writing mode to expand a seed idea, and personal narrative writing also serves as a strong foundation for other types of writing. When young writers feel confident, and are competent in writing a personal narrative, they can easily transfer components of the narrative to different types of writing. Just as important, many states require students to write in narrative format when completing their writing assessment. Successful teachers show children how to find a seed idea in their writer's notebook to expand and develop.

New Literacies

New literacies can also be integrated into the writing process. New literacies is simply a method of teaching reading, writing, listening, speaking, viewing, and representing in a way that doesn't use paper and pencil; instead, new literacies involve the skills of locating, evaluating, and synthesizing information from the Internet (Karchmer, Mallette, Kara-Soteriou, & Leu, 2005; Leu, Kinzer, Coiro, & Cammack, 2004; Street, 2003). In the area of writing, teachers throughout the country are using technology to model and demonstrate ways to draft (Lacina, 2008a). For example, sixth-grade teacher Lynette Mayo in the Fort Worth Independent School District in Texas uses a desktop computer to lead students through a think-aloud, in which she models and shows students her thinking process. Lynette thinks aloud how to begin a lead that catches the readers' attention. She types her lead on the computer, as students watch her. Then, as students draft their own leads on the class laptops, Lynette monitors their progress. When she notices a student having difficulty, she can "beam" them a question or comment to help scaffold instruction.

Similarly, Mrs. Kari Enge, an ESL teacher in Carrolton Farmers Branch School District in North Dallas, teaches her sixth graders how to publish their final draft through video and voice-overs using portable media players:

> For the past couple of years Mrs. Enge used portable media players in classroom instruction—and for individualized homework assignments. Not only does she create her own podcasts for students to work on developing English listening and vocabulary skills, but she has students go through the writing process and publish their writing projects by creating podcasts. (Lacina, 2008a, p. 248)

Throughout the school year, Mrs. Enge designs several podcasts for the students to listen to for homework. Through a grant program in her school district, Mrs. Enge has a classroom set of iPods that students check out each week. Many of the podcasts were created by Mrs. Enge; however, the school district also purchases the rights to use video streaming/podcasts, such as those created by United Streaming (http://streaming.discovery education.com/index.cfm). The quality of writing from this type of project is amazing, and even more important, students are engaged and interested in writing using this type of new literacy because outside of school iPods are part of their lives. Mrs. Enge emphasizes the benefits of using new literacies in writing instruction by stating, "I see my kids writing more, and they are more engaged. They go back and ask me about other podcasts. It is a memory maker and shows student growth" (p. 248).

Using Texts as Tools

Writers need tools to create and craft their writing. Writers use a variety of tools when they write, such as touchstone or mentor texts to help them craft writing, following the structure published writers use (Ray, 1999; Tropp & Van Sluys, 2008). Ray explains that teachers must first teach their students to read like writers. Writers need to be familiar with texts as readers, which means they need to spend a great deal of time reading and listening to books being read aloud to them. They also need to be able to respond to these stories, both in small groups and as a whole class. Once students are familiar with texts, teachers can then spend time pointing out how writers craft their writing, which means how they use words to create vivid mind pictures for readers, or how authors design a particular text structure to create a certain meaning. While examining the work of published authors, both as a whole class and then in small groups, teachers can show their students the authors' craft. For example, Ray describes how a fourth-grade teacher has students generate a list to note how Cynthia Rylant crafted her book, *The Relatives Came.* Students noted the following ways the author crafted her writing:

Structure:

- She writes it so that it makes a circle (*leaving Virginia, returning to Virginia*).

Ways With Words:

- She uses commas a lot.
- She puts periods at the ends of words that aren't sentences (*Miss them.*).
- She uses "funny" words together like *hugging time.*
- She uses dashes.
- She uses the same words a lot (*hugging, breathing,* etc.) (Ray, 1999, pp. 118–119).

Once students generate such lists after thoroughly analyzing a text and the author's crafting techniques, it is always important to discuss why the author did what he or she did. The goal of such an activity is for students to be able eventually to look at a text and read more than just the lines of the text. By creating an understanding of why an author uses words, phrases, or structure in a certain way, children can learn how to create and revise their own writing better. Finally, Ray (1999) notes the five parts to reading like a writer, which are essential to this process of analyzing text:

1. First children must *notice* the craft of the text—what makes the text different or interesting?

2. Second, students must *talk* about the text with others—and make a *theory* about why the author uses a particular crafting technique.

3. Then, children must give the crafting technique a *name.* By naming crafting techniques students can talk about this technique with their teachers and peers—and better analyze the technique.

4. Make the connection to *other texts.* How is this text similar to other texts read in class?

5. *Think about* how to use this technique in your own writing.

There are a variety of excellent examples in children's literature that can be used as models for crafting writing. Table 7.8 illustrates how teachers can show students how to examine an author's crafting in a text.

TABLE 7.8 Crafting Techniques

Crafting Name	Description	Example Texts
Close-Echo Effect	When an author unnecessarily repeats words very close together in order to call attention to the words or create a desired rhythm	"There is no night so dark, so black as night in the country." (*Night in the Country,* by Cynthia Rylant, 1991)
Repeating Details	Repeating specific details at different points in a text that works as a running theme throughout the books, tying everything together	A paper fan and a shiny black umbrella are details mentioned here and there throughout the text. (*Miz Berlin Walks,* by Jane Yolen, 2000)
Repeating Sentence Structures	Repetition of types of words or a specific text structure to connect sentences and add rhythm to the text	"The growl of traffic, the snort of trains . . . the cackle of coots, the quack of teals . . ." (*Secret Place,* by Eve Bunting, 1996)
Re-Say	The repetition of an idea that comes immediately after the idea has been presented; stopping to say something again; similar to a close echo	"like a dream, like a sandcastle . . ." (*Dreamplace,* by George Ella Lyon, 1998)
Striking Adjectives	Using strange or surprising adjectives	"Then it was hugging time. . . ." (*The Relatives Came,* by Cynthia Rylant, 2001)
Out-of-Place Adjectives	Putting the adjective in an unexpected place to highlight both the adjective and the noun it describes	"But one feather rained into my hand, and it was all over gold. . . ." (*Miz Berlin Walks*, by Jane Yolen, 2000)
Striking Verbs	Using strange or surprising verbs that do not seem to go with the subject	"But I hardly really sleep. . . ." (*The Lost and Found House,* by Michael Cadnum and Steve Johnson, 1997)
Intentional Vagueness	Using nonspecific pronouns and adjectives to describe a noun	"They are floating like feathers in a sky. . . ." (*The Whales,* by Cynthia Rylant, 1996)
Proper Nouns	Using names of specific people, places, or things to create sensory images	"I saw Oreos, Ruffles, and big bags of Snickers. . . ." (*Missing May,* by Cynthia Rylant, 2004)
Use of *And*	Used to give a thing or idea significance by isolating it in its own sentence	"And so I can remember too. . . ." (*What You Know First,* by Patricia Maclachlan, 1998)
Runaway Sentences	Purposely elongating sentences to convey a sense of panic, desperation, excitement, fear, etc.	"But my mother's hair, my mother's hair, like little candy circles all curly and pretty because she pinned it in pincurls all day,

Crafting Name	Description	Example Texts
		sweet to put your nose into when she is holding you, holding you and you feel safe. . . ." (*House on Mango Street*, by Sandra Cisneros, 1991)
Artful Sentence Fragments	Purposely using sentence fragments to clarify, describe, or list, the "understood" part of the sentence	"Then it's as it should be. Smooth as silk. Easy as air on the face. Right as falling water . . ." (*Home Run*, by Robert Burleigh and Mike Wimmer, 2003)
One-Sentence Paragraphs	Simple sentences made into their own paragraphs for effect	"He loved them both very much." (*Nana Upstairs & Nana Downstairs*, by Tomie dePaola, 1973)
Loop Ending	An ending that ends the story at the same place it began	*Grandfather Twilight*, by Barbara Berger (1984), and *If You Give a Mouse a Cookie*, by Laura Numeroff (1985)
Summary Ending	Repeats the main ideas of the story—a good way to tie up loose ends	*Green Eggs and Ham*, by Dr. Seuss (1960)
Mysterious Ending	Leaves the reader guessing and allows the reader to use their imagination to end the story	*The Giver*, by Lois Lowry (2006)
Sad-But-True Ending	Used for stories that need to end sad to remain "true"	*Charlotte's Web*, by E. B. White (1952), and *The Giver*, by Lois Lowry (2006)
Exploding Moments	Using details to "explode" a small moment in a text—integrates vivid imagery and specific word choice	*Hatchet*, by Gary Paulsen (1999)
Books With Vivid Pictures	Illustrations or pictures that evoke a strong image in the reader's mind	*Storm in the Night*, by Mary Stolz (1988)
Strong Characters	Characters with great presence or notability due to distinctive characteristics or vivid features	*The Long Goodbye*, by Raymond Chandler (1992)
Dialogue	Conversations between characters or an internal conversation a character has with themselves	*Amelia Bedelia* by Peggy Parish, Alexander (1963); *Alexander and the Terrible, Horrible, No Good, Very, Bad Day*, by Judith Viorst (1972); and *Ira Sleeps Over*, by Bernard Waber (1972)
Unforgettable Characters	A memorable character or characters	*Bedtime for Frances*, by Russell Hoban and Garth Williams (1960); *Ramona the Pest*, by Beverly Cleary (1968); and *Miss Maggie*, by Cynthia Rylant (1983)

SOURCE: Adapted from: Ray, K. W. (1998). *Wondrous Words: Writers and Writing in the Elementary Classroom*. Urbana, IL: National Council for Teachers of English.

Narrative Writing

Memoir writing is a great way to get started with text analysis, and to teach narrative writing. First, children must be familiar with the elements of a story. **Narrative writing** tends to include the following elements.

- **Plot**: This includes the sequence of events in a story, which in a narrative story includes a beginning, middle, and end. The book *Where the Wild Things Are,* by Maurice Sendak (1963), is a good book to show students the plot of a story.
- **Conflict:** Conflict can occur between different forces in the plot—and this is usually what keeps readers interested in reading more. Conflict can occur between a character and nature, between a character and society, between different characters, or conflict with another character. *Smoky Nights,* by Eve Bunting (1994), is an excellent picture book to show as an example of conflict between a character and society. The book describes one evening of the Los Angeles riots in the 1990s and a child's perspective of the event.
- **Setting**: Texts have different types of settings, some in which the setting is only briefly described—such as a backdrop setting. Folktales and some fairy tales use a backdrop setting because the setting is not an important part of the story. Such books may begin with "Once upon a time" and move right into discussing the characters and a conflict, without much or any mention of the setting, whereas an integral setting is given in great detail, by describing the location, weather, and time. A children's book that models an integral setting is Bunting's *Is Anybody There?* (1988). The integral setting described in this book states as follows:

It was the week before Christmas when I first got the idea that someone was watching our house.

   My name is Marcus Mullen. I'm thirteen years old, and I don't usually wimp out over just nothing. What made my creepy, crawly, eyes-on-the-back-of-my-neck feeling so silly was that it was morning. I mean, it wasn't even a dark and stormy night. The sun was shining and I was standing at the end of our driveway waiting for my friend, Robbie, to come by so we could walk to school together, the way we always do. The sky was a deep, calm blue. The thermometer on the porch said it was 76 degrees, typical for December 20 in Southern California. (pp. 1–2)

Beyond reading and discussing integral settings, teachers can guide student to create an integral setting map to distinguish the various elements of the integral setting. Using "the setting" as the focal point of the map, students can brainstorm: how the setting looks, how the setting smells, how the setting sounds, and how the setting feels (Buss & Karnowski, 2000). Students can use the senses to describe and compare a setting, letting their writing show their audience the integral setting elements within their writing.

There are a variety of excellent children's books teachers can read aloud to their students to familiarize them with memoir narratives (see Table 7.9).

Using mentor texts, such as those listed in Table 7.9, teachers teach their students to begin to read text like a writer. Mentor texts can guide students as they talk about the writer's notebook seed idea they would like to expand. A mentor text can also help students

TABLE 7.9   Children's Books and Memoirs
Childtimes (Greenfield & Little, 1993)
The House on Mango Street (Cisneros, 1991)
Snapshots From the Wedding (Soto, 1997)
We Had a Picnic This Sunday Past (Woodson, 1997)
Aunt Flossie's Hats (and Crabcakes Later) (Howard, 1991)
The Keeping Quilt (Polacco, 1998)
Walking the Log: Memories of a Southern Childhood (Nickens, 1994)
So Much (Cooke, 1994)
My Family / En Mi Familia (Garza, 1996)
My Mama Had a Dancing Heart (Gray, 1995)
When I Was Young in the Mountains (Rylant, 1982)
Tell Me Again About the Night I Was Born (Curtis, 1996)
What You Know First (Maclachlan, 1995)
My Rotten Redheaded Older Brother (Polacco, 1994)

envision the possibilities for text structure, organization, and development. Most important, reading the work of published authors helps students find ways to connect reading and writing, and to understand better the function of reading and writing beyond the classroom. In the next section of the chapter, you will read how an exemplary teacher integrates reading and writing instruction within her classroom to create a community of writers.

Inside the Classroom:
Alice Carlson Applied Learning Center, Fort Worth, Texas

Jan Lacina

Alice Carlson Applied Learning Center is a magnet school in Fort Worth Independent School District. The school's instructional philosophy is based on the work of John Dewey, in which there is an emphasis on real-world connections, project-based activities, and collaborative problem solving. The school is composed of students the state of Texas identifies as primarily at risk, which includes 91% of the students enrolled at Alice Carlson. Eighty-four percent of the students are also identified as economically disadvantaged. The school is racially diverse, composed of 50% White students, 29.3% Hispanic students, 15% African American students, 0.5% Native American students, and 5.2% Asian students. Any student in Fort Worth can attend a magnet school. Typically, a lottery format is followed in which students' names are drawn to select a magnet school's student population.

Alice Carlson is a unique and exemplary campus for many reasons. First, teachers teach students how to read, write, and think while incorporating the work of excellent published authors throughout the curriculum. Second, by preparing their students to think like authors, they prepare them for the state-mandated reading and writing tests. Students at Alice Carlson received "commended" status from the state of Texas for their excellent academic performance on this test.

Exemplary writing teachers connect reading and writing, and they model and demonstrate how writing is used in children's literature. Debbie Gerwick has been teaching elementary school for more than 20 years. She has been teaching at Alice Carlson since the 1990s, and she finds Alice Carlson a great place to teach since the school and the parents support teacher growth. For example, each year the school's PTA raises money for a special budget because they believe teachers should have the opportunity to be growing professional educators. From this budget, Mrs. Gerwick has been able to attend workshops by Lucy Calkins at Teachers College, Columbia University, and their nationally known writing project. As Mrs. Gerwick explains, "I have been teaching for 22 years, and it has really helped me to come back reinvigorated and excited." From classroom observations and interviews with her, it is clear that Mrs. Gerwick understands how to teach writing well to create a classroom community of writers.

It is the beginning of June in Mrs. Gerwick's fourth-grade classroom, and the students are in the middle of a unit of study on poetry. As students enter Mrs. Gerwick's class from P.E., she pulls a few students to the side to conference with them about math word problem explanations. She pulls Caleb to the side and says, "I loved it—I checked your extensions, and it was excellent. But, I have a question for you. . . ." The student then explains the word problem in his own words. After this is clarified, Mrs. Gerwick tells the class, "Please get out your writer's notebooks. Today we are going to continue our study of poetry." The children immediately take out their notebooks and walk to the front of the room, where they sit on the floor in front of Mrs. Gerwick as she prepares to hold a brief meeting about writing. To her left is a wall of leveled books and a wall full of anchor charts. Mrs. Gerwick points to a piece of chart paper titled "Poetry Is." While examining the list, Mrs. Gerwick and her students discuss the importance of using strong verbs and adjectives in poetry as a way to help readers create a mind picture when reading poetry.

Mrs. Gerwick: Can anyone think of poetry words to add to our list?

Anna: *Feel* . . . I like to read fantasy so that is why I chose that word.

Mrs. Gerwick: So, poetry can be about dreams. Whenever you think about poems, do they all sound the same?

Students: No.

Mrs. Gerwick: OK, turn now and talk to a friend about what you have noted about poetry.

As the students discuss what they know about poetry, Mrs. Gerwick rotates through the group, helping students who seem to struggle. After the students have had time to discuss, Mrs. Gerwick says,

Some haikus capture a sunset, and some poems tell more about a story. So, can you take things from your lives and think of ways to add imagery in which you created a picture in someone's head?

Then, Mrs. Gerwick writes on chart paper, "My friend <u>went</u> down the street." She says, "Strong verbs need images that are vivid, and specific language. Can you think of other verbs we can use to make this a stronger sentence?" Students brainstorm vivid verbs, such as: galloped, trotted, walked, skipped, and ran. After Mrs. Gerwick was convinced that the students understood how to create a strong verb, she said, "Now, return to your tables and read through your notebooks. Look for verbs that you can make stronger, and as a table—use the thesaurus to help your group."

Students then work diligently to come up with a list of stronger verbs from their notebooks, while working together to use a thesaurus.

Connecting Reading and Writing

Mrs. Gerwick is a successful writing teacher for many reasons, but one of the key components to her teaching is the connection between reading and writing. She explains this important connection:

> Kids have to be totally immersed with good literature, short stories, poems, picture books, and they have to be read to—to hear what good language sounds like. And then you have to take them from where they're at and move them forward. So, they may be writing five sentences the first day of school, and your goal is to try to get them to see that they have a lot more to say. I think just demonstrating writing for them and sharing writing, setting up a writer's notebook and showing them ways that they can collect things that they need to write about.

Mrs. Gerwick is a reader–writer herself, and her classroom includes an extensive variety of literature and genres. Likewise, writing is celebrated. Publications of student writing are on display, and the room is rich with literature and student writing. She shows students how published writers craft their writing so students can use published authors as models for their own writing. Because this is also significant in Mrs. Gerwick's philosophy and methods for teaching writing, she helps her students develop personal goals for writing. For example, Mrs. Gerwick finds that some students struggle to expand and develop their writing; she has these students count the lines they wrote at the beginning of the school year. Then she hands out a simple T-chart. If the student is writing 5 lines, their goal the next day would be to write 5 more lines than what they wrote earlier. Mrs. Gerwick emphasizes, "I try to tell them that their goal is to have an entry that is at least a page long within the first two weeks of school." Reading a wide variety of literature, modeling how to read like a writer, and setting personal goals make Mrs. Gerwick an exemplary writing teacher.

A Writer's Notebook

In Mrs. Gerwick's class, students keep a writer's notebook throughout the school year, both in school and for homework. Kaitlin, a student in this class, shares her notebook entry, "A Christmas Tradition" (see Figure 7.7). This is just one brief entry in her notebook, but because the entry was significant to Kaitlin personally, she decided to take this entry through the writing process and eventually publish it. Examine Figure 7.8 for her first draft.

FIGURE 7.7 Writer's Notebook Entry

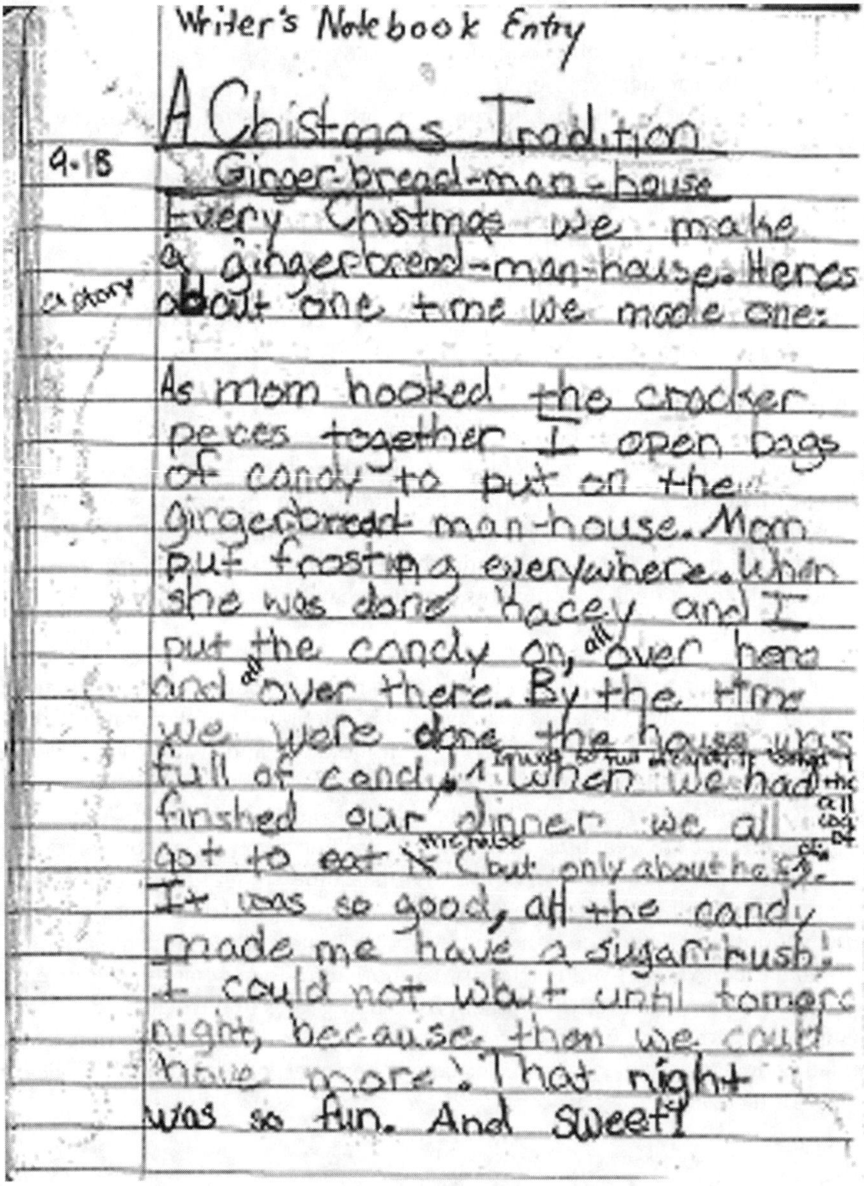

Writer's Notebook Entry

A Chistmas Tradition

9-18 Ginger-bread-man-house

Every Chistmas we make a gingerbread-man-house. Heres a story about one time we made one:

As mom hooked the cracker peices together I open bags of candy to put on the gingerbread man-house. Mom put frosting everywhere. When she was done kacey and I put the candy on, all over here and all over there. By the time we were done the house was full of candy. When we had finshed our dinner we all got to eat but only about he It was so good, all the candy made me have a sugar rush! I could not wait until tomore night, because then we could have more! That night was so fun. And sweet!

FIGURE 7.8   Writer's Notebook Entry Expanded

> a non ordinary
> Today was ~~an ordinary~~ day, it was a day
> for happiness and joy and family. Everyone was doing
> that ~~~~ because today was Christmas
> Eve! We always have a big party at my
> house. We talked and ate, and talked
> some more. Kacey, I and Minnie played
> games and chatted. Kacey and I went
> over to the table. We could eat wait.
> mom was frosting the ginger-bread-man-
> House. It was a family tradition, and my
> favorite. Suddenly, "Decoration time!" mom
> yelled. "Yeah" Kacey and I said. Everyone
> gathered around the table and looked at the
> house. "Man that ~~looks~~ really white" I thought.
> Finally, we all got the candy and covered the
> house. When we were done we stepped back to admire
> our work
> The house was full. It had mints, lolypops,
> and candycanes and more! "What a sugar
> rush I will get." I thought. Everyone wanted
> it now. But mom said to us, "Dinner is served
> first." Finally it came time to eat our
> gingerbread-man-house. "I want that one."
> I shouted. "But I want it." Kacey shouted.
> "Fine." I said angrily. "I'll have that one."
> "I wanted that piece, I wish I got it." I
> thought, as mom got our pieces and she

(Continued)

FIGURE 7.8 (Continued)

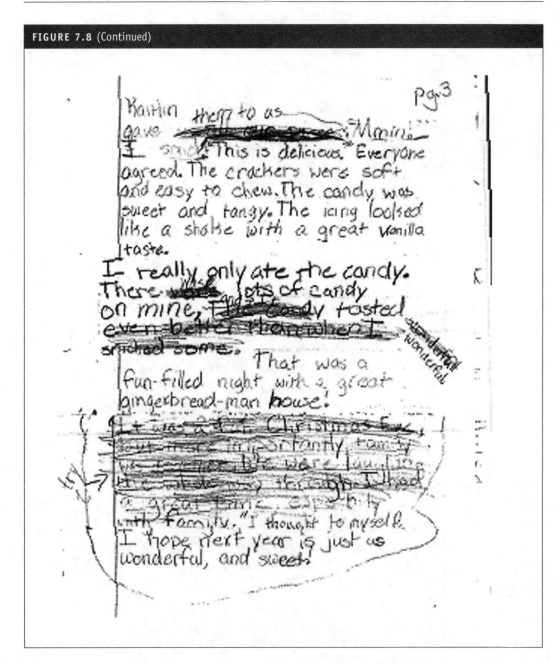

Teachers at Alice Carlson Applied Learning Center teach their students how to publish their writing by creating pictures to match the text using the software program KidPix. Kaitlin used KidPix to publish her final piece (see Figure 7.9).

FIGURE 7.9   Published Writing Using KidPix

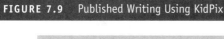

Ginger-bread-man-house

By Kaitlin Brunett

This book is dedicated to my mom

for making Christmas joyful each year

(Continued)

FIGURE 7.9 (Continued)

Today was a non-ordinary day, it was a day for happiness, joy, and family. Everyone was doing that, especially today, because today was Christmas Eve!! We always have a big party at my house. When everyone came we talked and ate and talked some more. Hunnie, Kacey, and I played games and chatted. Then Kacey and I ran to the table. We could not wait. Mom was frosting the ginger-bread-man-house! It's a family tratition, and my favorite.

Suddenly, "Decoration time!"mom yelled right out of the blue.
"Yeah!"Kacey and I yelled. Everyone gathered around the table. "Man, that looks really white,"I thought "candy is going everywhere." Finaly, we all got the candy and put it everywhere. When we were done, we steped back to admire our work.

The house was full. It had mints, lollypops,candycanes, and more! "What a sugar rush I will get."I thought. Everyone wanted a piece now. But mom said "Dinner is served first."

Finaly it came, time to eat the ginger-bread-man-house! "I want... that piece!" I shouted. "But I want that piece!!" Kacey shouted trying to sound louder than me. "Fine." I said angrily. "I'll have... that piece." I had found another piece with alot of candy. But I still wanted the other one.

(Continued)

FIGURE 7.9 (Continued)

Mom gave us our pieces."Mmmm!" I said. "This is delicious."
Everyone agreed. The crackers were soft and easy to chew. The
candy was sweet and tangy. The icing looked and tasted like a
vanilla shake.   I really only ate the candy. There was a lot of candy
on mine, and it tasted wonderful. that was a fun-filled night with a
great ginger-bread-man-house!! A great Christmas Eve too. Our
ginger-bread-man-house was a hit. Everyone loved it. I hope next
year is just as wonderful, and sweet!

Common Questions Teachers Have About Writing

Novice teachers often find conferencing with students about their writing a challenge—and many teachers find that they spend time telling students what to do to "fix" their writing, instead of spending the time conversing with the students about writing. Mrs. Gerwick faces the same challenge, even as a veteran teacher. For that reason, we asked Mrs. Gerwick to offer advice to teachers who are interested in refining how they teach writing, in order to better build a community of writers. The answers that follow include Mrs. Gerwick's recommendations for building community and developing writers to their writing potential.

1. How do you conference with your students?

Conferencing is where I feel like I struggle a lot. I tend to do more individual conferences, and sometimes I feel like it's more productive to do small-group conferencing just depending on where the kids are at. What I try to do is take their notebooks home once a week or once every two weeks, so I divide the class out into groups and try to take home half one week and half the next week so you can try to see how you could group them and what kinds of things they need. Just requires a lot of analysis to see what they need. They do have writing partners and Lucy [Calkins] believes that your writing partners should be pretty close as far as where they are in writing. Then, sometimes, like six months into the year, I might group the kids that have more success with writing and scoring higher with a kid who's struggling so they can give feedback to the kid who's struggling.

2. What's the role of the writing partner?

To respond and give them ideas about their writing. And I usually start out with a really simple checklist of things that they are to look for in their writing because as a teacher long ago I used to think, "Okay, sit down and start conferencing. Revise and edit your piece of writing," and, you know, they need some guidance to do that. Another thing I do when they write is I start the timer one minute before and ask them to reread and make any changes that stand out to them, and I try to zero in on kids. For example, they may have a sticky note in the front that will say, "I forget to put periods in," to try and help them remember. I try to embed everything in so they know that revising and editing is part of the process and not something you put off to the very end.

3. For those kids who are really struggling writers, how do you approach getting them started with a notebook?

Pretty much just the same way, trying to look at their lives to see what they can write about. Typically, those kids will say, "I don't have anything to write about." I try to make the kids see that writing about your life is not a trip to Six Flags. It is not like a trip to New York or a trip to Alaska. Its things like, "Today we played in the park and I saw an old man that did not have on shoes." It's those little things that they see and things that happen to them in their lives. What's your favorite food? What's you favorite meal? And I try to use literature to begin stories about family so they can think about that the things that they can write about are the things in their life that they know. And I share my own writer's notebook; I have like three now. I show them topic lists in there, just different kinds of things. When students see my writer's notebook, this generally pushes them on. It's a great strategy. If a teacher doesn't have one they can even ask someone else with one to come in and show, and a teacher that has never had one can do one with the kids. I typically start one with the kids. We've done a lot of timelines to help them focus and plan what they are going to do. We try to show them ways to focus and plan their writing.

Both novice and veteran teachers alike can learn from teachers like Mrs. Gerwick. One of the key reasons Mrs. Gerwick is successful as a writing teacher is because she values her students—and their writing. The tone in her classroom is one of collegiality (Calkins, 2005). She sits side by side with the child while conferencing about writing, instead of standing above the child looking down. Likewise, as emphasized by Calkins (2005), Mrs. Gerwick often explicitly tells and shows examples, thereby making such a conference memorable to students. She does that by showing examples of her own writing or examples of other students' writing. Lastly, conferencing is ongoing in her class, and she talks with her students about their writing across the content areas, not just during the literacy block of time.

Questions for Discussion

1. How does Mrs. Gerwick guide students through the writing process?

2. Notice how Mrs. Gerwick explains having students keep a writer's notebook. How can the writer's notebook serve as a way to develop "seed ideas"—as also mentioned in the section titled "Reading Research to Know"?

3. What are the key qualities that make Mrs. Gerwick an effective teacher?

Summary of Strategies Used

Debbie Gerwick uses many effective strategies to teach students writing. Similar to the International Reading Association's 2002 position statement describing excellent teachers, Mrs. Gerwick serves as a writing coach in the classroom. She confers with students in an ongoing way about their writing, motivates them, and helps them see themselves as writers. She talks with students about their writing—not "at" them. Lastly, she designs and teaches mini lessons to students when she notices that they are struggling in a particular area—and she is continually making informal assessments about where individual children are and how they can develop further as a writer. A writing coach helps students move forward to become fluent readers and writers, while also serving as a cheerleader and confidante. Both novice and veteran teachers can learn from excellent reading teachers like Mrs. Gerwick how to create better writing communities.

Case for Exploration:
Bruce Shulkey Elementary School, Fort Worth, Texas

Cecilia Silva

Eunice Davis is a second-grade teacher at Bruce Shulkey Elementary School in Fort Worth Independent School District. She is a veteran elementary teacher, and she describes her teaching philosophy as follows:

> I believe that every child has something that they want to say, that they want to share. So, I encourage children to do that. I encourage them to write from their personal experiences, from their academic standpoint, you know, content writing, poetry, we do lots of poetry here.

Mrs. Davis has a love for teaching reading and writing that has not waned over the years—but has grown stronger.

Like many urban schools, Bruce Shulkey reflects a diverse population. Approximately 20% are African American, and Hispanic and White students each constitute 40% of the student body. More than half of the children attending Bruce Shulkey are economically disadvantaged, and 22% of the students are enrolled in bilingual or ESL education programs. Parents at this school often participate in family activities, and the school has received the Golden Apple Award several years in a row because of this high rate of parent volunteerism.

Eunice Davis's class, Fort Worth Independent School District

Large-Group Discussion

Sitting on a rocking chair, Mrs. Davis initiates the writing workshop session by conducting a picture walk of *Galimoto* (Williams, 1991), a book she first introduced to the children at the beginning of the school year. Now, close to the end of the school year, Mrs. Davis and the students revisit the story, this time more closely examining the piece from a writer's perspective. "This week we are looking at how the book is put together," Mrs. Davis reminds the children.

Throughout the week the class has read and reread *Galimoto*. Today, the students are focusing on Kondi, the main character in the story. In this story, Kondi, who wants to construct his own galimoto—toy car—goes around the village collecting the scraps of materials he needs to accomplish the task. "Each time Kondi sees someone, he says what he wants and then he gets what he wants," a student remarks. "Yes, he gets what he needs to build the galimoto," someone else states. As Mrs. Davis continues to read the book, the children discuss how Williams, the author, developed a character that wants something and is able to show how the character gets what he wants. They note how the author has organized the narrative so there is a story within a story. "There is a complete story with every character Kondi sees," one of the students remarks.

After the reading, Mrs. Davis moves toward one of the wall charts posted at the front of the room. The class developed this particular wall chart—*Changing Settings*—earlier in the week to draw attention to the way Kondi moves through different settings in *Galimoto*. Mrs. Davis and the children discuss how in their own writing, similar to the way Williams has done, they are attempting to develop narratives where their main character knows what he or she wants and encounters other characters in different settings in order to get it.

Additional wall charts in Mrs. Davis's room highlight the various writing mini lessons the class has had over the week. In one of the charts the children have identified key elements of expressive writing. A second chart reflects a class discussion on words and adverbs that writers could use as an alternative to "said." A third chart reflects discussions on the various characters Kondi encounters as he moves toward obtaining what he wants in *Galimoto*.

The large-group session concludes as the students review one more of the wall charts: a rubric they are using to guide their narrative writing. The students generated the rubric earlier in the week and today they review how a good narrative should reflect the criteria they had previously selected.

"When you are at your tables keep the book open, you know you will not copy, but you will use it as a pattern," Mrs. Davis reminds the students as she distributes the writing folders prior to dismissing them back to work at their own tables.

Conferencing With Individual Students

Once the class has settled and the children are working at their tables, Mrs. Davis meets with individual students to confer about their writing. On this particular day, the conferences begin with a general discussion of the student's floor map or floor plan. The floor map, reflecting this week's analysis and mini lessons on *Galimoto,* is a graphic organizer that each student develops during the drafting phase of the writing workshop. It consists of a series of boxes that identify the settings and secondary characters that the main character will encounter in order to meet his or her wants. Once Mrs. Davis and the student confer about the floor map, the remainder of the writing conference focuses on the particular needs of each student. The following excerpts highlight six of the conferences that took place the day we visited Mrs. Davis's class. The conferences usually were short—about 3 to 4 minutes per student. The excerpts provide an overview of the conferences and how teachers conference with students about their writing.

Conference 1

This student's main character, Yoyo, wants to make a hat. Yoyo, she describes, has a basket and will be visiting other characters to obtain the parts she needs for the hat. Mrs. Davis listens as the student discusses her "floor plan." The conference concludes as Mrs. Davis suggests that in the future she does not include as much information in the floor map. The floor map, she says, serves to remind her of the settings the main character will visit to collect items for her basket, and does not need to include all of the details she has added to her graphic organizer.

Conference 2

This student is in the beginning stages of the drafting process and has only begun to develop a floor map. In the conference he talks about how his character wants to make a robot and brainstorms potential settings and some of the characters he will visit in the narrative. Mrs. Davis listens to his ideas and as the conference comes to an end, she reminds him to use the floor map to jot down some of these ideas. They also discuss how his floor plan might need two additional boxes in order to show how the main character builds the robot and plays with the robot.

Conference 3

The student starts the conference by talking about her main character—Memito—who is going to "make a birthday party." Aware that this student is a second language learner, Mrs. Davis accepts her statement and asks what Memito will need to plan for the party. The student talks about birthday parties she has attended while Mrs. Davis begins to make a list of the items Memito will need for the party on a yellow sticky note. The conference ends as the student and Mrs. Davis agree that she will think of the places that Memito will visit to get what he needs for the party and will add these to her floor plan.

Conference 4

This student has completed the floor plan and is working on his first draft. In his narrative, Mike, the main character, wants to catch a deadly snake. He briefly goes over the floor map with Mrs. Davis. He then read begins to read his draft: "It was a cold and foggy morning. . . ." "I like the lead-in sentence," Mrs. Davis responds. The student then discusses how in his draft Mike is about to encounter John, one of the secondary characters in the narrative. Mrs. Davis asks, "Is this where Mike tells him about his goal?" This conference ends as Mrs. Davis says, "Can't wait to see how you introduce his goal."

Conference 5

This student is also well into her first draft. Mrs. Davis and the student briefly go over her floor plan and talk about the characters in her story. She then reads part of the draft. In this draft, Chloe, the main character, has asked her mom for what she needs. "How she is going to get stuff she needs?" Mrs. Davis responds, "We want to be able to hear what she said to her mom." The remainder of this conference focuses on alternatives to "said" words.

Conference 6

With this student, an ELL student, the conference focuses on the secondary characters the main character will encounter in order to get what he wants—to make a car. Throughout this conference, Mrs. Davis makes references to *Galimoto,* as well as to other students' writing in order to further support the student in understanding how the main character collects what he needs throughout the narrative. As the conference comes to an end, the student apprehensively asks how many boxes he will need in his floor plan. "You need to have three," Mrs. Davis responds. Curious about this response, after class we had the opportunity to ask Mrs. Davis why she had required that this student add only three boxes to his floor plan given that other children we had observed had many more. Mrs. Davis explained that this was one way she could modify the curriculum for ELLs in her class-room. This way, she explained, ELLs could engage in the content and process while differentiating their product.

Group Sharing

"Anyone want to share what your have so far?" Mrs. Davis asks the students as they come to the end of the writing workshop. Many children raise their hands to participate in this activity. The teacher and students are attentive as each writer reads his or her draft. Most responses focus on points that had been highlighted in their earlier mini lessons surrounding *Galimoto*. The following comments were offered as several of the authors shared their drafts on this morning:

"She brought in the character and explained what she needs."

"When she meets a person, she uses dialogue."

"He brings in the characters and we can hear what they say when they talk."

Some of the responses are more general, reflecting writing discussions the students have had throughout the year.

"I heard a transitional word, she said *next*."

"I liked your description of the main character. You said everything about the character."

"You could see how the character leaves one scene and goes to another."

Mrs. Davis concludes the writing workshop by pointing out how, from the comments she heard in today's sharing session, she notices that the students have been paying close attention to the rubric they had discussed earlier in the day. The students are asked to put away their writing folders for today and reminded that they will have another opportunity to come back to their drafts on the following day.

Questions for Discussion

1. Based on the six different conferences that Mrs. Davis held with students, what do you notice about her role in the conferences? What differences did you notice between the students?

2. How does Mrs. Davis meet the writing needs of ESL students within her mainstream second-grade class?

3. What are the benefits of using literature in writing instruction, and how does Mrs. Davis integrate the two effectively in her class?

Concluding Thoughts

Debbie Gerwick and Eunice Davis use many effective strategies for teaching students writing. Similar to the International Reading Association's 2002 position statement describing excellent teachers, both teachers serve as writing coaches in the classroom. They confer with students about their writing, and motivate and engage them while helping independent and dependent writers alike to find ways to read text like a writer. Also similar to IRA's (2000) position statement on excellent teachers, both teachers use a variety of instructional strategies to teach writing. Mrs. Gerwick and Mrs. Davis teach writing mini lessons to students when they notice that students are struggling in a particular area—and both teachers are continually making informal assessments about where a child is and how they may develop further the child as a writer. Unlike Mrs. Wesvessel, the teacher from Lowry's (1979) popular book, *Anastasia Krupnik,* teachers like Mrs. Gerwick and Mrs. Davis are true writing coaches who look for the best in their students. All children deserve to have teachers like these excellent Fort Worth, Texas, teachers—and veteran and novice teachers can both learn from their effective, research-based teaching.

TERMS TO KNOW

Automaticity	New literacies
Beginning writing	Plot
Conflict	Publishing
Drafting	Revising
Editing	Seed idea
Emergent writing	Setting
Fluent writing	Setting a purpose for writing
Guided writing	Shared writing
High-frequency words	Word walls
Independent writing	Writer's notebook
Interactive writing	Writing process
Modeled writing	Writing workshop
Narrative writing	

RESEARCH THAT WORKS

Higgins, B., Miller, M., & Wegmann, S. (2006). Teaching to the test . . . not! Balancing best practice and testing requirements in writing. *The Reading Teacher, 60*(4), 310–319.

Lacina, J. (2006). Developing a writing workshop classroom: Collaboration between a charter school principal, second-grade teacher, and university professor. *Teacher Educator, 42*(1), 63–74.

Leu, D. J., Kinzer, C. K., Coiro, J. L., & Cammack, D. W. (2004). Toward a theory of new literacies emerging from the Internet and other information and communication technologies. In R. B. Ruddell & N. J. Unrau (Eds.), *Theoretical models and processes of reading* (5th ed., pp. 1570–1613). Newark, DE: International Reading Association.

Leu, D. J., Mallette, M. H., Karchmer, R. A., & Kara-Soteriou, J. (2006). Contextualizing the new literacies of information and communication technologies in theory, research, and practice. In R. A. Karchmer, M. A. Mallette, J. Kara-Soteriou, & D. J. Leu (Eds.), *Innovative approaches to literacy education* (pp. 1–12). Newark, DE: International Reading Association.

Myles, J. (2002, September). Second language writing and research: The writing process and error analysis in student texts. *TESL-EJ, 6, A-1.* Retrieved October 2006, from http://www-writing.berkeley.edu/TESl-EJ/ej22/a1.html

National Writing Project. (2003). *Because writing matters: Improving student writing in our schools.* San Francisco: Jossey-Bass.

Teale, W. H., Leu, D. J., Labbo, L. D., & Kinzer, C. (2002). The CTELL project: New ways technology can help educate tomorrow's reading teachers. *The Reading Teacher, 55,* 654–659.

WEB SITES

Annenberg Media: **http://www.learner.org/index.html** includes several streamed video clips of professional development session on how to teach writing in a workshop format. For example, titles include *Inside Writing Communities, Grades 3–5, Teaching Reading K–2 Workshop,* and *Write in the Middle: A Workshop for Middle School Teachers.*

A MiddleWeb Listserv Project: **http://www.middleweb.com/ReadWrkshp/JK45.html** offers upper-elementary teachers a wealth of information and resources for developing a writing workshop classroom. There is a discussion board in addition to examples of how one particular teacher, Julie Kendall, integrates literature and writing instruction within her classroom.

Writing Process Resources: **http://www.edzone.net/ ~ mwestern/ww.html** provides resources for teachers interested in the Six Trait Writing Model, including posters, lesson plan examples, and rubrics.

Young Authors' Workshop: **http://www.planet.eon.net/ ~ bplaroch/index.html** includes information and resources for upper elementary writers. The resources included on this Web site help guide young writers through the writing process.

CHAPTER 8

Literacy Across the Curriculum

Strategic Instruction in the Content Areas

Prior to reading, try to answer the following questions:

1. What are several ways teachers can integrate reading and writing throughout the curriculum?

2. Think of an exemplary teacher you have observed teaching. How did he or she ensure that students understood what they were reading in the content areas (math, science, social studies, etc.)?

Reading Research to Know

Teachers today must find unique ways to help students develop **content literacy** as students learn to comprehend difficult expository texts. Researchers define content literacy as the ability to read, write, and communicate effectively within each content area (Brozo & Simpson, 2007; Draper, Smith, Hall, & Siebert, 2005; Lacina & Watson, 2008; Sturtevant & Linek, 2004; Wood & Harmon, 2005). Content literacy is not a new concept, but a redefined one (Draper et al., 2005). Even though it is not a new concept, researchers documented for more than a decade that content area teachers, especially preservice teachers, often resist learning about literacy strategies while enrolled in content area reading courses (Bean, 1997; Fox, 1993; Hollingsworth & Teal, 1991; Lesley, 2005; Nourie & Lenski, 1998; O'Brien, Stewart, & Moje, 1995; Wilson, Konopak, & Readence, 1993), and preservice teachers often question college requirements to enroll in a content area literacy course (Lesley, 2005; Nourie & Lenski, 1998). Finding teachers who have the expertise to integrate content literacy can be a great challenge for teacher educators (Barry, 2002; Fisher & Ivey, 2005; Zimpherer, Worley, Sission, & Said, 2002).

Most teachers have trouble integrating content literacy because few have observed teachers who teach content literacy effectively, and many teachers report that they do not view literacy to be a high priority for content area teaching since they regard it as the specific responsibility of reading or English teachers (Lester, 2000). Teachers need to see and experience active literacy engagement and comprehension strategies when teaching elementary age students in order to better transfer strategy instruction into their future classrooms (Fisher & Ivey, 2005; L'Allier & Elish-Piper, 2007). Such active literacy engagement is especially important when children learn to read content texts. In the following section we discuss (a) why children have difficulty comprehending content texts, (b) the elements of expository texts, (c) the importance of explicitly teaching expository elements, and finally, (d) strategy instruction and the content areas.

Difficulty Reading Content Texts

There are a number of reasons why students have difficulty reading content texts. Elementary age children spend a great deal of time reading **narrative texts** in school (Duke, 2000), and in the early childhood years, their parents spend much time reading stories to them. The purpose of a narrative text is to entertain and interest an audience. There are many different types of narrative texts, such as fictitious, factual, science fiction, and romance. Some of the features of a narrative text include the following:

- Characters with distinct personalities
- Dialogue
- Descriptive language that brings the story to life

Narrative texts tend to follow a similar framework, which can be compared to the shape of a diamond. Like a diamond, a narrative text begins small because the author typically describes the setting and characters in the beginning of the text. As the plot thickens, the author builds a sense of suspense or conflict. For that reason, this section of the narrative can be compared to a diamond—since a diamond shape begins with a pointed tip, then widens and becomes more intricate and complex. In the narrative, the ending typically shows how the author resolves the conflict—and a closure is described. Some authors use a "loop ending" to show the similarities between the beginning and the end of the story. A good example of the loop ending is the book, *If You Give A Mouse a Cookie* (Numeroff, 1985). The author begins the book with the line "If you give a mouse a cookie, he's going to ask for a glass of milk." This same line is repeated at the end of the book. Similarly, the end of the diamond is comparable to the top of the diamond, pointed and concise—and also giving a sense of closure. Figure 8.1 shows the typical structure of a narrative text.

Parents may find that narrative texts are easier to read to young children, and they may also find that the children are more engaged reading such texts. Stories in which children can make personal connections to the main character encourage engagement during reading, and this particular element may influence parents' choices of books to read aloud to their children. Narrative texts typically have characters, a plot, and a

FIGURE 8.1   The Narrative Story Diamond

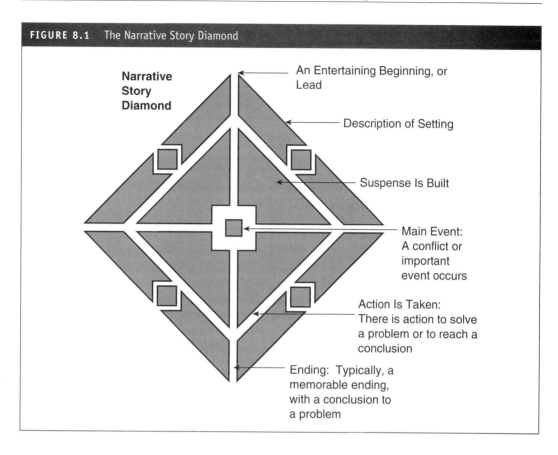

setting; whereas **expository texts**, or informational books, give factual information to the reader. Table 8.1 describes the organizational features found in nonfiction texts. Such organizational features vary, but by teaching students the most common features and uses of these organizational features, students will be better able to use them as a tool when reading.

TABLE 8.1   Nonfiction Text Organizational Features

Organizational Features	Description
Table of contents	The table of contents is located at the beginning of the book. It tells the reader what topics will be covered in the book, and often gives specific details about content covered in each chapter.
Headings	Headings are typically found at the beginning of a paragraph. They tell the reader what a paragraph, or a section of the text, will be about. Usually, headings are in a larger font or bolded.

(Continued)

TABLE 8.1 (Continued)	
Organizational Features	*Description*
Sidebars	Nonfiction texts often present important factual information in sidebars. Sidebars are boxed information located on the side of a page.
Captions	Captions are located beside or beneath illustrations. The caption tells the reader what the illustration represents.
Diagrams, charts, graphs, and tables	This nonfiction element summarizes or clarifies factual information in the text. Presented in a diagram, chart, graph, or table, information is shown to readers in a different way.
Glossary	The glossary includes all vocabulary, or specialized terms, emphasized throughout the book. Typically words that are highlighted or noted in bold font are defined in the glossary. The glossary is typically located at the end of a book.

Elements of Expository Texts

Researchers explain that **expository texts** are difficult for students to comprehend for many reasons (Hall, Sabey, & McClellan, 2005; Williams, Hall, & Lauer, 2004). Expository texts are nonfiction readings intended to inform or explain factual information to an audience. Expository text can vary in organizational features, and the variety of text organizational structures and features are often unfamiliar to children unless they are explicitly taught how to read expository text. For struggling readers, and for English language learners (ELLs) in particular, expository texts are a great challenge to read. Several factors make reading expository text difficult for ELLs. For example, ELLs may have limited exposure to English texts (Young & Hadaway, 2006), or they may have limited experience reading similar types of texts in their native language. Likewise, familiarity with English **text structures** may be a function of familiarity of common structures in their first language (Carrell, 1984). Additionally, researchers report that by fourth grade, there tends to be an overall decline in children's reading scores since they must now read to learn, instead of merely learning to read (Chall, Jacobs, & Baldwin, 1990; Chall & Snow, 1988; Hall et al., 2005). The fourth-grade slump, as defined by these researchers, can be avoided if more teachers explicitly teach students how to read and understand expository texts. By teaching all students, including ELLs, the components of expository texts, students will be better able to comprehend and remember information read in these texts (Goldman & Rakestraw, 2000; Pearson & Duke, 2002).

Since the 1980s, researchers have identified the most common organizational structures found in expository texts. For example, Anderson and Armbruster (1984) described six structures: description, temporal sequence of events, explanation of concepts, definition and example, compare and contrast, and problem–solution–effect. What is important to

Display of nonfiction books at Alice Carlson Elementary School, Fort Worth Independent School District

know is that most texts do not represent merely one organizational structure, but may use several (Meyer & Poon, 2001). Table 8.2 summarizes the five most common expository text structures found in children's textbooks, while noting trade books that exemplify such a text structure. The list of trade books noted in this table includes a wide variety of Orbis Picture Award winning books—in addition to other good examples of expository picture books.

TABLE 8.2 Trade Books and Expository Text Patterns		
Pattern	*Definition*	*Children's Book Examples*
Description	In expository text, the author describes a topic by listing characteristics and examples. The author may use phrases such as *for example, characteristics are, for instance, specifically,* and *in addition*.	Balestino, P. (1989). *The Skeleton Inside You* Dorros, A.(1987). *Ant Cities* Gibbons, G. (1994). *Nature's Green Umbrella* Gibbons, G. (1999). *Bats* Giblin, J. (2004). *Secrets of the Sphinx* Montgomery, S. (2004). *The Tarantula Scientist* Pringle, L. (2000). *Bats* Siy, A., & Kunkel, D. (2005). *Mosquito Bite* Teitelbaum, M. (1997). *The Colossal Book of Dinosaurs*
Sequence	The author lists items in a series, in steps, or in chronological or place order. The author may use the following words to signal a sequence of items: *first, second, third, next, last, then, finally*.	Bartoletti, S. (2005). *Hitler Youth: Growing Up in Hitler's Shadow* Blumberg, R. (2004). *York's Adventures With Lewis and Clark: An African-American's Part in the Great Expedition* Bolden, T. (2005). *Maritcha: A Nineteenth-Century American Girl* Cole, J. (1991). *My Puppy Is Born* Delano, M. (2005). *Genius: A Photobiography of Albert Einstein* Freedman, R. (2004). *The Voice That Challenged a Nation: Marian Anderson and the Struggle for Equal Rights* Gibbons, G. (199). *Pirates* Hampton, W. (1997). *Kennedy Assassinated! The World Mourns* Hoose, P. (2004). *The Race to Save the Lord God Bird* Knowlton, J. (1988). *Geography From A to Z* Legg, G. (1998). *From Egg to Chicken* Macdonald, F. (1996). *Exploring the World* Magloff, L. (2003). *Butterfly* McWhorter, D. (2004). *A Dream of Freedom: The Civil Rights Movement From 1954 to 1968*

Pattern	Definition	Children's Book Examples
		Schanzer, R. (2007). *George vs. George: The American Revolution as Seen From Both Sides* Warren, A. (2008). *Escape From Saigon: How a Vietnam Boy Became an American Boy* Webb, S. (2004). *Looking for Seabirds: Journal of an Alaskan Voyage*
Problem/Solution	The author states a problem, while listing possible solutions to the problem. Signal words that may indicate this text structure include: *problem is, solution is*, etc.	Bartoletti, S. (2005). *Hitler Youth: Growing Up in Hitler's Shadow* Blumberg, R. (2004). *York's Adventures With Lewis and Clark: An African-American's Part in the Great Expedition* Bolden, T. (2005). *Maritcha: A Nineteenth-Century American Girl* Cole, J. (1983). *Cars and How They Go* Crisp, M. (2003). *Everything Cat: What Kids Really Want to Know About Cats* Freedman, R. (2004). *The Voice That Challenged A Nation: Marian Anderson and the Struggle for Equal Rights* Hatkoff, I., Hatkoff, C., & Kahumbu, P. (2006). *Owen & Mzee: The True Story of a Remarkable Friendship* Hoose, P. (2004). *The Race to Save the Lord God Bird* Lauber, P. (1989). *The News About Dinosaurs* Levine, E. (1992). *If You Lived at the Time of the Great San Francisco Earthquake* McWhorter, D. (2004). *A Dream of Freedom: The Civil Rights Movement From 1954 to 1968* Seymour, S. (2002). *Danger! Volcanoes* Thimmesh, C. (2000). *Girls Think of Everything: Stories of Ingenious Inventions by Women* Warren, A. (2008). *Escape From Saigon: How a Vietnam Boy Became an American Boy* Webb, S. (2004). *Looking for Seabirds: Journal of an Alaskan Voyage*
Compare/Contrast	The author compares two or more things, which are alike or different. Signal words include: *in contrast, in comparison, alike*, and *on the other hand*.	Burleigh, R. (2004). *Seurat and La Grande Jatte: Connecting the Dots* Facklam, M. (2003). *Lizards: Weird and Wonderful* Gibbons, G. (1984). *Fire! Fire!* Jenkins, S. (2004). *Actual Size*

(Continued)

TABLE 8.2 (Continued)		
Pattern	*Definition*	*Children's Book Examples*
		Markle, S. (1991). *Outside and Inside You* Rauzon, M. J. (1993). *Horns, Antlers, Fangs and Tusks* Schanzer, R. (2007). *George vs. George: The American Revolution as Seen From Both Sides*
Cause and Effect	The author lists the causes and reasons why something happens. Signal words that may indicate a cause-and-effect structure include: *reasons why, as a result, consequently, therefore, thereby, leads to* and *therefore.*	Bartoletti, S. (2005). *Hitler Youth: Growing Up in Hitler's Shadow* Blumberg, R. (2004). *York's Adventures With Lewis and Clark: An African-American's Part in the Great Expedition* Bolden, T. (2005). *Maritcha: A Nineteenth-Century American Girl* Branley, F. (1986). *What Makes Day and Night?* Hatkoff, I., Hatkoff, C., & Kahumbu, P. (2006). *Owen & Mzee: The True Story of a Remarkable Friendship* Hoose, P. (2004). *The Race to Save the Lord God Bird* Maestro, G. (1992). *How Do Apples Grow?* McWhorter, D. (2004). *A Dream of Freedom: The Civil Rights Movement from 1954 to 1968* Showers, P. (2001). *What Happens to a Hamburger?* Taylor, B. (2001). *How to Save the Planet* Warren, A. (2008). *Escape From Saigon: How a Vietnam Boy Became an American Boy*

Explicitly Teaching Expository Elements

In addition to exposing children to a wide variety of excellent expository texts, teachers must also explicitly teach students strategies for reading expository texts. In Grades K–3, children read a wide range of narrative and blended texts; however, upper-elementary and middle school text book authors do not necessarily blend narrative features into content area texts, and most important, students must be able to read and comprehend a variety of texts to function in today's world. Researchers find that the greatest reason to use expository texts is to help students have less difficulty in comprehending expository texts later in school (Caswell & Duke, 1998; Chall et al., 1990; Chall & Snow, 1988).

Students at Starpoint School (Forth Worth, Texas) read nonfiction texts in small groups

Many children's literature authors are now blending expository and narrative text structures to interest more children in expository reading. Table 8.3 describes how such blending can take place in a children's book. The *Magic School Bus* series of books illustrates how such blending looks in a book. For example, in *The Magic School Bus: Inside a Hurricane* (Cole, 1996),

TABLE 8.3 Expository and Narrative Text Features		
Fiction Features	*Blending Fiction and Nonfiction Features*	*Nonfiction Features*
Beginning, middle, and end	Beginning, middle, and end	Introduction, body, and conclusion
Details	Characters	Details
Characters	Setting	Title and author
Setting	Problems and solutions	Important facts
Problems and solutions	Details	Learn information
Title and author	Important facts	
Interesting	Learn information	

factual information about the earth's atmosphere is presented, as well as narrative features, such as characters and an engaging lead, to interest children in the story while scientific information presented. Blending narrative and expository texts is an excellent way to expose young children to expository features. In order to teach such blending, teachers must find ways to explicitly teach the various text structures.

Teaching text structures requires three factors, according to Moss (2003). First, teachers must be knowledgeable about each structure, and be able to examine texts to categorize the type of structure. Second, teachers must select passages that clearly illustrate the text structure being taught, and model how to identify **signal words** and phrases within the text. Third, Moss recommends that teachers teach children a strategy they can use while reading, such as using a visual organizer like a comparison–contrast matrix or a semantic map, as discussed at the end of this chapter. By following the steps below, teachers can show students how to identify and categorize text structures:

1. Begin with a book children are familiar with and have read many times in class. Introduce the pattern and why the author used this pattern for the book. Point out the signal words used to indicate the text structure. For each text structure, introduce a book that illustrates that structure. Guide students to identify the pattern and the signal words used.

2. In small groups, distribute paragraphs taken from expository texts. Have each group read their text excerpt, identify the pattern, and circle the signal words that indicate the text structure.

3. As a whole class, discuss the small-group findings. Have a spokesperson from each group describe the rationale for selecting the particular text structure.

After examining text structures, students often find that a text fits in more than one pattern. Some books include both descriptive and sequence patterns. This is common, but what is most important is that students are noticing the signal words used to indicate a pattern.

Signal words are helpful to struggling readers and ESL students because these words help students decipher the particular text structure. For example, in the book *Exploring the World* (MacDonald, 1996), the authors tell the story of the first explorers to travel around the world. The text represents a sequencing pattern since the author uses such words as *first, before, then,* and *after*—and the content of the story is presented in chronological order. Figure 8.2 demonstrates how a teacher can show students how to notice signal words while reading this book.

A good example of the compare/contrast text pattern is in the book *George vs. George: The American Revolution as Seen From Both Sides.* In this book, author Rosalyn Schanzer (2004) uses such signal words as: *in contrast, neither, meanwhile, both sides,* and *on the other hand* to indicate a compare/contrast structure. Even more evident to the reader are the beautiful pictures throughout the book that also indicate a compare/contrast structure. For example, the author titles one section of the book "George vs. George 1774–1775," and in this section a cartoon with captions shows the thought processes of both Georges at the time of the Continental Congress in Philadelphia as they consider war. Books such as *George vs.*

FIGURE 8.2   Text Structure and Signal Words Used in the Book *Exploring the World*

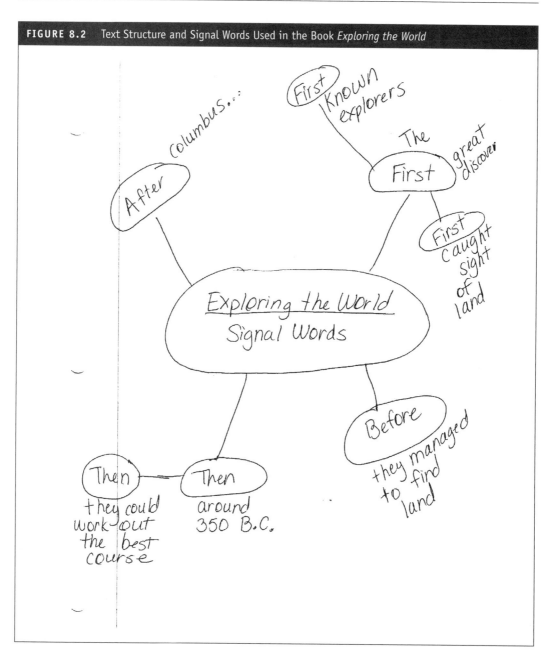

George: The American Revolution as Seen From Both Sides enable struggling readers and ELLs not only to find signal words, but to use pictures as a guide for comparing historical characters. In summary, being able to notice a particular pattern aids students in recalling important information from the expository text, and serves as a guide when retelling the main ideas and details to support those ideas. Teaching children strategies for reading expository texts allows them to comprehend difficult texts and paves the way for future reading success.

Cooperative Learning Structures

Several cooperative learning structures work well when teaching students to analyze and discuss text features. First, a **gallery walk** is an effective cooperative learning structure that encourages active engagement and discussion, which is especially important for ELLs. ELLs, especially students who are new to the United States, need to be given the opportunity to actively practice English. In a gallery walk students must read higher-level questions and determine how to answer such questions with their peers. This type of activity promotes listening, reading, writing, and speaking—all of which are important for ELLs who are developing academic language.

Teachers plan the gallery walk by posting higher-level questions that relate to content area text reading on butcher paper. Students are paired in small groups, and must walk around the room discussing their answers to the questions. Students then share their responses with the whole class. Examples of gallery walks in the science classroom are located at the following Web site: http://serc.carleton.edu/introgeo/gallerywalk.

A very popular cooperative learning structure, **think–pair–share**, is also especially helpful in encouraging students to think, reflect, and discuss text features and structures. With think–pair–share, the teacher poses a higher-level question and asks students to think silently about their answer for 1–2 minutes. Students then discuss their answer with a partner. Once answers are discussed in pairs, the teacher guides a whole-class discussion on the students' answers. In conclusion, there are many ways teachers can actively involve students in discussing and analyzing expository texts.

Comprehension Instruction

Effective content literacy teachers use many comprehension strategies to help facilitate students' understanding of a text, and such behaviors help children better understand what they read (McLaughlin & Allen, 2002). Ways in which students and teachers use comprehension strategies are highlighted in this section. Children use primarily eight comprehension strategies to understand what they are reading, but they also use these strategies for communicating what they learned through speaking and writing (Tompkins, 2007). These strategies include the following:

- Predicting (guessing what will happen next)
- Connecting (making text-to-text, text-to-self, or text-to-world connections while reading)
- Visualizing (finding a mental image to make reading meaningful)
- Questioning (readers ask questions while they read)
- Identifying big ideas (noticing important information in the text)
- Summarizing (combining main ideas and supporting details to summarize)

- Monitoring (readers supervise their own reading experience by finding ways to understand material they do not comprehend)
- Evaluating (evaluating the reading and experience)

Next, we describe how teachers and students apply comprehension strategies in the classroom.

Predicting

Teachers can model how to think aloud while they read an expository text; for example, how to predict or "guess" what will happen next. As they read, they identify sections of the text they did not understand, and model how they would reread the passage to help answer their questions about the passage. Students then make predictions about what will happen next, and confirm their predictions as they read.

Connecting

When teachers point to difficult words in the passage and then make connections to a prior lesson and to the **word wall** on display in the classroom—they are connecting the reading in a comprehension lesson. Word walls, which typically list words in alphabetical order, are used to define words or phrases found in class readings. Many teachers also include drawings or pictures of the words to help ESL students better understand a word's meaning. The word wall in the photo is in a one-way dual language class in which the primary language of instruction is Spanish. In this class, there are two word walls, one in English and one in Spanish

Visualizing

Teachers help students visualize while they read when they connect students' prior background knowledge to the current reading. For example, a teacher might ask fifth-grade students to visualize what they could do to keep warm in an unheated classroom. Students who visualize—create mental images—make this part of the text more memorable.

Questioning

Teachers encourage students to ask themselves questions while reading the text. For example, if a student does not understand a phrase in the text, the teacher may pose a question to help the student rethink the phrase in a new way.

Summarizing

Teachers often guide students through an oral summary of the text while pointing out the ways to use important details to support main ideas. Students can then combine these ideas to write a paragraph summary in which they combined big ideas to create a concise summary.

Spanish and English word walls in teacher Jessica Brown's class, Westcliff Elementary, Fort Worth, Texas

Strategy Instruction and the Content Areas

The difficulty of understanding expository texts was discussed earlier in this chapter. For more than a decade, researchers documented the success of strategy instruction in helping students better comprehend what they read in the content areas (Bean, 1997; Block, 1993; Durkin, 1978–1979; National Institute of Child Health and Human Development [NICHD], 2000; Neufeld, 2005; Pearson & Duke, 2002; Pearson & Fielding, 1991; Pressley, 1999; Pressley, Wharton-McDonald, Mistretta-Hampston, & Echevarria, 1998). Strategy instruction is specific, explicit instruction, and the teacher's explanation and modeling of the strategy are essential (Adams, 1990; Block, 1993; Kragler, Walker, & Martin, 2005; L'Allier & Elish-Piper, 2007; Pressley, 1999; Snow, Burns, & Griffin, 1998).

Exemplary teachers use a wide variety of reading and instructional strategies in content area instruction. For the purpose of this chapter, we decided to feature three common strategies used to teach reading in content area instruction. We observed teachers implement the following research-based strategies in classroom instruction, and below we provided brief descriptions of the strategies observed.

Sara Barnebee teaches a reading strategy using an interactive whiteboard, Fort Worth, Texas

ReQuest

ReQuest was originally designed for remedial instruction (Vacca & Vacca, 2008), but the strategy is a good one for content area instruction because it promotes active thinking about content during reading. Manzo (1969) suggests the following steps:

1. Read silently with your students. Students write down questions they have about the passage to later ask the teacher.

2. The teacher closes the book, and students ask their questions.

3. Now, there is an exchange of roles. The teacher asks the students questions about the text.

4. Last, the students make predictions about the rest of the text.

5. Students and the teacher read silently again, and then repeat numbers 1–4 above.

While recently observing Ms. Meaghan Burk teaching a social studies lesson, we noted ways in which she used ReQuest to help her students better comprehend a difficult text. Ms. Burk wanted to find a way to interest and engage students in learning about the Declaration of Independence, while also making sure that they comprehended the document. She decided to break the Declaration down and rewrite it in "kid language" so her students could better understand it. She also wanted to make sure students comprehended the individual sections of the Declaration, and so she chose to implement the ReQuest strategy in class. First, she described the ReQuest strategy to her class, and then she placed students in groups of three or four and gave them a modified version of the Declaration. She divided the Declaration into three easy parts (the Preamble, the Grievance, and the formal Declaration), and the class did three rounds of ReQuest. After each round, students received the next section of the modified Declaration, and the class completed a new round. For each round, Ms. Burk asked higher-level questions to elicit critical thinking and reflection. This lesson was a particular success since students were actively engaged and interacting continually with their peers while they learned important information about the contents of the Declaration of Independence.

Directed Reading-Thinking Activity

The directed reading-thinking activity, or **DR-TA**, is a strategy that encourages critical thinking about a text and actively engages students as they are guided by the teacher to think about what they are reading. The teacher uses frequent open-ended questions to help students think through the text (Vacca & Vacca, 2008). The example provided below illustrates in detail how Ms. Jennifer Scott used DR-TA to help second-grade students comprehend a book in a classroom where all of the students were deaf. Ms. Scott used sign language to demonstrate DR-TA. She chose DR-TA to help her students make predictions, connect to their prior background, and engage actively in thinking about a book.

Teacher: Now before we read a new *Biscuit* book, I want to ask you some questions. What do you think of when I say the word *trick?* For example, I think of pulling a rabbit out of a hat.

Student: Back . . . um back flips. And splits.

Teacher: Those are all tricks. What about dogs? What kind of tricks do dogs learn?

Student: Dogs jumping up for a treat. Dogs can learn back flips. I think they learn how to catch a ball.

Teacher: Great! Now I want you to look at the book we are reading today and tell me what you think it is going to be about. You can read the title and look and the picture to help you think of ideas.

Student: He might learn to jump. Look, he is going to learn how to catch a ball.

Teacher: How do you know he will learn to catch a ball?

Student: Because there is a ball in his mouth.

Teacher: Good. You all did a great job thinking about what might happen in the story. That is called making predictions. Are you ready to read?

The teacher read the book and commented on the pictures. She also asked the students questions about the book.

Teacher: OK. So what really happened in the story? What trick did Biscuit learn?

The teacher continued the ongoing questioning while she signed and read the book to the children. She monitored their understanding of the text while she helped them make connections and predictions during reading. DR-TA is a way for the teacher to ensure comprehension of reading while making reading interactive and engaging. Especially helpful for students who struggle with text—whether they are deaf or learning English as a new language—DR-TA is an effective strategy.

REAP

REAP is an effective strategy for upper elementary students as they try to understand a text they are reading (Eanet & Manzo, 1976). The teacher first models the REAP process and then guides students through a practice session of completing a REAP chart. Students complete a chart, using the following:

- R—read on your own and write down the title and the author's name.
- E—encode the text by writing down the main ideas in your own words.
- A—annotate the text by writing a summary of important points.
- P—ponder what you read by thinking about questions you may still have about the topic. Write down your questions.

We observed Mrs. Cindy Smith effectively teach a difficult concept, globalization, while using the REAP strategy. Mrs. Smith first introduced REAP when her class discussed the new vocabulary word, *globalization*. She displayed a Japanese sign for a McDonald's restaurant, and asked students what this picture meant to them. She then defined *globalization,* using the students' own words in the definition. After the students seemed to grasp globalization, she added the word and the class definition to the class word wall. Next, she said, "Today, we are going to learn a new reading strategy to help us better understand and recall information from a text. This strategy is called REAP." Mrs. Smith read aloud a short expository piece on globalization, as students followed along with their own copy of the text. Next, she displayed the REAP framework on the overhead, and guided students through recalling the components of REAP (see Figure 8.3).

FIGURE 8.3 REAP Example	
REAP	
R Title: The good and the bad of globalization	**E** Globalization is a way for countries to share economic resources.
A The author says that the wealthy get wealthier, and the poor get poorer.	**P** Globalization is changing the world. Question: How do we monitor globalization and how it impacts kids?

REAP offers a way to break a difficult expository piece into manageable chunks, and a way for students to recall important information from the text. Most important, students must summarize information they learn and identify main ideas from the text. When explicitly taught and modeled prior to independent practice, REAP provides students a framework for showing what they learned from reading an expository text.

Thematic Units

Thematic units are an effective way to connect learning across the curriculum, while emphasizing the importance of reading and writing. Because thematic units integrate meanings across content areas, readers and writers engaged in this type of curriculum can easily explore a variety of text structures and genres.

Tompkins (2007) suggests that students be involved in the planning of a thematic unit. Teachers can introduce a broad topic, and then have students generate questions about the topic. These questions became the basis for planning the thematic unit. A unit on weather, for example, can be framed around three "big" questions: (1) How does the weather change from day to day? (2) How does water in the air affect weather? (3) How does weather affect people? Framing a theme around big questions allows the teacher to identify the concepts that students will encounter in the unit (Kucer, Silva, & Delgado-Larocco, 1995). When exploring one of our big questions—How does water in the air affect weather?—students will encounter concepts such as water cycle, precipitation, condensation, evaporation, cloud, solid, liquid, and gas. For concepts related to other big questions in the weather unit please refer to Table 8.4. The identification of concepts that students will encounter during

TABLE 8.4	Weather Theme		
Big Questions	How does the weather change from day to day?	How does water in the air affect weather?	How does weather affect people?
Concepts	Weather, temperature, rain, snow, sleet, hail, cold, hot, tornado, hurricane, thunderstorm	Water cycle, precipitation, condensation, evaporation, cloud, solid, liquid, gas	Safety, shelter, adaptation, meteorologist, "wives' tales"

the unit allows the teacher to begin selecting **text sets**. A text set is a grouping of two or more books that are linked by a topic or concept but vary in terms of author, point of view, organizational structure, genre, or text type. Text sets in a weather unit can include fiction and nonfiction books, newspapers, magazines, audiotapes to place in a listening center, and multimedia material.

A thematic curriculum assists less proficient readers and ELLs in developing the background necessary to link language and meaning in order to facilitate reading comprehension. As a unit progresses, students use their new understandings to make inferences and formulate further predictions when engaged in reading throughout the theme.

Inside the Classroom:
Thurgood Marshall Elementary School, Buffalo, New York

Theresa Harris-Tigg

Thurgood Marshall Elementary School is situated in a large urban school district in Buffalo, New York. The district enrolls approximately 38,000 students in 70 facilities.

The Thurgood Marshall School serves a large population of African American students and parents. Ninety percent of the students are eligible for free and reduced-price lunch.

The teacher discussed in this vignette, Ms. Jenkins, was a nontraditional elementary teacher. She strayed away from just having her students identify and study dates and facts for multiple choice tests. She refused to have teacher-written notes on the board for students to copy and regurgitate on a test. Literacy skills were directly taught to her students and they were given ample time to use and practice these skills in every subject in her fifth-grade class. Her students not only learned the content knowledge deeply, but they were taught what, how, and when to use strategies that would ensure they learned at high levels.

Ms. Jenkins's fifth-grade class began the school day by reading an article on China from a *Junior Scholastic* magazine: "China's New Tomorrow: Amid a Booming Economy, Many Parents Are Struggling to Build a Brighter Future for Their Children." The wall at the front of the classroom was covered with three large Post-it sheets. One sheet had a paragraph written from the article. The second sheet had a drawing of a map of China, and the third sheet had a list of eight vocabulary words. The students were seated in groups of four to a table. The class was studying about the lives of children in modern-day China.

Today's social studies lesson began with a sharing of the day's agenda and goals. Ms. Jenkins began the class discussion by stating the day's agenda:

Today we are going to read and learn about the experiences of young people, like yourselves, who live in modern-day China. We will also learn how to use the strategy "to reread" a paragraph or section of a textbook when you don't understand it completely. When this strategy is applied, we will be able to monitor our own comprehension and make sure that we understand what we are reading. Sounds good? OK, let's begin.

The teacher directed the students' attention to the large yellow Post-it paper with a short passage from the magazine written on it. She read the passage out loud. While reading, the teacher identified sections of the passage where she did not understand what was going on from the reading. Ms. Jenkins used the **think-aloud** strategy to describe the sections she did not understand. She said,

As I am thinking [reading], I wonder why it is that the Chinese fifth graders sat in unheated classrooms dressed in winter coats to keep warm? I am not sure I understand the reason for that, so I will go back and reread the first part of the article to figure out why this is so.

When Ms. Jenkins reread passage, she identified words from the article that might give her a clue as to what was happening. Ms. Jenkins explained to the class,

The chapter includes words like: migrants, communist, authoritarian. We studied these words last week! How many of you remember these words? Please look at the word wall and review them again if you have forgotten [what] these words mean. Does your understanding of these words help us to figure out why the Chinese children were sitting in an unheated school in the city?

One of the students, Xavier, responded,

Sort of . . . because the children moved to the city from farms to get a better life and from being governed by a person who did not allow the people to move around in the country or live in the city.

Similarly, Jasmin responded,

Yeah, it says in the article that this was the winter months and the children had to bundle up because the building was not prepared for these students from the farming areas.

After this discussion, Ms. Jenkins called on pairs of students to read the next paragraph in **choral reading,** which means out loud and together. After each pair of students read the paragraph, Ms. Jenkins followed by asking her students what motivated one of the Chinese students to seek a specific profession. She asked, "Why did Yuan He want to be a scientist when she grows up?"

The students sat quietly. Many of the students began flipping back in the magazine looking for information that would help them to find an answer to their teacher's question. The teacher explained to the class that knowing when to reread is a useful strategy. She told her students that most readers do not retain everything they have read, even after reading a text selection more than one time.

Ms. Jenkins: Does anyone know why Yuan wanted to be a scientist? Brooklyn?

Brooklyn: I don't know, Ms. Jenkins.

The other students in Brooklyn's group suggested that they would help her find the answer by rereading the section for clues.

Betty: . . . about farming . . . it does not figure in her future plans.

Taylor: Her mother wants her to be a doctor or a lawyer so she can make more money.

Brooklyn: She will make big money being a scientist.

Ms. Jenkins: *[laugh]* So now we know why she wanted to be a scientist. And I bet if you go back and reread the sentences before and after that particular passage they might tell you another reason she wanted to be a scientist. So what was her point?

Belinda: China was changing in a lot of ways but it still has an authoritarian government. The people could not criticize their government but Yuan was worried about those families who could not leave the farms for a better life so she wanted to make their farming chores not so hard and better for them. She believed that studying her favorite subject, science, could help her to make changes in the farmlands.

Ms. Jenkins again called on pairs of students to read the next paragraph chorally in their groups. She informed the class that there was a lot of difficult and challenging information in the article. She suggested that while reading, if they felt they didn't know what was going on, they stop at a certain point and assess what they did understand.

Ms. Jenkins: Did anyone find this passage difficult and confusing?

One student, Albert, raised his hand and shared a sentence that was confusing to him.

Albert: *[reading from the article]* "The result is a society of stark contrasts."

Ms. Jenkins: What part did you find difficult? Where were you confused?

Albert: a . . . society

Ms. Jenkins: How can you clarify it for yourself?

Albert: I can reread the paragraph and try to understand it.

Ms. Jenkins: Excellent!

Albert and his group reread the passage together and discussed the term *society* as it related to the article. The students were not only engaged in finding the particular word in the article but in discussing its meaning.

Ms. Jenkins: Okay. Did rereading the paragraph clarify for you what the author meant by "a society of stark contrasts"?

Albert: Yes. The society is the people of China.

Ms. Jenkins: And what do you understand about the "stark contrast" part?

Albert: Well, the Chinese people have a lot of choices now. Choices in clothing and what to wear. They used to wear boring suits like their communist leader. So that's a big difference.

Lizzie: So contrast is the differences that are shown.

Finally, the students were asked to read the remainder of the article silently—and then to jot down on a sticky note the most important information they learned from the section of text. After waiting for a few moments and observing the students to determine when everyone had completed the task, Ms. Jenkins reminded the students about the importance of summarizing their learning from the article, and she asked for volunteers to read their sticky notes as a way to share a short summary. Lastly, Ms. Jenkins instructed the students to take out their notebooks and decide how they will write a summary of their reading.

Ms. Jenkins: I can summarize our reading today by identifying just the main ideas, or the important details in the chapter, and leaving out all the small things that are not important. Who would like to have a shot at summarizing our reading today?

Mark: Beijing is a dusty city in China.

Ms. Jenkins: Mark, is that an important idea? Was most of the article about the dust in the city of Beijing?

The student hesitated, and the teacher instructed him to keep thinking about what information was presented in the article and, perhaps, go back and reread to help with his summarization.

Mark: Oh, Beijing is a capital city of China. That is more important than the description of it being a dusty city.

Ms. Jenkins: Mark, what reading strategies did you use to comprehend?

Mark: I went to the information about Beijing and reread it. I thought about what is most important here.

Ms. Jenkins: Class, how did rereading help Mark's comprehension?

Trina: It helped him to look at the information again, think about and decide what part of the information is really important.

Ms. Jenkins: Thank you, Trina.

After the students wrote summaries in their notebooks, Ms. Jenkins asked them to share their notes with their group buddies to realize the scope of information they had learned in the lesson. The teacher concluded the lesson with a viewing of a movie about modern-day China.

Questions for Discussion

1. What did you find most interesting about this vignette?

2. Describe the effectiveness of Ms. Jenkins's approach to using literacy strategies and skills in her social studies lesson.

4. How were literacy strategies and skills explicitly taught by Ms. Jenkins?

5. Using this vignette, discuss how you would convince your colleagues of the importance of using literacy across the curriculum in their classes.

Summary of Strategies Used

Ms. Jenkins used many effective reading strategies to help her students better understand the material they read in social studies. Similar to the International Reading Association's 2002 position statement describing excellent teachers, it is clear that Ms. Jenkins understands reading development since she uses a variety of effective strategies to help students better comprehend what they are reading, such as think aloud, word walls, and the importance of teaching students how to summarize information. Likewise, similar to IRA's position statement describing the qualities of excellent teachers, Ms. Jenkins provides students with a variety of texts to read, and she explicitly teaches them how to read using research-based reading strategies. The strategies she uses are explained in detail in the next section of this chapter.

Case for Exploration: PS 17, Buffalo, New York

Theresa Harris-Tigg

The fourth graders in PS 17 in Buffalo, New York, sporadically and quickly entered the classroom and settled down to the sounds of light jazz softly infiltrating the busy room. The children hung their coats in the closet area and took their seats at their assigned group tables.

On the center wall facing the children, the teacher had written "Day 20: Clock Work."

> Melissa started reading her book at 5:30 p.m. and read until 10:15 p.m. How much time passed?

The students hurriedly wrote their computations on different colored Post-it notes and placed their work proudly on the wall. One male student marched back to his desk, as the other students returned to their desks.

After the students completed their work, the teacher, Ms. Cunningham, called everyone's attention to the front of the class. She instructed one female student to come up to the front of the class and invited her to sit on a stool placed next to a square table. Ms. Cunningham paper-clipped a piece of paper to the collar of the student's blouse. Located in the middle of the table were three unlike items. One item was an empty canister with a price tag of $2.00 taped to it. There was a second canister filled with markers and pens and a price tag of $7.50. The third item on the table was a hole-punch priced at $3.00. The final item for sale was the female student, priced at $4.00.

Teacher: What do you think about the things we have for sale today?

Students: *[many laughing]*

Teacher: What is wrong with this picture? Is she the most expensive item? What does that mean? When you first look at it, what is your first thought?

Student 1: Why is she being sold?

Student 2: Who will take care of her?

Teacher: Great. What other questions will you ask? What other things are you thinking? I am able to purchase markers, a hole-punch, and Daja at a store! Does that make any sense?

Student 3: No way!

Later on in the lesson, Ms. Cunningham asked the students what activities they participate in when they have free time. The students shared inside and outdoor activities and games they play. After a lively discussion about their free time, the teacher introduced a game called Mancala and read a brief history of the game's origin. It is a math game that children played in Africa. Using the globe, she showed the students how the game traveled from Africa, to Asia and finally to North America. Then she had the students observe the game at Addy's Web site (see p. 188). The students read on the screen the rules and game play moves. The teacher asked if there were any confusing words in the instructions. She reviewed with the students how to use context clues to make sense of the unfamiliar words.

Student 1: What does the word *deposit* mean?

Teacher: Read the sentence using the word.

Student 1: The player deposits one stone in each hole.

Teacher: Are there any words that might give you a clue about the word *deposit*?

Student 2:   In the hole; right?

Teacher: What does that phrase suggest the player is doing?

Student 3:   Putting the stone in the hole. Deposit means to put the stones in the holes.

Teacher: Good work.

Then the teacher had the students get in a circle on the floor. Ms. Cunningham played the game with one student to model the procedures. As the game progressed, she would, again, ask specific questions about what she was doing and what her opponent was doing. The students would respond chorally.

Teacher: How many stones did I deposit in my storage?

Students: One.

Teacher: Is that a good thing? Why?

Student 1:   Because the more you put . . . I mean deposit . . . in your own storage the better it is for you to win. The instructions said that the person with the most stones in their storage container wins.

Ms. Cunningham continued with process and procedural questions to make sure the students understood how to play the game and some tips for playing skillfully. Before allowing the students to play the game with partners on their own, Ms. Cunningham explained how to care for the pieces and the procedures to put the game away in storage. When they were allowed to play, the students counted the pieces by 2s and 5s to practice their multiplication facts and document how many stones were included with the game. Then students played the game with partners.

After the students finished two rounds of Mancala, the teacher asked each partnership to be responsible for making sure all the pieces of the game were counted and correct. She asked the students to count using various multiples to check for accuracy. Ms. Cunningham's final directive was to instruct each student to write a journal entry about his or her strategy for playing and winning this game. After the students completed the journal entry, volunteers read their entries aloud.

Literacy across the curriculum is an immediate focus in U.S. schools today. With English language arts (ELA) and math scores on standardized tests plummeting in urban schools, literacy across the curriculum becomes a major concern. The approaches used to promote literacy across the curriculum are widely discussed and vary by school district, individual schools, and teachers. Literacy across the curriculum is a mainstay in Ms. Cunningham's classroom. She provides a learning opportunity where students can see that reading, writing, speaking, listening, and critical listening skills are applicable in real life. In addition, the parallels between literacy and mathematics are made visible by Ms. Cunningham (Minton, 2007).

In the last period of the day, Ms. Cunningham taught social studies. There are several approaches to literacy across the curriculum. For our purposes here, Ms. Cunningham used very good examples of literacy across the curriculum approaches. This approach is called *thematic units* (Atwell, 1990; Fredericks, Meinbach, & Rothlein, 1993). In a thematic unit, the teacher designs instruction around a theme. In this case, Ms. Cunningham used the study of slavery as the theme for her math and social studies lessons.

Teacher: Where did slavery begin? Where did slavery end?

Students: *[No response]*

Teacher: Run your finger along the timeline to see what happened.

   [Students look at the teacher and imitate what she is doing.]

Teacher: Today, we are going to be studying my friend, Addy. Addy is very, very special. We are going to look at her life. The book is titled *Meet Addy: An American Girl,* by Connie Porter. The book is part of The American Girls Collection. [See more information about "American Girls" and interactive games online at http://www.americangirl.com/fun/agcn/addy/index.php? section = game]

   [The teacher is sitting on a stool, holding an Addy doll on her lap.]

Student: Ooo, I like that doll.

Teacher: Write the word "slavery" in your notebooks. What would be the genre for this book about Addy?

Student: Historical fiction.

Teacher: What does it actually mean to be a slave?

Student: She works for other people.

The teacher asked students to sit down on the rug to see the computer. The teacher is using Brain Pop, a computer program on the history of slavery. The teacher instructed the students to watch and listen to the program the first time. On the second viewing, the students were instructed to listen and take notes on key points of the presentation.

Teacher: That is very important! You want to make a note of that (pertaining to specific points in the presentation to enhance their note taking).

After viewing the presentation a second time, the students were asked to share their findings with the whole class.

Teacher: Very good, class. Now let me hear some of the things you wrote down from the presentation.

Students shared various aspects of the presentation.

Teacher: Students please put your selves in a circle. Let's just take a minute to think about some things here. What if it were you? Or your mom?

Teacher: Tell me some of the things Addy went through.

The teacher had a brown paper bag with problems written on slips of paper, and students drew a slip of paper out of the bag. One student read the problem. Then students went around the circle giving a solution to the problem:

First student:	What would you do if your mom was a slave?
Second student:	I would try to get her back.
First student:	What would you do if the master sold your brother?
Second student:	I would get money.
Teacher:	How would you get money?
Second student:	Work.
Third student:	I will try to trade me for my brother.
First student:	What would you do if you are a slave, unable to work, and are punished for it?
Second student:	I would try to escape.
Teacher:	What would be a way you could get away? *[No responses from students]*
Teacher:	How many would try to work anyway? *[Many hands went up.]*
Teacher:	Would you complain?
First student:	Yes.

The teacher then directed students to return to their desks and take out their social studies notebooks. She asked them to write information on the title, author, and genre of the book. After entries into notebooks were completed, the teacher began reading the first chapter of the book. She would stop for very specific and usual words.

Teacher:	What are corn husks?
Teacher:	What is a pallet? Oh, my grandmother would say that all the time.
Student:	Somewhere to sleep.

The teacher then called on a student to read. Students were called on to read in a round-robin fashion. After a number of students had read, the teacher concluded the chapter with an audiotape of the book.

Teacher:	Why might they want to change the language? The slaves did not read or write, right? How were they able to talk? Because they were going by what they heard. Do you think the Africans spoke English when they were brought here?
Students:	No.

After listening to the audiotape, students were asked to write chapter summaries in their notebooks. Students were given approximately 5 minutes to write a minimum of eight lines for their summaries. Very soft jazz was playing in the background.

Teacher: How should you begin your summaries?

Student: In this chapter . . .

Teacher: Good. What is a summary?

Student: Tell what happened in the story.

Teacher: If you are stuck, don't forget to use your toolbox.

At the end of class, students shared their summaries, and corrections were made.

Questions for Discussion

1. What did you find most interesting about this vignette?

2. What connections do you see between effective literacy instruction and math?

3. In what way did Ms. Cunningham develop a natural connection between literacy and social studies?

4. In what way did she develop a sense of community?

5. How can you integrate literacy across the curriculum in your classroom, or in a classroom you are familiar with?

6. In your own situation, or one that you have observed, would it be possible to teach this way? Why or why not?

Concluding Thoughts

Returning to the vignette, Ms. Jenkins provided the type of instructional support all students need. She actively involved students in the reading process, taught them reading strategies needed to comprehend difficult expository texts, and created a classroom community in which all students felt comfortable voicing their opinions. Teachers like Ms. Jenkins know a variety of ways to teach reading, as supported by IRA's *Excellent Reading Teachers Position Statement* (2000). Ms. Jenkins possessed the qualities that distinguish her as an excellent teacher, in particular the strength of knowing a variety of ways to teach reading within content area instruction.

TERMS TO KNOW

Content literacy

DR-TA

Expository texts

Gallery walk

Narrative texts

Signal words

Text sets

Text structure

Think aloud

Think–pair–share

Word wall

REAP

ReQuest

Thematic units

RESEARCH THAT WORKS

Atwell, J. (2004). *Tools for teaching content literacy.* Portland, ME: Stenhouse.

Gregg, M., & Sekeres, D. C. (2006). Supporting children's reading of expository text in the geography classroom. *Reading Teacher, 60*(2), 102–110.

Montelongo, J. A., & Hernández, A. C. (2007, March). Reinforcing expository reading and writing skills: A more versatile sentence completion task. *Reading Teacher, 60*(6), 538–546.

Rodgers, Y. V., Hawthorne, S., & Wheeler, R .C. (2007, September). Teaching economics through children's literature in the primary grades. *Reading Teacher, 61*(1), 46–55.

WEB SITES

Reading Quest for Social Studies: **http://www.readingquest.org/strat/** is an excellent Web site that provides instructions and charts to print. Charts highlighted include ABC Brainstorming, Concept of Definition Map, Comparison-Contrast Charts, Column Notes, and many more.

Mosaic Listserv Tools: **http://www.readinglady.com/mosaic/tools/tools.htm** is one of our favorite Web sites because of the plethora of tools available. The site is divided into the following sections: assessment, lesson plans, worksheets/reporting forms, staff development, writing, parents, and other. Downloadable rubrics and resources are located in each of these sections.

Glossary

Ability grouping: student groups based on students' abilities or reading levels; group members do not rotate

Academic language: language proficiency needed to perform well in school tasks

Activity centers: interest centers where the props are varied to promote the development of oral and written language; can be structured to represent environments (e.g., post office, library, bakery), to give students an opportunity to manipulate materials (e.g., blocks, water table), or a theme related to a content area

Adequate yearly progress (AYP): the required progress each school must attain if is not meeting state accountability standards. Schools that cannot demonstrate AYP risk being restaffed and/or losing federal money to support their school programs

After reading: the teacher and students discuss their predictions and revisit the text to point out problems that need to be solved

Alphabetic principle: the knowledge of letter–sound correspondence and spelling patterns

Anecdotal records: brief, focused teacher comments kept in chronological order and used to track student progress over time

Automaticity: the ability to recall and recognize a word quickly and accurately

Before reading: teacher chooses a text that presents few challenges for the students, introduces the story, and poses questions for the children to think about while they read

Beginning writing: the second stage of writing development; includes invented spelling with spacing and the use of invented spelling while applying spelling and grammar rules learned in school

Big books: oversized books that allow all children to see the print and illustrations and easily follow the reading

Bound morphemes: morphemes that must be attached to unbound morphemes (e.g., the bound morpheme /s/ is attached to the unbound morpheme /cat/ to signify plural)

Choral reading: a group of students, or even an entire class, reads a text or passage together

Chunks: distinct parts of the word that can be recognized without an analysis of the word

Cognates: words that have the same linguistic root and are similar in terms of spelling and meaning

Cognitive strategies: plans for carrying out mental operations

Concepts about print: the concept elements about language and print that young children develop as they interact with books (e.g., print carries a message; print is different from pictures)

Conflict: occurs between two different forces in the plot and keeps readers interested

Content literacy: the ability to read, write, and communicate effectively within each content area

Content-specific vocabulary: technical words that relate to a particular academic field

Context clues: using words before and after an unfamiliar word in text to determine the meaning of the unknown word or phrase

Conversational language: language proficiency required to carry on conversations in everyday situations

Culturally relevant books: relate to the student's background; cause children to become more engaged in reading the story while allowing them to more easily make predictions and inferences about the story being read

Demonstration: acting out an example or model

Differentiated reading instruction: teacher adapts instruction to individual learners; and teaches each student according to his or her ability

Directed reading-thinking activity (DR-TA): encourages critical thinking about a text while actively engaging students as the teacher guides them to think about the text by asking open-ended questions

Discourse: discussion

Drafting: writing or rewriting a text; usually occurs more than once in the writing process

During reading: the teacher assesses children's reading fluency and comprehension while they read, while also trying to help student connect to the text

Ebonics: African American Vernacular English

Echo reading: a less fluent reader "echoes" a more fluent reader

Editing: fixing the grammatical errors in text

Emergent writing: the earliest stage of writing development; consists of scribbling, one-letter writing, and invented spelling that children use without necessarily including spacing between words

Environmental print: the print encountered in familiar contexts in everyday life; for example, the word *McDonald's* on the sign for the restaurant or the word *Cheerios* on a cereal box; also environmental print in the classroom

Expository texts: informational books meant to give factual information to the reader

Flexible grouping: students grouped into temporary groups based on their level of independence in reading

Fluency: the ability to easily decode words and use appropriate intonation and expression while reading

Fluency development workshop: a hands-on method for teaching fluency developed by Ray Reutzel; includes explicit instruction about the elements of reading fluency, rich and varied modeling of fluent reading, guided oral reading practice, guided rereadings of the same text, assessment and self-monitoring of fluency progress, information on how to fix faltering reading fluency, and genuine audiences for oral reading

Fluent writing: the final stage of writing development; includes nearly conventional spelling

Frontloading: the process of introducing new vocabulary and discussing concepts before reading or writing about academic content

Frustrational-level texts: texts that students read with 89% or less accuracy

Gallery walk: a cooperative learning structure that encourages active classroom engagement and participation; teachers post higher-level questions that relate to content area text on butcher paper; students, paired in small groups, walk around the room discussing their answers to the questions, then share their responses with the whole class

General academic vocabulary: vocabulary that appears across multiple disciplines

Graded word lists: high-frequency words that need to be known for the student's grade level

Gradual release of responsibility: withdrawing the amount of teacher support as children become more independent readers and writers; the teacher gradually releases the responsibility of explicit teaching as students become more fluent readers and writers

Graphemes: letters

Graphic organizers: visual ways to organize information (e.g., Venn diagram)

Graphophonemic system of language: the knowledge of letter and sound relationships

Graphophonic cues: sound–letter patterns and other print conventions such as punctuation and directionality

Graphophonics: understanding the relation between letters (graphemes) and sounds (phonemes)

Guided reading: the teacher introduces a strategy to use when encountering difficult text before giving students in small groups a chance to practice with a book containing unfamiliar words

Guided writing: the teacher works with a small group of children to help them craft their writing based on the students' needs

Heuristic (Tell me why): Language used to learn about the environment (e.g., child says, "What is this?")

High-frequency words: words that appear often in written text but are difficult to remember because they have no meaning

Imaginative (Let's pretend): Language used to pretend (e.g., language children use when engaged in pretend play)

Independent-level texts: texts that students can read with 95% accuracy

Independent reading: a regularly occurring time students and teachers read self-selected materials

Independent writing: when children are able to move through the writing process, while practicing the writing strategies and skills they have learned

Informal reading inventory (IRI): an assessment that provides teachers with information about a student's reading level without diagnosing the child

Informative (I've got something to tell you): Language used to impart information (e.g., giving a report or writing a paper)

Instructional conversations: allow teachers to explore instructional goals while supporting children's participation in discussions

Instructional-level texts: texts that students can read with 90%–94% accuracy

Instrumental: language used to meet needs (I want; e.g., child says "bottle" while pointing at and reaching for a bottle)

Interactional: language used to build personal relations (you and me; e.g., child says, "I love you")

Interactive writing: students take turns writing down a text they compose while the teacher helps them with any difficulties; once the writing is finished, the students and teacher read the text repeatedly

Labels and directions: support literacy development by helping students understand how reading and writing are used on a daily basis for a wide range of needs

Language experience approach: the teacher provides students an experience, then the teacher transcribes students' statements about the experience; the teacher reads the written statements back to the students, then has the students read and reread the passage

Language functions: the wide variety of needs that language serves

Language-rich classroom environment: a setting that is bursting with oral and written language

Language systems: children use their language system to construct meaning when reading or writing; their prior background knowledge and experiences influence the messages they interpret

Leveled-text sets: a collection of books that that may relate to a particular theme or topic; can include a variety of genres, such as narrative texts, expository texts, poetry, and more; leveled texts are on the independent reading level of particular readers who can read the texts sets independently

Literacy centers: provide individuals or small groups of children with time to participate independently in reading and writing activities by supplying materials and an opportunity to work collaboratively and use language to communicate

Literature: refers to books that children read

Literature circles: small groups of students who read and discuss books that they self-select from teacher-provided text sets

Modeled writing: the teacher shows students what it means to be a fluent writer by demonstrating thought processes involved for one aspect of the writing process

Morning message: a time that allows students to share important life events while the teacher transcribes and draws attention to specific aspects of writing (e.g., same beginning or ending letters)

Morphemes: the smallest unit of meaning in a language

Morphological: using the understanding of morphemes to predict the meanings of words

Morphology: a study of structure or form, including, for example, words and language

Narrative texts: a fictitious, factual, science fiction, or romance text created to entertain and interest an audience; it includes characters with distinct personalities, dialogue, and descriptive language that bring the story to life

Narrative writing: includes plot, conflict and setting, and characters that are well developed; these are some of the elements of a story

New literacies: a way to teach reading, writing, listening, speaking, viewing, and representing that doesn't use paper and pencil

Nonlinguistic representation: a picture or graphic organizer that explains the meaning of words or text

Non–Standard English: a dialect of English that is considered socially inferior (e.g., Ebonics)

Onset: the part of the syllable that precedes the vowel sound in oral language

Partner reading: when two children take turns reading and rereading a text or passage

Personal: language used to express individuality ("Here I come," or a child says "pretty girl" when referring to herself)

Phonemes: the smallest units of sound that can signal differences in meaning

Phonemic awareness: child's ability to recognize that a spoken word is composed of individual sounds—or phonemes

Phonics: focus on learning the alphabetic principle that involves knowledge of letter–sound correspondence and spelling patterns

Phonological awareness: the ability to understand the different sounds letters make

Phonological systems of language: the rules that govern how sounds can be combined in any particular language

Phonology: the sounds of a language

Plot: the events in a story; in a narrative text the plot has a beginning, middle, and end

Pragmatic system of language: what the reader knows about the purposes or functions of reading

Print-rich environment: a place where students are exposed to a wide range of words and books in a variety of contexts

Progress monitoring: teachers regularly check their students' progress in accuracy, rate, and expression by having them read three grade-level passages aloud; the results are graphed to track progress

Publishing: writers celebrate and showcase their writing by sharing it with others and/or illustrating their text

Read-alouds: when a teacher or caregiver reads a story aloud to a child, while also supporting readers in acquiring concepts about print

Reading aloud: teacher or student reads a text out loud to others, then actively discusses it; this is the most highly recommended activity for encouraging the development of language and literacy

Reading comprehension: understanding a text's meaning

Real discussion: occurs when teachers support children in exploring ideas and engaging in more talk while providing children with opportunities to decide when to speak and to address their peers directly

Realia: the objects a classroom teacher uses to help students better understand the vocabulary terms being targeted

REAP: *r*eading, *e*ncoding, *a*nnotating, *p*ondering; teacher models the strategy, then guides students through a practice session of reading on their own and writing down the title and author's name, encoding the text by writing down the main ideas in their own words, annotating the text by writing a summary of important points, and pondering what they have read by listing questions they may still have

Readers Theater: a story is broken into individual parts based on the characters; a fun and engaging way to read and to improve fluency for young children

Regulatory: language used to control others (Do as I tell you; e.g., child says "bye-bye" while taking his dad's hand and moving toward the door)

ReQuest: designed for remedial instruction but works well for content area instruction; teacher reads silently with the students while they write down their questions about the passage, the teacher closes the book and students ask their questions, the teacher then asks students questions about the text, and lastly, the students make predictions about the rest of the text

Revising: writers share their writing with a writing group of their peers and/or with their teacher, and give feedback on their peers' writing

Rime: the vowels and consonants after the onset

Round-robin reading: students read orally from a text and move from student to student in the classroom as each student reads aloud from the text

Running records: notes taken on a child's performance while the child reads a text unassisted; used to analyze, record, and score a child's reading behaviors

Schemata: cognitive framework that helps people organize and interpret information

Seed idea: an idea that a writer may want to expand by taking it through the writing process

Semantic: relating to meaning in a language

Semantic cues: students use their background knowledge and context of the text to evaluate whether what they are reading makes sense in the context in which it appears

Semantics: govern the meaning relations among words, phases, or sentences, and understanding that different words usually have different meanings and may evoke different feelings

Setting: where a story takes place; location, weather, and time

Setting a purpose for writing: choosing a topic, determining the audience, and organizing writing ideas during prewriting

Shared reading: the teacher does most of the reading but children contribute to repeated lines or words throughout the reading

Shared writing: the children tell the teacher what and how to write while the teacher models the thought processes for writing

Sight words: words seen most often in text

Signal words: words that help students decipher the particular text structure, such as *first, before, then,* and *after*

Sustained silent reading (SSR): usually a brief (30 minutes) time during the school day when students silently read a book of their choice

Simultaneous interaction: the classroom is split into partners and each partner shares what he or she knows; this way half of the class is interacting simultaneously instead of one child sharing with the entire class

Sound–letter correspondence: understanding the correspondence between letters in written language and sounds in oral language

Standard English: the variety of English that is socially accepted and used by the dominant groups in U.S. society

Stigmatized dialects: dialects that are devalued in schools, business, government, and the media

Strategic reading: using mental plans of action that support constructing meaning

Syntactic cues: students use prior knowledge of English language structure and grammar to evaluate whether what they are reading sounds right

Syntactic system of language: how words are arranged in a sentence

Syntax: the order of words in a language (e.g., the red house instead of the house red)

Text sets: a grouping of two or more books that are linked by a topic or concept but vary in terms of author, point of view, organizational structure, genre, or text type

Text structure: the organization of written material

Thematic units: effective way to connect learning across the curriculum, while emphasizing the importance of reading and writing by integrating meanings across content areas

Think-alouds: while reading a text out loud to the students, the teacher demonstrates this strategy by periodically stopping and voicing what is going on inside his or her head

Think–pair–share: students think, reflect, and discuss text features and structures

Unbound morphemes: morphemes that can stand alone (such as *dog*)

Visuals: pictorial portrayals of messages

Whole-class instruction: a whole-class reading lesson in which all students are expected to read the same piece of literature at the same pace

Wide reading programs: programs that provide fixed times during the day for children to engage in self-selected reading materials (e.g., DEAR, SSR)

Word map: a strategy commonly used to help students further define new concepts and examine their characteristics

Word meaning: developing (a) a new concept or (b) a new word for a familiar concept

Word recognition: the ability to recognize the written form of a word

Word utility: the range of frequency and usage a word might have

Word walls: large wall or whiteboard spaces divided into sections for each letter in the alphabet where high-frequency words are displayed

Writer's notebook: a place for younger children to draw pictures and for older children to record ideas for stories

Writing process: a recursive process involving setting a purpose for writing, drafting, revising, editing, and publishing

Writing workshop: a time block of about an hour that allows students to write about what is important to them while the teacher pulls small groups to teach mini lessons targeting those students' needs

Zone of proximal development: the difference between what children can do with the guidance of an adult and what they can do by themselves

References

Adams, M. (1990). *Beginning to read: Thinking and print.* Cambridge: MIT Press.

Afflerbach, P. (2004, September). *High stakes testing and reading assessment* (National Reading Conference Policy Brief). Presentation at the University of Maryland.

Afflerbach, P. (2008). *Understanding and using reading assessment K–12.* Newark, DE: International Reading Association.

Aiex, N. K. (1990). Debate and communication skills. Bloomington, IN: ERIC Clearinghouse on Reading, English and Communication. (ERIC Document Reproduction Service No. ED 321 334)

Alanis, I. (2007). Developing literacy through culturally relevant texts. *Socials Studies and the Young Learner, 20*(1), 29–32.

Alderson, J. C., & Urquhart, A. H. (1988). This test is unfair: I'm not an economist. In P. Carrell, J. Devine, & D. Eskey (Eds.), *Interactive approaches to second language reading* (pp. 168–182). New York: Cambridge University Press.

Allen, H. (2002). *On the same page.* Portland, ME: Stenhouse.

Allen, J. (2007). *Inside words: Tools for teaching academic vocabulary grades 4–12.* Portland, ME: Stenhouse.

Allington, R. (Ed.). (2002). *Big brother and the national reading curriculum: How ideology trumped evidence.* Portsmouth, NH: Heinemann.

Allington, R. L. (2006). *What really matters for struggling readers: Designing research-based programs.* Boston: Pearson Education.

Allington, R. L., & Johnston, P. H. (2000). What do we know about effective fourth-grade reading teachers and their classrooms? *CELA Research Report.* Retrieved August 31, 2009, from http://www.eric.ed.gov/ERICDocs/data/ericdocs2sql/content_storage_01/0000019b/80/16/a8/e6.pdf

American Federation for Teachers. (2007). *Meeting the challenge: Recruiting and retaining teachers in hard-to-staff schools.* Washington, DC: American Federation for Teachers.

Anders, P. L., Hoffman, J. V., & Duffy, G. G. (2000). Teaching teachers to teach reading: Paradigm shifts, persistent problems, and challenges. In M. L. Kamil, P. B. Mosenthal, P. D. Pearson, & R. Barr (Eds.), *Handbook of reading research* (Vol. 3, pp. 719–742). Mahwah, NJ: Lawrence Erlbaum.

Anderson, R. C. (1994). Role of reader's schema in comprehension, learning, and memory. In R. B. Ruddell, M. R. Ruddell, & H. Singer (Eds.), *Theoretical models and processes of reading* (4th ed.; pp. 483–495). Newark, DE: International Reading Association.

Anderson, T. H., & Armbruster, B. B. (1984). Studying. In P. D. Pearson (Ed.), *Handbook of reading research* (pp. 657–679). New York: Longman.

Ashton, P. T., & Webb, R. B. (1986). *Making a difference: Teacher's sense of efficacy and student achievement.* New York: Longman.

Atwell, N. (1987). *In the middle: Writing, reading, and learning with adolescents.* Portsmouth, NH: Boynton/Cook.

Atwell, N. (1990). *Coming to know: Writing to learn in the intermediate grades.* Portsmouth, NH: Heinemann.

Au, K. H., Caroll, J. H., & Scheu, J. A. (1997). *Balanced literacy instruction: A teacher's resource book.* Norwood, MA: Christopher-Gordon.

Barry, A. L. (2002). Reading strategies teachers say they use. *Journal of Adolescent & Adult Literacy, 46*(2), 132–141.

Bean, T. W. (1997). Preservice teachers' selection and use of content area literacy strategies. *Journal of Educational Research, 90*(3), 154–163.

Beck, I. L., & McKeown, M. G. (2001). Text talk: Capturing the benefits of read-aloud experiences for young children. *Reading Teacher, 55*(1), 10–20.

Beck, I. L., & McKeown, M. G. (2003). Different ways for different goals, but keep your eye on the higher verbal goals. In R. K. Wagner, A.E. Muse, & K. R. Tannenbaum (Eds.), *Vocabulary acquisition: Implications for reading comprehension* (pp. 182–204). New York: Guilford.

Beck, I. L., McKeown, M. G., & Kucan, L. (2002). *Bringing words to life: Robust vocabulary instruction.* New York: Guilford.

Blachowicz, C. L. Z., & Fisher, P. (2000). Vocabulary instruction. In M. L. Kamil, P. B. Mosenthal, P. D. Pearson, & R. Barr (Eds.), *Handbook of reading research* (Vol. 3, pp. 503–523). Mahwah, NJ: Lawrence Erlbaum.

Blachowicz, C. L. Z., & Fisher, P. (2009). *Teaching vocabulary in all classrooms* (4th ed.). Upper Saddle River, NJ: Pearson.

Blachowicz, C. L. Z., Fisher, P. J. L., Ogle, D., & Watts-Taffe, S. (2006). Vocabulary: Questions from the classroom. *Reading Research Quarterly, 41*(4), 524.

Blair, T. R., Rupley, W. H., & Nichols, W. D. (2007). The effective teacher of reading: Considering the "what" and "how" of instruction. *Reading Teacher, 60*(5), 432–438.

Block, C. C. (1993). Strategy instruction in a student-centered classroom. *Elementary School Journal, 94*(2), 137–153.

Block, C. C., Gambrell, L. B., & Pressley, M. (2002). *Improving comprehension instruction: Rethinking research, theory, and classroom practice* (Jossey-Bass Education Series). San Francisco: Jossey-Bass.

Block, C. C., & Pressley, M. (2003). Best practices in comprehension instruction. In L. M. Morrow, L. B. Gambrell, & M. Pressley (Eds.), *Best practices in literacy instruction* (2nd ed., pp. 111–126). New York: Guilford.

Bloodgood, J. W. (1999). What's in a name? Children's name writing and literacy acquisition. *Reading Research Quarterly, 34*(3), 342–367.

Bravo, M. A., Hiebert, E. H., & Pearson, P. D. (2003). Tapping the linguistic resources of Spanish–English bilinguals: The role of cognates in science. In R. K. Wagner, A.E. Muse, & K. R. Tannenbaum (Eds.), *Vocabulary acquisition: Implications for reading comprehension* (pp. 140–156). New York: Guilford.

Briggs, K. L., & Thomas, K. (1997). *Patterns of success: Successful pathways to elementary literacy in Texas spotlight schools.* Austin: Texas Center for Educational Research.

Bright, R. (1995). *Writing instruction in the intermediate grades: What is said, what is what is done, what is understood.* Newark, DE: International Reading Association.

Brozo, W. G., & Simpson, M. L. (2007). *Content literacy for today's adolescents: Honoring diversity and building competence* (5th ed.). Upper Saddle River, NJ: Merrill Prentice Hall.

Bukowiecki, E. M. (2007). Teaching children how to read. *Kappa Delta Pi Record, 43*(2), 58–65.

Bus, A., & Van IJzendoom, M. (1995). Mothers reading to their 3-year-olds: The role of mother–child attachment security in becoming literate. *Reading Research Quarterly, 30,* 998–1015.

Buss, K., & Karnowski, L. (2000). *Reading and writing literary genres: Literacy genres.* Newark, DE: International Reading Association.

Button, K., Johnson, M. J., & Furgerson, P. (1996). Interactive writing in a primary classroom. *The Reading Teacher, 49,* 446–454.

Calkins, L. (1994). *The art of teaching writing.* Portsmouth, NH: Heinemann.

Calkins, L. (2001). *The art of teaching reading.* White Plains, NY: Longman.

Calkins, L. (2005). *One to one: The art of conferring with young writers.* Portsmouth, NH: Heinemann.

Cappellini, M. (2005). *Balancing reading & language learning.* Portland, ME/Newark, DE: Stenhouse/International Reading Association.

Carrasquillo, A., Kucer, S. B., & Abrams, R. (2004). *Beyond the beginnings.* Clevedon, UK: Multilingual Matters.

Carrell, P. L. (1984). The effects of rhetorical organization on ESL readers. *TESOL Quarterly, 17*(4), 441–469.

Carrell, P. L. (1987). Content and formal schemata in ESL reading. *TESOL Quarterly, 21*(3), 461–481.

Carrell, P. L., Eisterhold, J. C. (1988). Schema theory and ESL reading pedagogy. In P. Carrell, J. Devine, & D. Eskey (Eds.), *Interactive approaches to second language reading* (pp. 73–92). New York: Cambridge University Press.

Carrick, M. L. (2006). Readers theatre across the curriculum. In T. Raskinski, C. Blachowicz, & K. Lems (Eds.), *Fluency instruction: Research-based best practices* (pp. 209–228). New York: Guilford.

Cassidy, J., & Cassidy, D. (2005). What's hot, what's not for 2005. *Reading Today, 22*(3), 1.

Cassidy, J., & Cassidy, D. (2005/2006). What's hot, what's not for 2006. *Reading Today, 23*(3), 1.

Cassidy, J., & Cassidy, D. (2007, February). What's hot, what's not for 2007. *Reading Today, 24*(1), 1.

Cassidy, J., & Cassidy, D. (2008, February). What's hot, what's not for 2008. *Reading Today, 25*(4), 1, 10, 11.

Caswell, L. J., & Duke, N. K. (1998). Non-narrative as a catalyst for literacy development. *Language Arts, 75,* 108–117.

Cazden, C. B. (1974). Play with language and metalinguistic awareness: One dimension of language experience. *Urban Review, 7,* 28–29.

Cazden, C. B. (1988). *Classroom discourse: The language of teaching and learning.* Portsmouth, NH: Heinemann.

Chall, J. (1967). *Learning to read: The great debate.* New York: McGraw-Hill.

Chall, J. S., Jacobs, V. A., & Baldwin, L. E. (1990). *The reading crisis: Why poor children fall behind.* Cambridge, MA: Harvard University Press.

Chall, J. S., & Snow, C. E. (1988). School influences on the reading development of low-income children. *Harvard Educational Letter, 4*(1), 1–4.

Clay, M. (1979). *Reading: Patterning of complex behavior* (2nd ed.). Auckland, New Zealand: Heinemann.

Clay, M. (1991). *Becoming literate: The construction of inner control.* Portsmouth, NH: Heinemann.

Clay, M. M. (2006). *An observation survey of early literacy achievement.* Portsmouth, NH: Heinemann.

Csikszentmihalyi, M. (1990). Literacy and intrinsic motivation. *Daedalus, 119*(2), 115–140.

Cook-Gumperz, J. (Ed.). (2006). *The social construction of literacy.* Cambridge, UK: Cambridge University Press.

Cummins, J. (2000). *Language, power and pedagogy: Bilingual children in the crossfire.* Clevedon, UK: Multilingual Matters.

Cunningham, A. E. (2005). Vocabulary growth through independent reading and reading aloud to children. In E. H. Hiebert & M. L. Kamil (Eds.), *Teaching and learning vocabulary: Bringing research to practice* (pp. 45–68). Mahwah, NJ: Lawrence Erlbaum.

Cunningham, P. M. (2000). *Phonics they use.* New York: Longman.

Daniels, H. (1994). *Literature circles: Voices and choice in the student-centered classroom.* Portland, ME: Stenhouse.

Darling-Hammond, L. (1997). *Doing what matters most: Investing in quality teaching.* New York: National Commission on Teaching and America's Future.

Day, J. P. (2000). *The acquisition of exemplary teaching capacity: Teacher voices on teacher learning.* Manuscript submitted for publication.

de la Luz Reyes, M. (1991). A process approach to literacy using dialogue journals and literature logs with second language learners. *Research in the Teaching of English, 25,* 291–313.

Delpit, L. (1997). The silenced dialogue: Power and pedagogy in educating other people's children. In A. H. Halsey, H. Lauder, P. Brown, & A. S. Wells (Eds.), *Education: Culture, economy and society* (pp. 582–594). Oxford, UK: Oxford University Press.

Dickinson, D. K., & Neuman, S. B. (Eds.). (2006). *Handbook of early literacy research* (Vol. 2). New York: Guilford.

Dickinson, D. K., & Tabors, P. O. (Eds.). (2001). *Beginning literacy with language.* Baltimore, MD: Brookes.

Diffily, D., Donaldson, E., & Sassman, C. (2001). *The Scholastic book of early childhood learning centers (Grades PreK–K).* New York: Scholastic Professional Books.

Doctoroff, S. (2001). Adapting the physical environment to meet the needs of all young children for play. *Early Childhood Education Journal, 28*(2), 105–109.

Dolch, E.W. (1936). A basic sight word vocabulary. *Elementary School Journal,* 456–460.

Dolch, E. W. (1939). *A manual for remedial reading.* Champaign, IL: Garrard.

Dolch, E. W. (1941). *Teaching primary reading.* Champaign, IL: Garrard.

Dolch, E. W. (1945). *A manual for remedial reading* (2nd ed.). Champaign, IL: Garrard.

Dolch, E. W. (1951). *Teaching primary reading* (2nd ed.). Champaign, IL: Garrard.

Dolch, E. W. (1960). *Teaching primary reading* (3rd. ed.). Champaign, IL: Garrard.

Draper, R. J., Smith, L. K., Hall, K. M., & Siebert, D. (2005). What's more important—literacy or content? Confronting the literacy–content dualism. *Action in Teacher Education, 27*(2), 12–21.

Dressler, C., & Kamil, M. (2006). First- and second language-literacy. In D. August & T. Shanahan (Eds.), *Developing literacy in second-language learners* (pp. 197–238). Mahwah, NJ: Lawrence Erlbaum.

Duffy, G. G. (1997). Powerful models or powerful teachers? An argument for teacher-as-entrepreneur. In S. Stahl & D. Hayes (Eds.), *Instructional models in reading* (pp. 351–365). Mahwah, NJ: Lawrence Erlbaum.

Duffy, G. G., Roehler, L. R., & Herrmann, B. A. (1988). Modeling mental processes helps poor readers become strategic readers. *Reading Teacher, 41,* 762–767.

Duke, N. (2000). 3.6 minutes per day: The scarcity of informal texts in first grade. *Reading Research Quarterly, 35*(2), 202–224.

Durkin, D. (1978–1979). What classroom observation reveals about reading comprehension instruction. *Reading Research Quarterly, 14,* 481–533.

Dyson, A. H. (1993). *Social worlds of children learning to write in an urban primary school.* New York: Teachers College Press.

Dyson, A. H., & Freedman, S. W. (1990). *On teaching writing: A review of the literature* (Occasional Paper No. 20). Berkeley, CA: Center for the Study of Writing.

Eanet, M., & Manzo, A. (1976). R.E.A.P.—A strategy for improving reading/writing study skills. *Journal of Reading, 19,* 647–652.

Echevarría, J., Vogt, M., & Short, D. (2008). *Making content comprehensible for English learners.* Boston: Pearson.

Eder, D. (1983). Ability grouping and student's academic self-concepts: A case study. *Elementary School Journal, 84,* 149–161.

Ellis, R. (1984). *Classroom second language development: A study of classroom interaction and language acquisition.* New York: Pergamon.

Farber, B. (1984). Stress and burnout in suburban teachers. *Journal of Educational Research, 77,* 325–331.

Farstrup, A. E., & Samuels, S. (Eds.). (2008). *What research has to say about vocabulary instruction.* Newark, DE: International Reading Association.

Fiene, J., & McMahon, S. (2007). Assessing comprehension: A classroom-based process. *Reading Teacher, 60*(5), 406–417.

Fisher, D., & Ivey, G. (2005). Literacy and language as learning in content-area classes: A departure from "Every teacher a teacher of reading." *Action in Teacher Education, 27*(2), 3–11.

Fisher, D., Rothenberg, C., & Frey, N. (2007). *Language learners in the English classroom.* Urbana, IL: National Council of Teachers of English.

Fives, H., Hamman, D., & Olivarez, O. (2007). Does burnout begin with student teachers? Analyzing efficacy, burnout, and support during the student-teaching semester. *Teaching and Teacher Education, 23,* 916–934.

Fletcher, J. M., & Francis, D. J. (2004). Scientifically based educational research: Questions, designs, and methods. In P. McCardle & V. Chabra (Eds.), *The voice of evidence in reading research* (pp. 59–80). Baltimore, MD: Brookes.

Fletcher, R. (1996). *A writer's notebook: Unlocking the writer within you.* New York: Avon Books for Young Readers.

Fletcher, R., & Portalupi, J. (2001). *Craft lessons: Teaching writing K–8.* Portland, ME: Stenhouse.

Fountas, I., & Pinnell, G. (1996). *Guided reading: Good first teaching for all children.* Portsmouth, NH: Heinemann.

Fountas, I., & Pinnell, G. (2001). *Guiding readers and writers Grades 3–6: Teaching comprehension, genre, and content literacy.* Portsmouth, NH: Heinemann.

Fountas, I., & Pinnell, G. (2005). *Leveled books: Matching texts to readers for effective teaching.* Portsmouth, NH: Heinemann.

Fountas, I., & Pinnell, G. (2006). *Teaching for comprehending and fluency.* Portsmouth, NH: Heinemann.

Fox, D. L. (1993). The influence of context, community, and culture: Contrasting cases of teacher knowledge development. In D. J. Leu & C. K. Kinzer (Eds.), *Examining central issues in literacy research, theory, and practice* (Forty-Second Yearbook of the National Reading Conference, pp. 345–366). Chicago: National Reading Conference.

Francis, D. J., Lesaux, N., & August, D. (2006). Language of instruction. In D. August & T. Shanahan (Eds.), *Developing literacy in second-language learners: Report of the National Literacy Panel on Language-Minority Children and Youth* (pp. 365–413). Mahwah, NJ: Lawrence Erlbaum.

Fredericks, A., Meinbach, A., & Rothlein, L. (1993). *Thematic units: An integrated approach to teaching science and social studies.* New York: HarperCollins.

Freeman, D., & Freeman, Y. (2004a). Connecting students to culturally relevant texts. *Talking Points, 15*(2), 7–11.

Freeman, D., & Freeman, Y. (2004b). *Essential linguistics.* Portsmouth, NH: Heinemann.

Freeman, D. E., & Freeman, Y. S. (2006). *Teaching reading and writing in Spanish and English.* Portsmouth, NH: Heinemann.

Freeman, Y. S., & Freeman, D. (2009). *Academic language for English language learners and struggling readers.* Portsmouth, NH: Heinemann.

Freeman, Y. S., Freeman, D. E., & Mercuri, S. (2005). *Dual language essentials for teachers and administrators.* Portsmouth, NH: Heinemann.

Freppon, P. A., & Dahl, K. L. (1998). Balanced instruction: Insights and considerations. *Reading Research Quarterly, 33,* 240–251.

Frey, B. B., Lee, S. W., Tollefson, N., Pass, L., & Massengill, D. (2005). Balanced literacy in an urban school district. *Journal of Educational Research, 98*(5), 272–280.

Friesen, D., Prokop, C. M., & Sarros, J. C. (1988). Why teachers burnout? *Educational Research Quarterly, 12,* 9–19.

Fry, E. (2004). *The vocabulary teacher's book of lists.* San Francisco: Jossey-Bass.

Galda, L., & Cullinan, B. E. (2000). Reading aloud from culturally diverse literature. In D. S. Strickland & L. M. Morrow (Eds.), *Beginning reading and writing* (pp. 134–142). New York: International Reading Association and Teachers College Press.

Gambrell, L. B., Block, C. C., & Pressley, M. (2002). Introduction. In C. C. Block, L. B. Gambrell, & M. Pressley (Eds.), *Improving comprehension instruction* (pp. 1–7). San Francisco: Jossey-Bass.

García, G. E. (1991). Factors influencing the English reading test performance of Spanish-speaking Hispanic children. *Reading Research Quarterly, 26*(4), 371–392.

Gay, G. (2001). Preparing for culturally responsive teaching. *Journal of Teacher Education, 53,* 106–115.

Gee, J. P. (2008). What is academic language? In A. S. Rosebery & B. Warren (Eds.), *Teaching science to English language learners* (pp. 57–70). Arlington, VA: National Science Teachers Association.

Genesee, F. (1987). *Learning through two languages.* Rowley, MA: Newbury House.

Genesee, F. (1994). *Educating second language children: The whole child, the whole curriculum, the whole community.* New York: Cambridge University Press.

Gersten, R., Baker, S. K., & Shanahan, T. (2007). *Effective literacy and English language instruction for English language learners in the elementary grades: IES practical guide.* Washington, DC: National Center for Educational Evaluation and Regional Assistance.

Gibbons, P. (2002). *Scaffolding language, scaffolding learning.* Portsmouth, NH: Heinemann.

Gill, S. R. (2006). Teaching rimes with shared reading. *Reading Teacher, 60*(2), 191–193.

Gitlin, A., Buendía, E., Crossland, K., & Doumbia, F. (2003). The production of margin and center: Welcoming–unwelcoming of immigrant students. *American Educational Research Journal, 40*(1), 91–122.

Godley, A., Sweetland, J., Wheeler, R. S., Minnici, A., & Carpenter, B. (2006). Preparing teachers for dialectally diverse classrooms. *Educational Researcher, 35*(8), 30–37.

Goldman, S. R., & Rakestraw, J. A. (2000). Structural aspects of constructing meaning from text. In M. L. Kamil, P. B. Mosenthal, P. D. Pearson, & R. Barr (Eds.), *Handbook of reading research* (Vol. 3, pp. 311–336). Mahwah, NJ: Lawrence Erlbaum.

Good, R. H., Kaminski, R. A., Simmons, D., & Kame'enui, E. J. (2001). Using dynamic indicators of basic early literacy skills (DIBELS) in an outcomes-driven model: Steps to reading outcomes. *OSSC Bulletin, 44*(1), 1–24.

Goodlad, J. I., & Oakes, J. (1988). We must offer equal access to knowledge. *Educational Leadership, 45*(5), 16–22.

Goodman, K. (1965). A linguistic study of cues and miscues in reading. *Elementary English Journal, 42,* 39–44.

Graves, D. H. (1994). *A fresh look at writing.* Portsmouth, NH: Heinemann.

Greenfield, P. M. (1997). You can't take it with you: Why ability assessments don't cross cultures. *American Psychologist, 52,* 1115–1124.

Gumperz, J. J., & Cook-Gumperz, J. (2006). Interactional sociolinguistics in the study of schooling. In J. Cook-Gumperz (Ed.), *The social construction of literacy* (pp. 50–75). Cambridge, UK: Cambridge University Press.

Gunning, T. G. (2009). *Assessing and correcting reading and writing difficulties* (4th ed.). New York: Allyn & Bacon.

Haberman, M. (1995). *Star teachers of children of poverty.* West Lafayette, IN: Kappa Delta Pi.

Hacquebord, H. (1994). L2 reading in the content areas: Text comprehension in secondary education in the Netherlands. *Journal of Research in Reading, 12*(2), 83–98.

Hakuta, K., Butler, Y. G., & Witt, D. (2000). *How long does it take English language learners to attain proficiency?* Santa Barbara: University of California Linguistic Minority Research Institute (LMRI). Retrieved March 27, 2008, from http://repositories.cdlib.org/lmri/pr/hakuta/

Hall, K. M., Sabey, B. L., & McClellan, M. (2005). Expository text comprehension: Helping primary-grade teachers use expository texts to full advantage. *Reading Psychology, 26,* 211–234.

Halliday, M. A. K. (1973). *Explorations in the functions of language.* New York: Elsevier.

Harp, B. (1989). What do we know about ability grouping? When the principal asks. *Reading Teacher, 42*(6), 430–431.

Hart, B., & Risley, T. R. (1995). *Meaningful differences in the everyday experiences of young American children.* Baltimore, MD: Brookes.

Hartman, D. K. (1995). Eight readers reading: The intertextual links of proficient readers reading multiple passages. *Reading Research Quarterly, 30*(3), 520–561.

Harvey, S., & Goudvis, A. (2007). *Strategies that work: Teaching comprehension to enhance understanding* (2nd ed.). Portland, ME: Stenhouse.

Hasbrouck, J., & Tindal, G. (1992). Curriculum-based oral reading fluency norms for students in grades 2–5. *Teaching Exceptional Children, 24*(3), 41–44.

Hasbrouck, J., & Tindal, G. (2006). Oral reading fluency norms. A valuable assessment tool for reading teachers. *Reading Teacher, 59*(7), 636–644.

Heacox, H. (2007). *Differentiated instruction in the regular classroom.* Minneapolis, MN: Free Spirit.

Hiebert, E. H. (1983). An examination of ability grouping for reading instruction. *Reading Research Quarterly, 18,* 231–255.

Hiebert, E. H., & Kamil, M. L. (Eds.). (2007). *Teaching and learning vocabulary: Bringing research to practice.* Mahwah, NJ: Lawrence Erlbaum.

Hoffman, J., & Pearson, P. D. (1999). *What your grandmother's teacher didn't know that your granddaughter's teacher should.* Austin: University of Texas at Austin Press.

Holdaway, D. (1979). *The foundations of literacy.* Sydney, Australia: Ashton Scholastics.

Hollingsworth, S., & Teal, K. (1991). Learning to teach reading in secondary math and science. *Journal of Reading, 35,* 190–194.

Hoyt, L. (2002). *Make it real: Strategies for success with informational texts.* Portsmouth, NH: Heinemann.

International Reading Association. (1997). *The role of phonics in reading instruction: A position statement of the International Reading Association.* Newark, DE: Author. Retrieved October 18, 2008, from the International Reading Association's Web site: http://www.reading.org/resources/issues/positions_phonics.html

International Reading Association. (2000). *Excellent reading teachers: A position statement of the International Reading Association.* Newark, DE: Author.

International Reading Association. (2002). *Evidence-based reading instruction: Putting the National Reading Panel Report into practice.* Newark, DE: Author.

International Reading Association. (2007). New reports fault management of Reading First program. *Reading Today, 24*(5), 1. Retrieved October 18, 2008 from the International Reading Association's Web site: http://www.reading.org/General/Publications/ReadingToday/RTY-0704-readingfirst.aspx

Isbell, R. (1995). *The complete learning center book.* Beltsville, MD: Gryphon House.

Jia, G. (2003). The acquisition of the English plural morpheme by native Mandarin Chinese-speaking children. *Journal of Speech, Language and Hearing Research, 46*(6), 1297–1311.

Jiménez, R. T., García, G. E., & Pearson, D. (1996). The reading strategies of bilingual Latina/o students who are successful English readers: Opportunities and obstacles. *Reading Research Quarterly, 31*(1), 90–112.

Johnson, D., & Johnson, R. (1985). The internal dynamics of cooperative learning groups. In R. Slavin, S. Sharon, S. Kagan, R. Hertz-Lazarowitz, C. Webb, & R. Schmuck (Eds.), *Learning to cooperate, cooperating to learn* (pp. 103–124). New York: Plenum.

Kagan, S., & Kagan, M. (2009). *Kagan cooperative learning.* San Clemente, CA: Kagan.

Karchmer, R. A., Mallette, M. H., Kara-Soteriou, J., & Leu, D. J. (2005). Innovative approaches to literacy education: Using the Internet to support new literacies. Newark, DE: International Reading Association.

Keene, E. O., & Zimmerman, S. (2007). *Mosaic of thought* (2nd ed.). Portsmouth, NH: Heinemann.

Keene, E. O., & Zimmerman, S. (1997). *Mosaic of thought: Teaching comprehension in a reader's workshop.* Portsmouth, NH: Heinemann.

Kelley, M., Clausen-Grace, N. (2006). R[5]: The Sustained Silent Reading makeover that transformed readers. *Reading Teacher, 60*(2), 148–156.

Kelly, P. R. (1990). Guiding young students' response to literature. *Reading Teacher, 43*(7), 464–470.

Kendall, J., & Khuon, O. (2005). *Making sense: Small-group comprehension lessons for English language learners.* Portland, ME: Stenhouse.

Kersaint, G., Lewis, J., Potter, R., & Meisels, G. (2007). Why teachers leave: Factors that influence retention and resignation. *Teaching and Teacher Education, 23,* 775–794.

Kim, J. S. (2008). Research and the reading wars. *Phi Delta Kappan, 89*(5), 372–375.

Klein, S. P., Hamilton, L. S., McCaffrey, D. F., & Stecher, B. M. (2000). *What do test scores in Texas tell us?* Santa Monica, CA: RAND Corporation.

Knapp, M. S. (1995). *Teaching for meaning in high poverty classrooms.* New York: Teachers College Press.

Kokoski, T., & Patton, M. M. (1997). Beyond homework: Science and mathematics backpacks. *Dimensions in Early Childhood, 25*(2), 11–16.

Koretz, D., & Barron, S. I. (1998). *The validity of gains on the Kentucky Instructional Results Information System (KIRIS).* Santa Monica, CA: RAND Corporation.

Kragler, S., Walker, C. A., & Martin, L. E. (2005). Strategy instruction in primary content textbooks. *Reading Teacher, 59*(3), 254–261.

Krashen, S. D. (2004). *The power of reading* (2nd ed.). Portsmouth, NH: Heinemann.

Krashen, S. D. (2006). Free reading. *School Library Journal, 52*(9), 42–45.

Kuby, P., & Aldridge, J. (2004). The impact of environmental print instruction on early reading ability. *Journal of Instructional Psychology, 31*(2), 106–114.

Kucer, S. B. (1995). Guiding bilingual students "through" the literacy processes. *Language Arts, 72,* 20–29.

Kucer, S. B. (2009). *Dimensions of literacy* (3rd ed.). Mahwah, NJ: Lawrence Erlbaum.

Kucer, S. B., & Silva, C. (1999). The English literacy development of bilingual students within a transition whole-language curriculum. *Bilingual Research Journal, 23,* 345–371.

Kucer, S. B., & Silva, C. (2006). *Teaching the dimensions of literacy.* Mahwah, NJ: Lawrence Erlbaum.

Kucer, S. B., Silva, C., & Delgado-Larocco, E. L. (1995). *Curricular conversations: Themes in multilingual and monolingual classrooms.* York, ME: Stenhouse.

L'Allier, S. K., & Elish-Piper, L. (2007). "Walking the walk" with teacher education candidates: Strategies for promoting active engagement with assigned readings. *Journal of Adolescent & Adult Literacy, 50*(5), 338–353.

LaBerge, D., & Samuels, S. J. (1974). Toward a theory of automatic information processing in reading. *Cognitive Psychology, 6,* 293–323.

Lacina, J. (2007). Reading, writing, & technology: Recommendations for generation 1.5 middle school students. *Focus on Middle School, 17*(3), 1–8.

Lacina, J. (2008a). Learning English with iPods. *Childhood Education, 84*(4), 247–249.

Lacina, J. (2008b). Sheltered English instruction: A model for English language learners in all content areas. In J. Lacina & P. Watson (Eds.), *Focus on literacy: Effective content teachers for the middle grades* (pp. 125–144). Olney, MD: Association for Childhood Educational International.

Lacina, J., Griffith, B., & Hagan, L. (2006). Developing a writing workshop classroom: Stories from a charter school principal, 2nd grade teacher, and university professor. *Teacher Educator, 42*(1), 63–75.

Lacina, J., & Watson, P. (2002). Joining the writing club: Everyone is welcome. *Childhood Education, 78*(2), 107–108.

Lacina, J., & Watson, P. (Eds.). (2008). *Focus on literacy: Effective teachers for the middle grades.* Olney, MD: Association for Childhood Education International.

Ladson-Billings, G. (1994). *The dreamkeepers: Successful teachers of African American children.* San Francisco: Jossey-Bass.

Lapp, D., Flood, J., & Roser, N. (2000). Still standing: Timeless strategies for teaching the language arts. In D. S. Strickland & L. M. Morrow (Eds.), *Beginning reading and writing* (pp. 183–193). New York: International Reading Association and Teachers College Press.

Lenski, S. D., Ehlers-Zavala, F., Daniel, M. C., & Sun-Irminger, X. (2006). Assessing English-language learners in mainstream classrooms. *Reading Teacher, 60*(1), 24–31.

Lesley, M. (2005). Looking for critical literacy with postbaccalaureate content area literacy students. *Journal of Adolescent and Adult Literacy, 48*(4), 320–334.

Lester, J. H. (2000). Secondary instruction: Does literacy fit in? *High School Journal, 83,* 10–16.

Leu, D. J., Jr., Kinzer, C. K., Coiro, J. L., & Cammack, D. W. (2004). Toward a theory of new literacies emerging from the Internet and other information and communication technologies. In R. B. Ruddell & N. J. Unrau (Eds.), *Theoretical models and processes of reading* (5th ed., pp. 1570–1613). Newark, DE: International Reading Association.

Levine, L. N. (2005). Teacher collaboration for the achievement of all learners. *TEIS News, 20*(2). Retrieved July 2005, from http://www.tesol.org/s_tesol/article.asp?vid=167&DID=4136&sid=1&cid=738&iid=4131&nid=3091

Lindholm-Leary, K. (2002). *Dual language education.* Clevedon, UK: Multilingual Matters.

Literacy Task Force. (1997). *A reading revolution: How we can teach every child to read well.* Retrieved August 21, 2009, from http://www.leeds.ac.uk/educol/documents/000000153.htm

Little, J. W. (1982). Norms of collegiality: Workplace conditions of school success. *American Education Research Journal, 19*(3), 325–340.

Lortie, D. C. (1975). *Schoolteacher: A sociological study.* Chicago: University of Chicago Press.

Lowery, L. (1996). *Georgia O'Keeffe.* Minneapolis, MN: Carolrhoda Books.

Lowry, L. (1979). *Anastasia Krupnik.* Boston: Houghton Mifflin.

Malik, A. A. (1990). A psycholinguistic analysis of the reading behavior of EFL-proficient readers using culturally familiar and culturally nonfamiliar expository text. *American Educational Research Journal, 27*(1), 205–223.

Manzo, A. (1969). The ReQuest procedure. *Journal of Reading, 13,* 23–26.

Marr, M. B., & Gormley, K. (1982). Children's recall of familiar and unfamiliar text. *Reading Research Quarterly, 18*(1), 89–104.

Martinez, M., Roser, N. L., & Strecker, S. (1998/1999). "I never thought I could be a star": A Readers Theatre ticket to fluency. *Reading Teacher, 52,* 326–334.

Marzano, R. (2004). *Building background knowledge for academic achievement.* Alexandria, VA: Association for Supervision and Curriculum Development.

Marzano, R. (2005). *Building academic vocabulary.* Alexandria, VA: Association for Supervision and Curriculum Development.

Mathis, S. (1986). *The hundred penny box.* New York: Newbury Puffin.

McCardle, P., & Chhabra, V. (Eds.). (2004). *The voice of evidence in reading research.* Baltimore, MD: Brookes.

McCarrier, A., Pinnell, G. P., & Fountas, I. C. (2000). *Interactive writing: How language and literacy come together, K–2.* Portsmouth, NH: Heinemann.

McGregor, T. (2007). *Comprehension connections.* Portsmouth, NH: Heinemann.

McIntyre, E. (2007). Story discussion in the primary grades: Balancing authenticity and explicit teaching. *Reading Teacher, 60*(7), 610–620.

McLaughlin, M., & Allen, M. B. (2002). *Guided comprehension in action: Lessons for the classroom.* Newark, DE: International Reading Association.

Mercuri, S., Freeman, Y. S., & Freeman, D. (2002). *Closing the achievement gap.* Portsmouth, NH: Heinemann.

Metsala, J. L. (1997). Effective primary-grades literacy instruction = balanced literacy instruction. *Reading Teacher, 50,* 518–521.

Meyer, B. J. F., & Poon, L. W. (2001). Effects of the structure strategy and signaling on recall of text. *Journal of Educational Psychology, 93,* 141–159.

Minton, L. (2007). *What if your abc's were your 123's? Building connections between literacy and numeracy.* Thousand Oaks, CA: Corwin.

Mohr, K. A. J., & Mohr, E. S. (2007). Extending English-language learners' classroom interactions using the Response Protocol. *Reading Teacher, 60*(5), 440–450.

Moll, L. (1988). Some key issues in teaching Latino students. *Language Arts, 65,* 465–472.

Morrow, L. M. (2009). *Literacy development in the early years: Helping children read and write.* Boston: Allyn & Bacon.

Morrow, L. M., & Rand, M. (1991). Preparing the classroom environment to promote literacy during play. In J. F. Christie (Ed.), *Play and early literacy development.* Albany: State University of New York Press.

Moss, B. (2003). *Exploring the literature of fact: Children's nonfiction trade books in the elementary classroom.* New York: Guilford.

Moustafa, M. (1997). *Beyond traditional phonics.* Portsmouth, MH: Heinemann.

Nagy, W. (2003). Metalinguistic awareness and the vocabulary-comprehension connection. In R. K. Wagner, A. E. Muse, & K. R. Tannenbaum (Eds.), *Vocabulary acquisition: Implications for reading comprehension* (pp. 53–77). New York: Guilford.

National Association for the Education of Young Children & International Reading Association. (2000). Learning to read and write: Developmentally appropriate practices for young children. In S. B. Neuman, C. Copple, & Y. S. Bredekamp (Eds.), *Learning to read and write: Developmentally appropriate practices for young children* (pp. 3–26). Washington, DC: National Association for the Education of Young Children.

National Association for the Education of Young Children & International Reading Association. (2005). *Where we stand on learning to read and write.* Retrieved August 16, 2008, from the National Association for the Education of Young Children Web site: http://208.118.177.216/about/positions/pdf/WWSSLearningToRead AndWriteEnglish.pdf

National Commission on Teaching and America's Future. (2003). *No dream denied: A pledge to America's children.* Washington, DC: Author.

National Council for Teachers of English (NCTE). (1997). *Ideas plus: Book 15.* Urbana, IL: National Council for Teachers of English.

National Institute for Child Literacy, & National Institute of Child Health and Human Development. (2001). *Put reading first: The research building blocks for teaching children to read.* Washington, DC: Government Printing Office.

National Institute of Child Health and Human Development. (2000). *Report of the National Reading Panel. Teaching children to read: An evidence-based assessment of the scientific research literature on reading and its implications for reading instruction* (NIH Publication No. 00–4769). Washington, DC: Government Printing Office.

Nesbitt, K. (2005). "Food fight." In *When the teacher isn't looking and other funny poems.* Minnetonka, MN. Meadowbrook Press. Retrieved May 22, 2009, from http://www.gigglepoetry.com/poem.aspx? PoemID = 192&CategoryID = 43

Neufeld, P. (2005). Comprehension instruction in content area classes. *Reading Teacher, 59*(4), 302–312.

Neuman, S. B. (1999). Books make a difference: A study of access to literacy. *Reading Research Quarterly, 34*(3), 286–311.

Neuman, S. B. (2006). The knowledge gap: Implications for early education. In D. K. Dickinson & S. B. Neuman (Eds.), *Handbook of early literacy research* (Vol. 2, pp. 29–40). New York: Guilford.

Neuman, S. B., Copple, C., & Bredekamp, S. (2000). *Learning to read and write: Developmentally appropriate practices for young children.* Washington, DC: National Association for the Education of Young Children.

Nourie, B., & Lenski, S. (1998). The (in)effectiveness of content literacy instruction for secondary preservice teachers. *Clearing House, 71,* 372–374.

Nystrand, M. (1997). *Opening dialogue: Understanding the dynamics of language and learning in the English classroom.* New York: Teachers College Press.

Oakes, J. (1986). Keeping track: Part 1. The policy and practice of curriculum inequality. *Phi Delta Kappan, 68*(1), 12–17.

Oakes, J. (1988). Beyond tracking. *Educational Horizons, 65*(1), 32–35.

O'Brien, D. G., Stewart, R. A., & Moje, E. B. (1995). Why content literacy is difficult to infuse into the secondary school: Complexities of curriculum, pedagogy, and school culture. *Reading Research Quarterly, 30,* 442–463.

Opitz, M. F. (1998). *Flexible grouping in reading: Practical ways to help all students become better readers.* New York: Scholastic.

Opitz, M. F., & Ford, M. P. (2001). *Reaching readers: Flexible and innovative strategies for guided reading.* Portsmouth, NH: Heinemann.

Orellana, M. F., & Hernandez, A. (1999). Talking the walk: Children reading urban environmental print. *Reading Teacher, 52*(6), 612–619.

O'Shea, L. J., Sindelar, P. T., & O'Shea, D. J. (1987). The effects of repeated readings and attentional cues on the reading fluency and comprehension of learning disabled readers. *Learning Disabilities Research, 2,* 103–109.

Paris, S. G., & Carpenter, R. D. (2003). FAQs about IRIs. *Reading Teacher, 56*(6), 578–580.

Payne, D. C., & Schulman, M. B. (1998). *Getting the most out of morning message and other shared writing lessons.* New York: Scholastic.

Pearson, P. D. (2004). The reading wars. *Educational Policy, 18*(1), 216–252.

Pearson, P. D., & Duke, N. K. (2002). Comprehension instruction in the primary grades. In C. C. Block & M. Pressley (Eds.), *Comprehension instruction: Research-based best practice* (pp. 247–258). New York: Guilford.

Pearson, P. D., & Fielding, L. (1991). Comprehension instruction. In P. D. Pearson, E. Barr, P. Mosenthal, & M. Kamil (Eds.), *Handbook of reading research* (Vol. 2, pp. 815–860). Mahwah, NJ: Lawrence Erlbaum.

Pearson, P. D., & Gallagher, M. C. (1983). The instruction of reading comprehension. *Contemporary Educational Psychology, 8*(3), 317–344.

Pederson, E., Faucher, T. A., & Eaton, W. W. (1978). A new perspective on the effects of first-grade teachers on children's subsequent adult status. *Harvard Educational Review, 48,* 1–31.

Pellegrini, A. D., & Galda, L. (1991). Longitudinal relations among preschoolers' symbolic play, metalinguisic verbs, and emergent literacy. In J. F. Christie (Ed.), *Play and early literacy development.* Albany: State University of New York Press.

Pellegrini, A. D., & Galda, L. (2000). Children's pretend play and literacy. In D. S. Strickland & L. M. Morrow (Eds.),, *Beginning reading and writing* (pp. 58–65). New York: International Reading Association and Teachers College Press.

Peregoy, S. F., & Boyle, O. F. (2005). *Reading, writing, and learning in ESL.* Boston: Pearson/Allyn & Bacon.

Perry, T., & Delpit, L. (1998). *The real Ebonics debate: Power, language, and the education of African-American children.* Boston: Beacon.

Petrakos, H., & Howe, N. (1996). The influence of the physical design of the dramatic play center on children's play. *Early Childhood Research Quarterly, 11,* 63–77.

Phythian-Sence, C., & Wagner, R. K. (2007). Vocabulary acquisition: A primer. In R. K. Wagner, A. E. Muse, & K. R. Tannenbaum (Eds.), *Vocabulary acquisition: Implications for reading comprehension* (pp. 1–14). New York: Guilford.

Pikulski, J. J., & Shanahan, T. (Eds.). (1982). *Approaches to the informal evaluation of reading.* Newark, DE: International Reading Association.

Pilgreen, J. (2000). *The SSR handbook: How to organize and manage a sustained silent reading program.* Portsmouth, NH: Heinemann.

Powell-Mikle, A., & Patton, M. M. (2004). Meaningful learning with African American families: The freedom quilt FunPacks. *Childhood Education, 80*(4), 187–190.

Pressley, M. (1999). Self-regulated comprehension processing and its development through instruction. In L. B. Gambrell, L. M. Morrow, S. B. Neuman, & M. Pressley (Eds.), *Best practices in literacy instruction* (pp. 90–97). New York: Guilford.

Pressley, M., Disney, L., & Anderson, K. (2007). Landmark vocabulary instructional research and the vocabulary instructional research that makes sense now. In R. K. Wagner, A. E. Muse, & K. R. Tannenbaum (Eds.), *Vocabulary acquisition: Implications for reading comprehension* (pp. 205–232). New York: Guilford.

Pressley, M., Gaskins, I., & Fingeret, L. (2006). Instruction and development of reading fluency in struggling readers. In S. J. Samuels & A. E. Farstrup (Eds.), *What research has to say about fluency instruction* (pp. 47–69). Newark, DE: International Reading Association.

Pressley, M., Mohan, L., & Raphael, L. M. (2007). How does Bennett Woods Elementary School produce such high reading and writing achievement? *Journal of Educational Psychology, 99*(2), 221–240.

Pressley, M., Rankin, J., & Yokoi, L. (1996). A survey of instructional practice of primary teachers nominated as effective in promoting literacy. *Elementary School Journal, 96,* 363–384.

Pressley, M., Wharton-McDonald, R., Mistretta-Hampston, J. M., & Echevarria, M. (1998). The nature of literacy instruction in ten Grade 4/5 classrooms in upstate New York. *Scientific Studies of Reading, 2,* 159–194.

RAND Reading Study Group. (2002). *Reading for understanding: Towards an R & D program in reading comprehension.* Santa Monica, CA: RAND Corporation.

Raphael, T., Highfield, K, & Au, K. (2006). *QAR now.* New York: Scholastic.

Rasinski, T. V. (2000). Speed does matter in reading. *Reading Teacher, 54,* 146–151.

Rasinski, T. V. (2003). *The fluent reader: Oral reading strategies for building word recognition, fluency, and comprehension.* New York: Scholastic.

Rasinski, T. (2006, April). Reading fluency instruction: Moving beyond accuracy, automaticity, and prosody. *Reading Teacher, 59*(7), 704–706.

Ray, K. W. (1999). *Wondrous words: Writers and writing in the elementary classroom.* Urbana, IL: National Council of Teachers of English.

Ray, K. W., & Laminack, L. L. (2001). *The writing workshop. Working through the hard parts (and they're all hard parts).* Urbana, IL: National Council of Teachers of English.

Reutzel, D. R. (2003). Organizing effective literacy instruction: Grouping strategies and instructional routines. In L. M. Morrow, L. B. Gambrell, & M. Pressley (Eds.), *Best practices in literacy instruction* (2nd ed.). New York: Guilford.

Reutzel, D. R. (2006). "Hey teacher, when you say 'fluency,' what do you mean?": Developing fluency in elementary classrooms. In T. Raskinski, C. Blachowicz, & K. Lems (Eds.), *Fluency instruction: Research-based best practices* (pp. 62–85). New York: Guilford.

Rosenbaum, J. (1980). *Making inequality: The hidden curriculum of high school tracking.* New York: Wiley.

Rosenblatt, L. (1978). *The reader, the text, the poem: The transactional theory of the literary work.* Carbondale: Southern Illinois University Press.

Roskos, K. A., Tabors, P. O., & Lenhart, L. A. (2004). *Oral language and early literacy in preschool.* Newark, DE: International Reading Association.

Routman, R. (1994). *Invitations: Changing as teachers and learners K–12.* Portsmouth, NH: Heinemann.

Ruddell, R. B. (1995). Those influential literacy teachers: Meaning negotiation and motivation builders. *Reading Teacher, 48,* 454–463.

Rule, A. C., & Barrera, M. T., III. (2003). Using objects to teach vocabulary words with multiple meanings. *Montessori Life, 15*(3), 14–17.

Samuels, S. J. (1970). The method of repeated readings. *Reading Teacher, 32,* 403–408.

Samuels, S. J. (1979). The method of repeated readings. *Reading Teacher, 4,* 403–408.

Samuels, S. J. (2002). Reading fluency: Its development and assessment. In A. Farstrup & S. Samuels (Eds.), *What research has to say about reading instruction* (2nd ed., pp. 166–183). Newark, DE: International Reading Association.

Samuels, S. J., & Farstrup, A. (Eds.). (2006). *What research has to say about fluency instruction.* Newark, DE: International Reading Association.

Samuels, S. J., & Flor, R. (1997). The importance of automaticity for developing expertise in reading. *Reading and Writing Quarterly, 13*(2), 107–122.

Schifini, A. (1997). Reading instruction for pre-literate and struggling older students. *Scholastic Literacy Research Paper, 3*(13).

Schleppegrell, M. J., & Colombi, M. C. (2002). Theory and practice in the development of advanced literacy. In M. J. Schleppegrell & M. C. Colombi (Eds.), *Developing advanced literacy in first and second languages: Meaning and power* (pp. 1–19). Mahwah, NJ: Lawrence Erlbaum.

Schreiber, P. A. (1980). On the acquisition of reading fluency. *Journal of Reading, 12,* 177–186.

Schumm, J. S. (2006). *Reading assessment and instruction for all learners.* New York: Guilford.

Shanahan, T. (2004). Critiques of the National Reading Panel report: Their implications for research for research, policy, and practice. In P. McCardle & V. Chhabra (Eds.), *The voice of evidence in reading research* (pp. 235–265). Baltimore, MD: Brookes.

Shanahan, T., & Beck, I. L. (2006). Effective literacy teaching for English-language learners. In D. August & T. Shanahan (Eds.), *Developing literacy in second-language learners: Report of the National Literacy Panel on Language-Minority Children and Youth* (pp. 415–488). Mahwah, NJ: Lawrence Erlbaum.

Sindelar, P. T., Monda, L. E., & O'Shea, L. J. (1990). The effects of repeated readings on instructional and mastery level readers. *Journal of Educational Research, 83*(4), 220–226.

Sipe, L. R. (2002). Talking back and taking over: Young children's expressive engagement during storybook read-alouds. *Reading Teacher, 55*(5), 476–483.

Slavin, R. E. (1987). Cooperative learning and the cooperative school. *Educational Leadership, 45*(3), 7–13.

Smith, F. (1997). *Reading without nonsense* (3rd ed.). New York: Teachers College Press.

Smith, J., & Elley, W. (1997). *How children learn to write.* New York: Richard C. Owen.

Smolkin, L. B., & Donovan, C. A. (2001). The context of comprehension: The information book read aloud, comprehension acquisition, and comprehension instruction in a first grade classroom. *Elementary School Journal, 102*(2), 97–122.

Snow, C. E., Burns, M. S., & Griffin, P. (Eds.). (1998). *Preventing reading difficulties in young children.* Washington, DC: National Academy Press.

Soderman, A., & Farrell, P. (2008). *Creating literacy-rich preschools and kindergartens.* New York: Pearson, Allyn & Bacon.

Staab, C. (1986). What happened to the sixth graders: Are elementary students losing the need to forecast and to reason? *Reading Psychology, 7*(4), 289–296.

Stahl, S. A., & Nagy, E. (2006). *Teaching word meanings.* Mahwah, NJ: Lawrence Erlbaum.

Stanovich, K. E., & West, R. F. (1989). Exposure to print and orthographic processing. *Reading Research Quarterly, 24,* 402–433.

Steffensen, M. S., Joag-Dev, C., & Anderson, R. C. (1979). A cross cultural perspective on reading comprehension. *Reading Research Quarterly, 15,* 10–29.

Stevens, K. (1982). Can we improve reading by teaching comprehension? *Journal of Reading, 25*(4), 326–329.

Street, B. (2003). What's "new" in new literacy studies? Critical approaches to literacy in theory and practice. *Current Issues in Comparative Education, 5*(2). Retrieved June 1, 2007, from http://www.tc.columbia.edu/cice/archives/5.2/52street.pdf

Sturtevant, E., & Linek, W. M. (2004). *Content literacy: An inquiry-based case approach.* Upper Saddle River, NJ: Pearson.

Sulzby, E., Barnhart, J., & Hieshima, J. (1989). *Forms of writing and rereading from writing: A preliminary report* (Technical Report No. 20). Retrieved October 8, 2008, from http://www.eric.ed.gov/ERICDocs/data/ericdocs2sql/content_storage_01/0000019b/80/1e/0b/7f.pdf

Sweet, A. P., Guthrie, J. T., & Ng, M. M. (1998). Teacher perception and student reading motivation. *Journal of Educational Psychology, 90,* 210–223.

Tafuri, N. (2001). *Silly little goose.* New York: Scholastic.

Taylor, B. M., Pearson, P. D., Clark, K. F., & Walpole, S. (1999). *Beating the odds in teaching all children to read.* Ann Arbor, MI: Center for the Improvement of Early Reading Achievement.

Teale, W. (1984). Reading to young children: Its significance for literacy development. In H. Goelman, A. Oberg, & F. Smith (Eds.), *Awakening to literacy* (pp. 110–121). Portsmouth, NH: Heinemann.

Temple, C., Nathan, R., Burris, N., & Temple, F. (1988). *The beginning of writing* (2nd ed.). Boston: Allyn & Bacon.

TESOL. (2006). *TESOL revises PreK–12 English language proficiency standards.* Alexandria, VA: Author. Retrieved October 20, 2008, from http://www.tesol.org/s_tesol/sec_document.asp?CID=1186&DID=5349#levels

Tharp, R., & Gallimore, R. (1991). *The instructional conversation: Teaching and learning in social activity* (Research Report 2). Santa Cruz, CA: University of California, National Center for Research on Cultural Diversity and Second Language Learning.

Tharp, R. G. (1997). *The five generic principles: Current knowledge about effective education of at-risk students.* Santa Cruz, CA: University of California, Center for Research on Education Diversity and Excellence.

Thomas, K. F., & Barksdale-Ladd, M. A. (1995). Effective literacy classrooms: Teachers and students exploring literacy together. In K. A. Hinchman, D. J. Leu, & C. K. Kinzer (Eds.), *Perspectives on literacy research and practice* (Forty-Fourth Yearbook of the National Reading Conference). Chicago: National Reading Conference.

Tierney, R. J., & Pearson, P. D. (1994). Learning to learn from text: A framework for improving classroom practice. In R. B. Ruddell, M. R. Ruddell, & H. Singer (Eds.), *Theoretical models and processes of reading* (4th ed., pp. 496–513). Newark, DE: International Reading Association.

Tolchinsky, L. (2006). The emergence of writing. In C. A. MacArthur, S. Graham, & J. Fitzgerald (Eds.), *Handbook of writing research* (pp. 83–95). New York: Guilford.

Tompkins, G. (2009). *Literacy for the 21st century: A balanced approach* (5th ed.). Upper Saddle River, NJ: Prentice Hall.

Tompkins, G. E. (2004). *Teaching writing: Balancing process and product.* Upper Saddle River, NJ: Pearson.

Tompkins, G. E. (2007). *Literacy for the 21st century: Teaching reading and writing in prekindergarten through Grade 4* (2nd ed.). Upper Saddle River, NJ: Pearson.

Tovani, C. (2005). The power of purposeful reading. *Educational Leadership, 63*(2), 48–51.

Tropp, L. T., & Van Sluys, K. (2008). Being and becoming: Multilingual writers practice. *Language Arts, 85*(4), 265–274.

Tschannen-Moran, M., Woolfolk-Hoy, A., & Hoy, W.K. (1998). Teacher efficacy: Its meaning and measure. *Review of Educational Research, 68,* 202–248.

U.S. Department of Education. (2008). *Student reading skills improvement grants.* Retrieved October, 2008, from the U.S. Department of Education Web site: http://www.ed.gov/policy/elsec/leg/esea02/pg4.html

U.S. Department of Education, National Center for Educational Statistics. (2003). *National assessment of educational progress.* Washington, DC: Author.

Vacca, R. T., & Vacca, J. L. (2008). *Content area reading: Literacy and learning across the curriculum* (9th ed.). Boston: Pearson.

Vaughn, S., & Linan-Thompson, S. (2004). *Research-based methods of reading instruction: K–3.* Alexandria, VA: Association for Supervision and Curriculum Development.

Vygotsky, L. S. (1978). *Mind in society.* Cambridge, MA: Harvard University press.

Wagner, R. K., Muse, A. E., & Tannenbaum, K. R. (Eds.). (2007). *Vocabulary acquisition: Implications for reading comprehension.* New York: Guilford.

Waller, W. (1961). *The sociology of teaching.* New York: Russell & Russell.

Walpole, S., & McKenna, M. C. (2006). The role of informal reading inventories in assessing word recognition. *Reading Teacher, 59*(6), 592–594.

Weaver, C. (2002). *Reading process and practice.* Portsmouth, NH: Heinemann.

Webster, J. (Ed.). (2004). *Collected works of M. A. K. Halliday: Vol. 4.* London: Continuum.

Wells, G. (1985). *The meaning makers.* Portsmouth, NH: Heinemann.

Wharton-McDonald, R., Pressley, M., & Hampston, J. M. (1998). Literacy instruction in nine first-grade classrooms: Teacher characteristics and student achievement. *Elementary School Journal, 99,* 101–128.

Williams, J. P., Hall, K. M, & Lauer, K. D. (2004). Teaching expository text structure to young at-risk learners: Building the basics of comprehension instruction. *Exceptionality, 12*(3), 129–144.

Wilson, E. K., Konopak, B. C., & Readence, J. E. (1993). A case study of preservice secondary social studies teachers' beliefs and practices about content area reading. In D. J. Leu & C. K. Kinzer (Eds.), *Examining central issues in literacy research, theory, and practice* (Forty-Second Yearbook of the National Reading Conference, pp. 335–343). Chicago: National Reading Conference.

Witherell, N. L. (2007). *The guided reading classroom.* Portsmouth, NH: Heinemann.

Wolfram, W., & Schilling-Estes. (2006). *American English* (2nd ed.). Malden, MA: Wiley-Blackwell.

Wong Fillmore, L., & Snow, C. (2000). *What teachers need to know about language.* U.S. Department of Education, Office of Educational Research and Improvement. Retrieved September 27, 2008, from http://faculty.tamu-commerce.edu/jthompson/Resources/FillmoreSnow2000.pdf

Wood, K., & Dickinson, T. (2000). *Promoting literacy in Grades 4–9.* Boston: Allyn & Bacon.

Wood, K. D., & Harmon, J. M. (2005). *Strategies for integrating reading and writing in middle and high school classrooms.* Westerville, OH: National Middle School Association.

Worthy, J., & Hoffman, J. V. (1996). Critical questions. *Reading Teacher, 49*(8), 656–657.

Wuthrick, M. A. (1990). Blue Jay's win! Crows go down in defeat! *Phi Delta Kappan, 71*(7), 553–555.

Young, T. A., & Hadaway, N. (2006). *Supporting the literacy development of English learners: Increasing success in all classrooms.* Newark, DE: International Reading Association.

Zimpherer, F., Worley, M., Sission, M., & Said, R. (2002). Literacy education and reading programs in the secondary school: Status, problems, and solutions. *NASSP Bulletin, 86,* 3–17.

Children's Book References

Armstrong, W. H. (1969). *Sounder.* New York: HarperCollins.

Balestino, P. (1989). *The skeleton inside you.* New York: Crowell.

Banks, L. R. (1980). *The Indian in the cupboard.* New York: Avon Books.

Bartoletti, S. (2005). *Hitler Youth: Growing up in Hitler's shadow.* New York: Scholastic.

Berger, B. (1984). *Grandfather twilight.* New York: Philomel.

Blumberg, R. (2004). *York's adventures with Lewis and Clark: An African-American's part in the great expedition.* New York: HarperCollins.

Bolden, T. (2005). *Maritcha: A nineteenth-century American girl.* New York: Harry N. Abrams.

Branley, F. (1986). *What makes day and night?* New York: Collins.

Bunting, E. (1988). *Is anybody there?* New York: Lippincott.

Bunting, E. (1994). *Smoky nights.* Orlando, FL: Harcourt Brace.

Bunting, E. (1996). *Secret place.* Boston: Houghton Mifflin.

Burleigh, R. (2003). *Home run: The story of Babe Ruth.* San Diego: Voyager Books.

Burleigh, R. (2004). *Seurat and La Grande Jatte: Connecting the dots.* New York: Harry N. Abrams.

Cadnum, M. (1997). *The lost and found house.* New York: Viking Juvenile.

Chandler, R. (1992). *The long goodbye.* New York: Vintage.

Cisneros, S. (1991). *The house on Mango Street.* New York: Vintage.

Cleary, B. (1968). *Ramona the pest.* New York: William Morrow.

Cleary, B. (1983). *Dear Mr. Henshaw.* New York: HarperCollins.

Cole, J. (1983). *Cars and how they go.* New York: Crowell.

Cole, J. (1991). *My puppy is born.* New York: William Morrow.

Cole, J. (1996). *The magic school bus: Inside a hurricane.* New York: Scholastic.

Cooke, T. (1994). *So much.* Cambridge, MA: Candlewick Press.

Creech, S. (1994). *Walk two moons.* New York: Scholastic.

Crisp, M. (2003). *Everything cat: What kids really want to know about cats.* Chanhassen, MN: NorthWord Press.

Curtis, J. L. (1996). *Tell me again about the night I was born.* New York: HarperCollins.

Delano, M. (2005). *Genius: A photobiography of Albert Einstein.* Washington, DC: National Geographic.

DePaola, T. (1973). *Nana upstairs & Nana downstairs.* New York: Putnam.

Donnelly, J. (1989). *Moonwalk.* New York: Random House.

Dorros, A. (1987). *Ant cities.* New York: HarperCollins.

Dower, L. (2001). *Caught in the Web (from the files of Madison Finn, Book 4).* New York: Volo Books.

Facklam, M. (2003). *Lizards: Weird and Wonderful.* New York: Little, Brown.

Fradin, D. B. (2003). *Who was Thomas Jefferson?* New York: Penguin.

Freedman, R. (2004). *The voice that challenged a nation: Marian Anderson and the struggle for equal rights.* New York: Clarion Books.

Garza, C. L. (1996). *My family/En mi familia.* San Francisco: Children's Book Press Libros Para Ninos.

Gibbons, G. (1984). *Fire! Fire!* New York: Crowell.

Gibbons, G. (1994). *Nature's green umbrella.* New York: Morrow.

Gibbons, G. (1999). *Bats.* New York: Holiday House.

Gibbons, G. (1999). *Pirates: Robbers of the high seas.* Boston: Little, Brown.

Giblin, J. (2004). *Secrets of the sphinx*. New York: Scholastic.

Gilman, P. (1993). *The wonderful pigs of Jillian Jiggs*. New York: Scholastic.

Gray, L. M. (1995). *My mama had a dancing heart*. New York: Orchard Books.

Greenfield, E., & Little, L. (1993). *Childtimes: A three-generation memoir*. New York: HarperCollins.

Hampton, W. (1997). *Kennedy assassinated! The world mourns: A reporter's story*. Cambridge, MA: Candlewick Press.

Hatkoff, I., Hatkoff, C., & Kahumbu, P. (2006). *Owen & Mzee: The true story of a remarkable friendship*. New York: Scholastic.

Hoban, R., & Williams, G. (1960). *Bedtime for Frances*. New York: Harper.

Hoose, P. (2004). *The race to save the Lord God bird*. New York: Farrar, Strauss & Giroux.

Howard, E. F. (1991). *Aunt Flossie's hats (and crabcakes later)*. New York: Houghton Mifflin.

Jenkins, S. (2004). *Actual size*. New York: Houghton Mifflin.

Knowlton, J. (1988). *Geography from A to Z*. New York: Crowell.

Kramer, S. A. (2003). *Who was Ferdinand Magellan?* New York: Penguin.

Lauber, P. (1989). *The news about dinosaurs*. New York: Bradbury Press.

Legg, G. (1998). *From egg to chicken*. New York: F. Watts.

Levine, E. (1992). *If you lived at the time of the great San Francisco earthquake*. New York: Scholastic.

Lowery, L. (1996). *Georgia O'Keeffe*. Minneapolis, MN: Carolrhoda Books.

Lowry, L. (1979). *Anastasia Krupnik*. New York: Random House.

Lowry, L. (2006). *The giver*. New York: Delacorte/Random House.

Lyon, G. E. (1998). *Dreamplace*. New York: Scholastic.

Macdonald, F. (1996). *Exploring the world*. Devon, UK: Toulouse Books.

MacLachlan, P. (1995). *What you know first*. New York: HarperCollins.

Maestro, G. (1992). *How do apples grow?* New York: HarperCollins.

Magloff, L. (2003). *Butterfly*. New York: DK Publishing.

Majoor, M. (2000). *Inside the Hindenburg*. Toronto, ON, Canada: McArthur/Boston: Little, Brown.

Markle, S. (1991). *Outside and inside you*. New York: Bradbury Press.

Martin, B. (2008). *Brown bear, brown bear, what do you see?* (3rd ed.). New York: Henry Holt.

McDonough, Y. Z. (2003). *Who was Wolfgang Amadeus Mozart?* New York: Penguin.

McWhorter, D. (2004). *A dream of freedom: The civil rights movement from 1954 to 1968*. New York: Scholastic.

Montgomery, S. (2004). *The tarantula scientist*. Boston: Houghton Mifflin.

Moss, M. (1995). *Amelia's notebook*. Middleton, WI: Pleasant Company.

Naylor, P. R. (2000). *Shiloh*. New York: Aladdin.

Nesbitt, K. (2005). *When the Teacher Isn't Looking: And Other Funny School Poems*. Minnetonka, MN: Meadowbrook Press.

Nickens, B. (1994). *Walking the log: Memories of a Southern childhood*. New York: Rizzoli.

Numeroff, L. (1985). *If you give a mouse a cookie*. New York: HarperCollins.

O'Dell, S. (1960). *Island of the blue dolphin*. New York: Random House.

Parish, P. (1963). *Amelia Bedelia*. New York: Harper & Row.

Paulsen, G. (1999). *Hatchet*. New York: Scholastic.

Polacco, P. (1994). *My rotten redheaded older brother*. New York: Simon & Schuster.

Polacco, P. (1998). *The keeping quilt*. New York: Simon & Schuster.

Polacco, P. (1998). *Thank you, Mr. Falker*. New York: Philomel.

Porter, C. (1993). *Meet Addy: An American girl*. Middletown, WI: Pleasant Co.

Pringle, L. P. (2000). *Bats: Strange and wonderful*. Honesdale, PA: Boyds Mills Press.

Raskin, E. (1978). *The Westing game*. New York: Penguin.

Rauzon, M. J. (1993). *Horns, antlers, fangs and tusks*. New York: Lothrop, Lee & Shepard Books.

Ride, S., & Okie, S. R. (1986). *To space and back*. New York: HarperCollins.

Riordan, R. (2005). *The lightning thief*. New York: Miramax Books.

Ruckman, I. (1984). *Night of the twisters*. New York: HarperCollins.

Rylant, C. (1982). *When I was young in the mountains.* New York: Dutton.

Rylant, C. (1983). *Miss Maggie.* New York: Dutton.

Rylant, C. (1991). *Night in the country.* New York: Atheneum.

Rylant, C. (1993). *The relatives came.* New York: Simon & Schuster Children's.

Rylant, C. (1996). *The whales.* New York: Blue Sky Press.

Rylant, C. (2004). *Missing May.* New York: Scholastic.

Schanzer, R. (2007). *George vs. George: The American revolution as seen from both sides.* Washington, DC: National Geographic Children's Books.

Sendak, M. (1963). *Where the wild things are.* New York: Harper & Row.

Shea, G. (1997). *First flight.* New York: HarperCollins.

Showers, P. (1992). *How you talk.* New York: HarperCollins.

Showers, P. (2001). *What happens to a hamburger?* New York: HarperCollins.

Simon, S. (2002). *Danger! Volcanoes.* New York: SeaStar Books.

Siy, A., & Kunkel, D. (2005). *Mosquito bite.* Watertown, MA: Charlesbridge.

Soto, G. (1997). *Snapshots from the wedding.* New York: Putnam.

Speare, E. G. (1983). *Sign of the beaver.* New York: Bantam Doubleday.

Spinelli, J. (1990). *Maniac Magee.* London: Little, Brown.

Stolz, M. (1988). *Storm in the night.* New York: Harper & Row.

Suess, Dr. (1960). *Green eggs and ham.* New York: Beginner Books/Random House.

Sutherland, T. T. (2003). *Who was Harry Houdini?* New York: Penguin.

Tafuri, N. (2001). *Silly little goose.* New York: Scholastic.

Taylor, B. (2001). *How to save the planet.* New York: F. Watts.

Teitelbaum, M. (1997). *The colossal book of dinosaurs.* New York: Modern Publications.

Thimmesh, C. (2000). *Girls think of everything: Stories of ingenious inventions by women.* Boston: Houghton Mifflin.

Thompson, G. (2003). *Who was Helen Keller?* New York: Penguin.

Viorst, J. (1972). *Alexander and the terrible, horrible, no good, very bad day.* New York: Atheneum.

Waber, B. (1972). *Ira sleeps over.* Boston: Houghton Mifflin.

Warren, A. (2008). *Escape from Saigon: How a Vietnam boy became an American boy.* New York: Farrar, Strauss & Giroux.

Webb, S. (2004). *Looking for seabirds: Journal of an Alaskan voyage.* Boston: Houghton Mifflin.

White, E. B. (1952). *Charlotte's web.* New York: Harper.

Williams, K. L. (1991). *Galimoto.* New York: Mulberry Books.

Wojciechowska, M. (1964). *Shadow of a bull.* New York: Aladdin.

Woodson, J. (1997). *We had a picnic this Sunday past.* New York: Hyperion Books for Children.

Yolen, J. (2000). *Miz Berlin walks.* New York: Putnam.

Index

About the Authors

Julie Ankrum (Ph.D.) serves as an assistant professor of teacher education and literacy at the University of Pittsburgh at Johnstown. She teaches literacy courses at both the elementary and secondary level. Her research interests include exemplary practices in literacy instruction and teacher preparation.

Theresa Harris-Tigg (aka Ama Serwa Akoto) (Ph.D.) is an assistant Professor in English, coordinator of English education (7–12), and current chair of the Teacher Education Council (TEC) at Buffalo State college. She is a former Buffalo Public School District High School reading/ELA support specialist and has 15 years of classroom experience as a secondary English teacher, and former clinical faculty member at State University of New York, Buffalo, and Bryant & Stratton College. She is the president of the Metro Buffalo Alliance of Black School Educators (MBABSE), and a member of the National Council of Teachers of English (NCTE) and of the National Coalition (NCBI). Her research interests are in urban education and culturally responsive pedagogy.

Robyn Knicely has worked in Lorain City Schools in Northeast Ohio as a teacher and a literacy specialist for the past 25 years. She is currently working on her doctoral degree in literacy at the University of Akron and plans to complete her dissertation in the area of fluency.

Jan Lacina (Ph.D.) has focused her research and teaching on reading and writing instruction and how mainstream and ESL teachers collaborate to meet the academic needs of English language learners (ELLs). She teaches undergraduate and graduate literacy courses at Texas Christian University. She is coauthor of *Helping English Language Learners Succeed in Pre-K–Elementary Schools,* published by TESOL, and she is an editor/author of *Focus on Literacy: Effective Content Teachers for the Middle Grades.* She has published in numerous journals, including *Balanced Reading Instruction, Childhood Education, Language Arts, Voices From the Middle, The Teacher Educator,* and *Teacher Education Quarterly.* She has published chapters in the *Handbook of Research on Reading* and in *Comprehension Instruction* (2nd edition), and several other books. She is currently serving as the associate editor for the *Journal of Research in Childhood Education* (JRCE). Prior to teaching at the college level, Jan taught ESL in Texas and Kansas.

Catherine McMillan (Ph.D.) is the principal of Franklin Elementary School in Madison, Wisconsin, where she also teaches in the graduate program at Edgewood College. She was principal at Hawthorne School in Madison, Wisconsin, at the time of this research.

Sandra Mercuri (Ph.D.) is an assistant professor at the University of Texas, Brownsville. She teaches courses in bilingual education and biliteracy and is working on research on the development of academic language across the content areas and the effect of long-term professional development for teachers of English learners. She has published articles in professional journals about bilingual learners and the application of second language theories in classroom practice in the

TESOL Quarterly, Talking Points, and the National Association of Bilingual Education (NABE) journal as well as professional journals in Spanish. She has also coauthored the books *Closing the Achievement Gap* and *Dual Language Essentials* with Yvonne and David Freeman and *Research-Based Strategies for English Language Learners* with Denise Rea.

James Salzman is an associate professor at Cleveland State University.

Cynthia M. Schmidt (Ph.D.) is an assistant professor at the University of Missouri–Kansas City, where she is involved in preparing teachers for urban classrooms. She teaches undergraduate and graduate courses in literacy and reading education. Her research interests include teacher education and critical literacy, literacy development, reading assessment, and instruction for diverse learners, including English language learners.

Jeanne Schrumm (Ph.D.) is a professor of reading education at University of Miami in Coral Gables, Florida. She is a professor in residence at Henry S. West Laboratory School where she directs a reading tutorial program. Her primary research interest is in teaching struggling readers in general education settings.

Cecilia Silva (Ph.D.) has pursued research interests including the integration of language, literacy, and concept development. She is a coauthor of *Teaching the Dimensions of Literacy* and of *Curricular Conversations: Themes in Multilingual and Monolingual Classrooms.* She is a contributing author to *On Our Way to English* and a member of the Advisory Committee for the *Oxford Picture Dictionary for the Content Areas.* She is a former member of the Reading Commission (National Teachers of English Reading Commission); she teaches undergraduate and graduate courses in second language acquisition and bilingual education at Texas Christian University. She began her career as a bilingual elementary teacher in California. Over the past 20 years she has worked with teacher preparation programs.

The Early Childhood through Sixth Grade Undergraduate Program (EC-6) at Texas Christian University, in which both Jan Lacina and Ceclila serve, received the International Reading Association's (IRA) *Certificate of Distinction* for 2009–2016.

Patience Sowa (Ph.D.) is an associate professor of education at Zayed University in the United Arab Emirates. She teaches general education and literacy courses. Her research interests include the preparation of preservice teachers to teach English language learners, literacy for English language learners, and bilingual and multicultural issues in schools.

Donna Witherspoon (Ed.D.) is retired from the Greater Latrobe School District in southwestern Pennsylvania, where she was an elementary teacher and administrator. She taught undergraduate and graduate education classes at Indiana University of Pennsylvania and Gannon University. She currently works as an educational consultant.

Supporting researchers for more than 40 years

Research methods have always been at the core of SAGE's publishing program. Founder Sara Miller McCune published SAGE's first methods book, *Public Policy Evaluation*, in 1970. Soon after, she launched the *Quantitative Applications in the Social Sciences* series—affectionately known as the "little green books."

Always at the forefront of developing and supporting new approaches in methods, SAGE published early groundbreaking texts and journals in the fields of qualitative methods and evaluation.

Today, more than 40 years and two million little green books later, SAGE continues to push the boundaries with a growing list of more than 1,200 research methods books, journals, and reference works across the social, behavioral, and health sciences. Its imprints—Pine Forge Press, home of innovative textbooks in sociology, and Corwin, publisher of PreK–12 resources for teachers and administrators—broaden SAGE's range of offerings in methods. SAGE further extended its impact in 2008 when it acquired CQ Press and its best-selling and highly respected political science research methods list.

From qualitative, quantitative, and mixed methods to evaluation, SAGE is the essential resource for academics and practitioners looking for the latest methods by leading scholars.

For more information, visit **www.sagepub.com**.